DALY

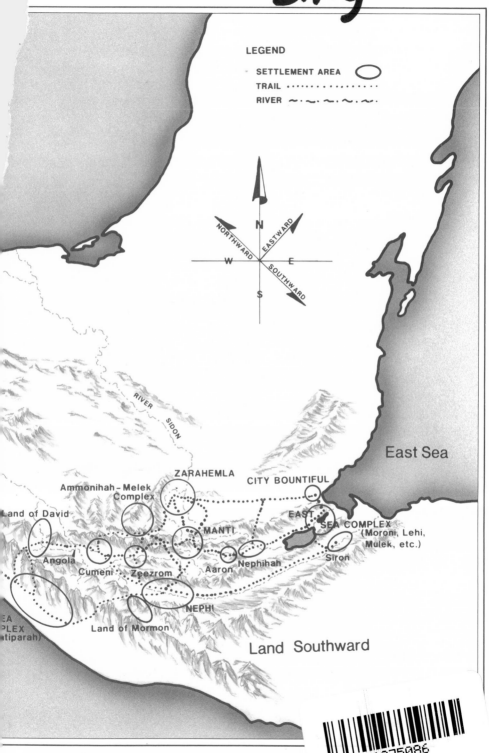

WATT

# DECIPHERING THE GEOGRAPHY OF THE BOOK OF MORMON

Settlements and Routes in Ancient America

## F. RICHARD HAUCK

Appendixes Prepared by
Vaughn E. Hansen
and
F. Richard Hauck
Graphics Prepared by Brad Weber

Deseret Book Company
Salt Lake City, Utah

First printing January 1988

---

**Library of Congress Cataloging-in-Publication Data**

Hauck, Richard, 1938–
        Deciphering the geography of the Book of Mormon / by Richard Hauck
        p.   cm.
        Bibliography: p.
        Includes index.
        ISBN 0-87579-128-X
        1. Book of Mormon—Geography.   I. Title.
BX8627.H37   1987                                        87-32943
289.3'22—dc19                                               CIP

---

Printed in the United States of America

10   9   8   7   6   5   4   3   2

The geographer must conceive of the places of the earth as parts of a system, related to each other at different levels of interaction.

*Fred Lukermann, Geographer*

# CONTENTS

# FIGURES

# PREFACE

This book has been prepared as a study guide to the geography and history of the Book of Mormon. My foremost objective has been to document the settlement and route networks of the Book of Mormon and to demonstrate the ancient American setting of those geographic associations.

Two very separate and diverse audiences are addressed in this book. The primary audience consists of those who are interested in using this information as a guide for their personal study of the geography and history of the Book of Mormon.

A second audience includes those whose interest is scientific. These readers are curious about the theory and technique used to reconstruct the Book of Mormon settlement and route networks.[1]

The Book of Mormon is an important historical document and a powerful theological text. My hopes in publishing this study are twofold: first, that I have done justice to the subject matter; second, that anyone spending time with this study guide will acquire a greater appreciation for the Book of Mormon.

As a professional archeologist, my training and experience have been devoted to gathering and using fragmentary evidence to reconstruct the activities and settlement patterns of ancient cultures.

Archeological training and diverse field experience are crucial to this task, as is an understanding of the various settlement concepts used to analyze ancient human occupations and population distributions. My perspective as a field archeologist stems from such a diverse background. Previous training in Mesoamerica (see Hauck 1973, 1975, and Matheny et al., 1983) and current experience as an archaeological consultant in the Intermountain West have expanded my appreciation for using concepts from a variety of scentific disciplines to help analyze ancient settlement patterns.

Having this background and interest, I began research in 1979 on what I initially thought was a short-term, personal examination of the Book of Mormon using a theoretical approach developed by geographers for studying human settlements as systems. This systems approach examines the interaction and relationships between settlements, transportation routes, and cultural technology and environment for any given people, time, and place. The preliminary probe of the Book of Mormon using this approach provided such positive results that it led to an intensive research program that has been underway since 1981. This volume and several other complementary publications presently in preparation are the current results of this research program.

The basis for this work rests on the assumption that, since the Book of Mormon purports to be a history of real people and their settlements, its place and route associations can be reconstructed from its internal information using systems analysis. Such reconstruction of an actual history will reveal a consistent pattern of associations between places mentioned in the text. Conversely, should the book be fictitious, such analysis will reveal major discrepancies in its settlement system. Simply stated, it would have been impossible for Joseph Smith in the 1820s to have fabricated such an elaborate history spanning 3,000 years of human experience and not incorporate identifiable errors within its complex and fragmentary geography.

I realized early in the research that in order to maintain an objective perspective, this reconstruction could be shaped only by descriptions specifically stated in the Book of Mormon. To follow the usual and convenient method of developing a model through associating textual places with specific sites or ancient localities anywhere in the Americas would be to base the evaluations on subjective biases. Such an error could lead to suppositions that, if incorrect, would only further warp the development of the analysis. Only after the settlement systems had been identified and reconstructed into an abstract, geometric model was an actual, physical correlation of the places in the Book of Mormon attempted in the Americas; only then was the model compared with the terrain of the American continent. Beginning with the tip of South America, the original, theoretical model was gradually worked north to the Arctic. Only one locality on the continent met the topographic conditions identified within the book. The model fit into the portion of ancient America that is known as southern Mesoamerica, comprising portions of the modern nations of Mexico, Belize, and Guatemala.

In 1981 the first field evaluations of the theoretical model within its theoretical setting in Mesoamerica were made with gratifying results. Upon completion in 1986 of the sixth consecutive annual field season using the model to identify ancient Book of Mormon settlement patterns in Mexico and Guatemala, there is good reason for optimism. Although field work is in its infancy, satisfaction can be taken in knowing that the correlation of the text to its setting has advanced substantially beyond the general theory stage where it has existed for more than 150 years. This does not mean that all the cultural and geographic factors are now understood. Archeologists face years of difficult field research before that level of understanding can be achieved.

The understanding provided in this research effort can be summarized in the following statements:

1. A comprehensive model has been established based strictly on the locational data in the Book of Mormon.

2. This model contains such a high level of internal consistency that it could not have been fabricated in the nineteenth century and must therefore be an abstraction of an ancient settlement system.

3. The physical environment of the model correlates with a portion of Mesoamerica.

4. The model has been taken into the field, resulting in the correlation of key topographic and cultural locations with ancient settlements and fortifications described in the Book of Mormon.

The settlement pattern and locational models reconstructed in this volume need not be blindly accepted. Data basic to the model are offered for independent study and testing by anyone desiring to make the effort. Appendix A, the starting point for this endeavor, has been prepared by Dr. Vaughn E. Hansen, a civil engineer. In the fall of 1982, following a discussion of this approach and model, Dr. Hansen decided to test the validity of this research. He did so by independently following the same procedures that have been outlined above. First, he extracted from the text all the references to each specific place and then reconstructed settlement associations using all the bits and pieces of evidence available. Neither of the models was developed by correlating text places with known sites and places in the Americas. To do so at that initial stage would have required assumptions that the researcher was not prepared to make. At the conclusion of his work, Dr. Hansen had reconstructed a basic settlement model of the land southward that was essentially identical to the original model that I used in 1981 to initiate field studies.

The perspective for this approach and the research contained in this volume are mine, although many technical concepts have been drawn from various disciplines. This work has been independently developed, although many individuals have participated in the various reviews and have provided suggestions. Funding for the field studies was aided by family and associates in the Ancient America Foundation based in Salt Lake City. I shall always be grateful to many associates and friends in Guatemala, including archeologist Edwin Shook, who graciously shared with me his home, library, and experience; President Gary Elliott, president of the LDS mission in Guatemala City, for his interest and encouragement; Cordell Anderson for his hospitality and assistance; and Lee and Joyce White for their support, hospitality, and friendship.

I give special thanks to all who reviewed the various drafts of this manuscript and supplied valuable critical assistance. Those individuals include Bryce Montgomery, B.S. — geologist; Lawrence Harmon, Ph.D. — geographer; Bruce Warren, Ph.D; Raymond Matheny, Ph.D.; T. Michael Smith, M.A.; V. Garth Norman, M.A.; and H. Blaine Phillips II, M.A. — archeologists; Paul Cheesman, D.R.E, and Bryan Weston, Ph.D. — educators; Macoy and Lynn McMurray — attorneys; and Vaughn E. Hansen, Ph.D. — civil engineer.

My deepest appreciation goes to a variety of individuals who have contributed in many different ways to this research program and publication. These include Brad Weber, who drafted the graphics; personnel in the firm Hansen, Allen, and Luce, who provided cartographic advice and assistance; and to my associates and family, who shared the trials and triumphs of these past field seasons: T. Michael Smith; Joyce and Lee White; Donell and Vaughn Hansen; and Greg, Forrest, and Laura Hauck. I especially extend my gratitude to my parents and to my wife, Laura, for their countless hours of editorial assistance, and to my family for their patience and their personal sacrifices during my long absences from them.

I am deeply indebted to my friend Vaughn Hansen, whose support, counsel, and personal sacrifice sustained much of this research and writing.

The research within this volume has been prepared for the Mormon Studies Division of the Ancient America Foundation. All royalties are dedicated to future research conducted by that foundation.

F. RICHARD HAUCK, PH.D.
FALL 1987

## NOTES

1. Addendum to Chapter 4: The Theoretical Background for this Study is a specialized introduction that addresses these scholarly questions by discussing the theoretical foundation of systems theory and spatial analysis. The archeological application of these theoretical approaches is also summarized in that addendum. The analyses of the Book of Mormon area settlement model are also provided as an addendum rather than in the main body of the document because of the statistical information (see Addendum to Chapter 8: Statistical Characteristics of the Area Settlement Model). Individuals interested in understanding the technical background may wish to refer to the first addendum before reading chapter 4, "Symbols, Paths, and Routes." The second addendum follows the reconstruction of the area model developed in chapter 8.

# 1

# THE BOOK OF MORMON AND ANCIENT AMERICA

Recent archaeological and geographical field investigations show that the migration accounts in the Book of Mormon involve the ancient settlement of the Olmec and Maya homelands of Mexico and Central America. This chapter is a synopsis of the correlations developed in the later chapters.

Long before the Pilgrims stepped ashore at Plymouth Rock, before Columbus arrived in the Caribbean, and even before the Vikings dropped anchor in Newfoundland's bays, complex civilizations existed on the American continent. These ancient civilizations in Mexico, Central America, and Peru rivaled the advanced cultures of the Old World in grandeur and knowledge. Modern research has established that extensive ethnic, cultural, and linguistic diversity existed among the ancient inhabitants of the New World. These cultures were not all of common origin. They did not all travel the same route to the Americas, nor did they arrive at the same time. Rather, over thousands of years, numerous distinct groups departed from many homelands to travel a variety of land and ocean routes leading to the American continent. One of the great mysteries of our time concerns the origins, migration routes, and cultural development of the ancient inhabitants of the New World.

Expeditions into the jungles and mountains of Mexico and Guatemala are currently providing answers about the ancient inhabitants of this area. These answers are coming from a surprising source—the Book of Mormon, whose own setting has been an enigma for over 150 years. For the first time since its publication in 1830, the Book of Mormon has been successfully used to predict the location on the American continent of ancient ruins described within its pages.

Using a model of the geography developed from the Book of Mormon, archeologists have discovered the remains of fortified settlements established by the Nephite commander Moroni about 2,000 years ago. For the first time, we have been able to examine the fortified trenches and walls that surround ancient Manti, Zeezrom, and Cumeni. For the first time, archeologists have visited the ancient lands of Nephi and Zarahemla with a knowledge of what occurred at those places so many years ago. For the first time, the Nephite temple complex in the ancient land of Bountiful has been viewed with a knowledge of the purpose for which it was initially constructed.

What has made the difference? How is it that now, after such a long period of silence, the Book of Mormon has been unlocked and its setting in the Americas identified and studied? The answer is simple: The geographic information on the book's settlements and routes has always been available in the pages of that text; but the information has never been analyzed as an integral system. A comprehensive network of Book of Mormon settlements and routes has never been reconstructed because the potential for a systems approach has neither been previously recognized nor employed.

Since 1830, when the Book of Mormon was first published, numerous attempts have been made to identify its location on the American continent. These worthy efforts require appreciation, for they have intensified the desire for understanding. Possibly the most important contribution to emerge from the variety of published and unpublished studies on Book of Mormon geography has been the continued probing and questioning of the book itself.

A recent study by John L. Sorenson has established the cultural correlation of Book of Mormon peoples with the ancient inhabitants of southern Mesoamerica.[1] Dr. Sorenson, an anthropologist and past chairman of the Department of Anthropology and Archeology at Brigham Young University, concludes his work *An Ancient American Setting for the Book of Mormon* by stating:

> The Book of Mormon shows so many striking similarities to the Mesoamerican setting that it seems to me impossible for rational people willing to examine the data to maintain any longer that the book is a mere romance or speculative history

written in the third decade of the nineteenth century in New York State. . . .

Our knowledge from scholarship on life and culture in Mexico and Central America in early times allows us to envision concretely how Book of Mormon armies fought, dissenters dissented, and farmers farmed. We also begin to see some of the whys of the ancient situation: secret societies, kinship and tribes, trade and conquest, migration and missions. . . . As a result of this explication of the setting, readers ought to become convinced that the Book of Mormon is an extremely complex record that deserves far more careful study than it has received in the past (1985: 354-55).

The study provided in the following chapters demonstrates that the Book of Mormon is a viable geographical and historical research document that provides extensive information pinpointing its setting on the American continent. The Book of Mormon contains geographical and cultural information that is internally consistent; no conflict exists among its numerous complex references. This study is therefore a demonstration of how all the fragmented, scattered geographical data contained in the book actually fit together to form the intricate network of the Book of Mormon settlement system in ancient Mexico and Guatemala.

This new breakthrough in our understanding of the Book of Mormon is the result of intensive analyses of its locational and historical information that were started in 1979. By 1981, a geographical model consisting of a network of settlements and routes was taken into the field to correlate with the ruins, terrain, and coastlines of southern Mesoamerica. Since then, expeditions into southern Mexico and Guatemala (see figure 1) have further advanced the correlation of the book with the topography. These informal archeological investigations have identified a series of large, fortified settlements in specific geographical locations described in the Book of Mormon. Field work has validated the theory that the book's setting coincides with the ancient homeland of the Olmec and Maya peoples.

The demonstration of how the Book of Mormon answers some of the questions about the ancient settlement of Mesoamerica begins with a discussion of the ancient Olmec civilization of Mesoamerica.

The Olmec peoples of the gulf coastal lowlands were the

3

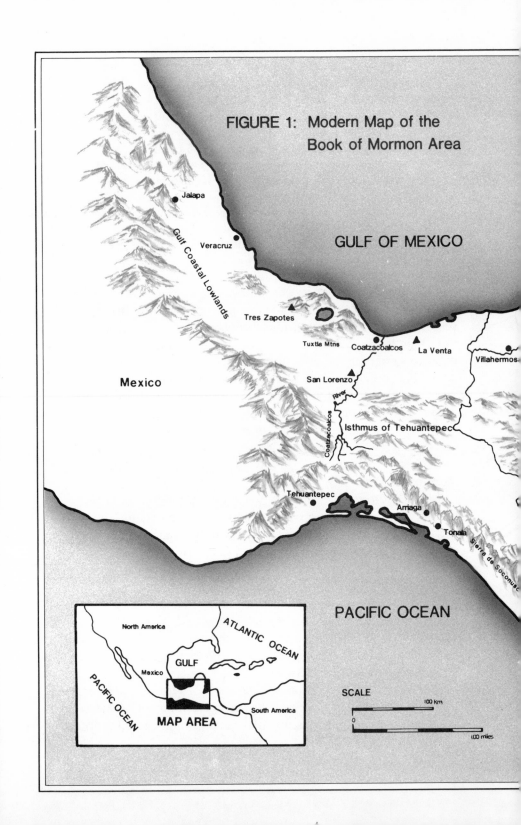

FIGURE 1: Modern Map of the Book of Mormon Area

GULF OF MEXICO

Jalapa

Veracruz

Gulf Coastal Lowlands

Tres Zapotes

Tuxtla Mtns    Coatzacoalcos    La Venta

Villahermosa

Mexico

San Lorenzo

Coatzacoalcos River

Isthmus of Tehuantepec

Tehuantepec

Arriaga

Tonala

Sierra de Soconusco

PACIFIC OCEAN

North America

ATLANTIC OCEAN

GULF

Mexico

PACIFIC OCEAN

South America

MAP AREA

SCALE

0    100 km

100 miles

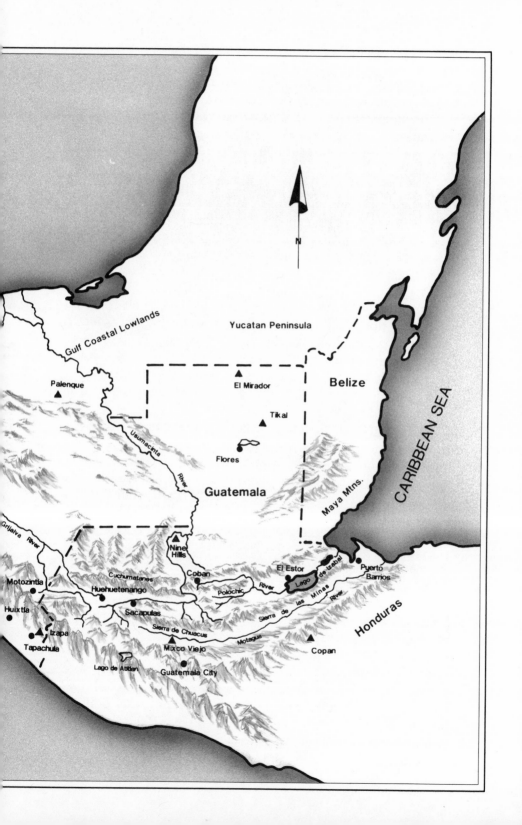

earliest literate civilization of the Americas. Their Old World origin has not been established; however, Olmec art and architecture suggest an Asian, possibly Near Eastern, homeland. This civilization achieved its peak in political, artistic, and economic influence between 2000 and 1000 B.C. The Olmec culture declined after that period and disappeared from the archeological record before 400 B.C. Even after its demise as a political power, the Olmec cultural contribution continued as a major influence in Mesoamerican developments for centuries afterward.

The Olmec development bears a striking similarity to the history of the Jaredite people as abridged in the segment of the Book of Mormon known as the book of Ether. Perhaps as early as 3000 B.C., these people migrated to an undisclosed location in the Americas from their Near Eastern homeland. Their complex civilization flourished until sometime between 300 and 600 B.C., when they were destroyed by civil war. Centuries after their political destruction, the philosophy of the Nehor cult, which possibly originated within the Jaredite culture, continued to influence the thinking and development of the later peoples that occupied those lands.

The geographic model of the Book of Mormon developed in the following chapters places the Jaredite homeland directly within the heartland of the Olmec civilization on Mexico's gulf coast. The Jaredite area of occupation, as demonstrated in the model, extended from the general locality of Jalapa southeastward past Veracruz and the Tuxtla Mountains to the general locality of the modern city Coatzacoalcos in the Isthmus of Tehuantepec. The Jaredite peoples probably landed their barges and waded ashore somewhere along this Gulf coastline. During their nearly 2,500 years of occupation, this Olmec-Jaredite culture became highly diversified both socially and economically, for they established a flourishing civilization with extensive trade networks and colonies elsewhere in Mexico and Central America.

Intrigue and savage warfare among prominent, ambitious individuals competing for political control of the kingdom were continuous sources of disruption throughout the history of the Olmec-Jaredite peoples. After the first millennium B.C. the political unrest intensified. Sometime between 600 and 300 B.C. a major civil war erupted between the protagonists of the two dominant political and ideological factions. Coriantumr, the ruler, fought a series of contenders to retain control of the capital at ancient Moron, which was apparently situated in the general region of modern Jalapa, Mexico. The struggle for domination became so intense that the localized feud gradually deteriorated into a destructive scorched-earth mode of intensive civil war.

The geographic model of the greater land northward shows that, as the conflict intensified, the contending forces carried the battle southeastward away from Moron into other Jaredite-Olmec population centers. Over the years, local peoples were forced to choose sides and enter the foray. As later populations, settlements, and lands were decimated, the conflict expanded into newer territories where casualties could be replaced and necessary sustenance could be found. The geographic model demonstrates that this series of battles alternated between coastal and inland sites as the combatting armies gradually worked their way south and eastward through the populated areas. Eventually they arrived in the region of the Isthmus of Tehuantepec, where the final battle was planned. The geographic model developed in chapter 6 correlates the hill Ramah with the Tuxtla Mountains complex west of the modern gulf coastal city of Coatzacoalcos, Mexico.

A four-year period followed—a time used by the opposing armies to recruit soldiers from the remaining populations. Eventually the concluding battle was fought on Ramah, bringing to an end this bloody civil war.

The war was not all that ended on Ramah; the very social fabric of the Olmec-Jaredite civilization and its complex political-economic structure were destroyed on that desolate hill.

Coriantumr, the leader of the dominant political faction, survived that last battle for a short time. Separate accounts in the Book of Mormon suggest that Coriantumr lived long enough to meet the people of Zarahemla. The record is unclear whether Coriantumr witnessed their early sixth century B.C. arrival from Palestine on the shores of the Gulf or whether this people had settled at Zarahemla long before Coriantumr spent the final nine months of his life in their company.

The geographic model developed in chapters 5, 6, and 7 and its correlation with Mesoamerica in chapter 8 indicate that the people of Zarahemla arrived by ship in the Gulf of Mexico and subsequently sailed to the mouth of the Usumacinta River. The colony then proceeded up that large river to the vicinity of the archeological site of Nine Hills, where the rapids halt further travel up the river. It was in that general locality, at a place they called Zarahemla, where this colony, now called Mulekites, evidently settled some time during the first half of the sixth century B.C.

Almost contemporaneously with the arrival of the people of Zarahemla was the landing of a separate group that also came from the Near East. This party was led by Lehi, a Hebrew prophet, who departed with his extended family from Jerusalem during the reign of King Zedekiah about 600 B.C. The main content of the Book of Mormon is an abbreviated history of Lehi's descendants spanning 985 years of cultural development in southern Mesoamerica. This historical account has a strong theological orientation, for it was prepared by Lehi's successors, who also were Old Testament–style religious leaders.

Unlike the debarkation of the Mulekite and Jaredite colonies on the Gulf of Mexico, Lehi's party came ashore some 300 miles to the southeast on the Pacific coast. This spatial study identifies this west sea locality as the land of Judea in the west sea land of Bountiful also called "the place of their fathers' first inheritance." (Alma 22:28.) This locality was evidently named Judea in remembrance of the colony's Old World homeland. A special temple complex was later erected at the site to commemorate the historic significance of the locality.

The geographic model correlates the locality of Lehi's landing with Tapachula, a Mexican city adjacent to the Guatemalan border. Indeed, archeological research on the architecture and art of the nearby ancient site of Izapa suggests that this location was developed as a commemorative shrine by Lehi's descendants. Construction of the sacred site may actually have begun during Lehi's lifetime while the original colony resided in the area. Although most of the development of the site occurred during the first century B.C., its artwork demonstrates a philosophical continuity that spans the intervening four hundred years. Bas-relief stone sculptures erected during the various stages of site development symbolically depict sacred concepts, such as the tree of life, blood atonement through a divine sacrifice, judgment and punishment of the wicked, premortal life, and resurrection. These concepts were the important religious themes of Lehi's day, as evidenced in the writings of Nephi, and they continued to have great influence on Lehi's successors throughout the course of Nephite history.

Izapa's 25 centuries of preservation, the correlation of its art with primary themes in the Book of Mormon, and its geographic identification with the land of Judea, as developed in the following chapters, all show the existence of an extremely significant cultural identity.

After Lehi's death, a segment of the colony led by his son Nephi migrated inland to settle in the land of Nephi. The geographic model correlates the land of Nephi with the locality of Mixco Viejo, a historic Maya site in the Motagua River valley of south-central Guatemala.

The following 300 to 360 years of history provide little geographical information. About 225 B.C., Mosiah and his followers abandoned the land of Nephi and settled among the people of Zarahemla on the Usumacinta River. The basic course they traveled via the modern cities of Rabinal and Coban north into the Peten basin eventually became the most important overland route of southern Mesoamerica. This system of trails was the Nephi-Manti-Gideon-Zarahemla route utilized throughout the history of the Book of Mormon as the primary travel corridor between the northern lands of Zarahemla inhabited by the Nephite peoples and the southern lands of Nephi inhabited by the Lamanites, a dissident culture that broke away from the original Nephite colony. This transportation corridor continued to be used by the Maya Indians after the Nephite demise. During the Classic Maya period, this route was just a segment of the extensive trail system that connected the Maya center of Kaminaljuyu (located in modern Guatemala City) with the Maya settlements of northern Yucatan via the Peten basin (see Hauck 1975).

Following the end of the Classic Maya period of occupation in the Peten basin, the overland trail system received less use; Maya trade then became oriented to coastal networks. However, the southern portion of this trail system continued to be used, for it was followed by the Spanish conquistadors and padres during the 16th and 17th centuries. From Coban north, the ancient route has not been a primary transportation corridor for centuries. Today it is possible to use both modern and colonial roads and travel segments of this route between Guatemala City, Granados, and Coban.

Only during the past 25 years has an alternate land route to the east via Rio Dulce been opened. This eastern route has helped curtail the centuries of isolation that have existed between northern and southern Guatemala following the Mayan abandonment of the Peten region at the close of the Classic period in ca. A.D. 900.

Someone unfamiliar with the geography and rugged terrain of Guatemala might wonder why the loss of this inland transportation route results in the isolation of two regions that are only about 150 miles apart. This question can be answered by studying the complex mountain system that bisects the country. An extensive east-west chain of mountains containing peaks that range over 10,000 feet in elevation is a major barrier separating the northern Guatemalan lowlands from the southern highlands. Spanning the continent, these elevations extend westward from the Caribbean, or east sea in the Book of Mormon, to the Pacific, or west sea.

The Book of Mormon refers to this chain of mountains as the narrow strip of wilderness. This rugged terrain was the primary barrier between the Nephites at Zarahemla on the north and their enemies, the Lamanites, at Nephi to the south.

A field examination of this mountain barrier makes apparent why the narrow strip of wilderness was the most important terrain feature discussed in the Book of Mormon. This narrow highland can be crossed only at a few highly strategic locations. It was at these strategic mountain locations where the Nephites between 74 and 60 B.C. fought the most documented war recorded in the Book of Mormon. The points of conflict during the various engagements of this war extended eastward from the Pacific, where Antiparah and Judea were situated, to the fortifications at Moroni near the Caribbean Sea. In the interior, Book of Mormon highland defenses adjacent to the narrow strip of wilderness included Cumeni, Zeezrom, Manti, and Nephihah.

Cumeni has been identified as a Preclassic site at the headwaters of the Grijalva River near modern Huehuetenango. It defended the entrance to the ancient highland trade route that linked the basin with the gulf coast via the colonial city of San Cristobal de las Casas. This site also defended the route leading down into the Grijalva depression and the important lateral route that linked the Huehuetenango basin westward with Judea on the Pacific coast. Eastward, this same lateral route led past Zeezrom to eventually connect with Manti and the main north-south trail.

Using the geographic model to identify the site of Zeezrom, a correlation has been located on the Chixoy or Negro River, which is an important headwater tributary of the Sidon or Usumacinta River. This defensive site is near the modern town of Sacapulas. Zeezrom was the first line of defense protecting the entrance to the north-bound route that extended beyond the present site of Nebaj into the Peten basin.

Manti was situated in the highlands north of the narrow strip of wilderness and near the Sidon River. This important fortified settlement on the Nephi-Zarahemla route has been identified at the colonial-modern site of Coban. Manti was important not only in its defense of Zarahemla, but because of its position in controlling travel along the important lateral corridor that linked the east sea, or Caribbean–Lago de Izabel, defenses with the west sea defenses at Judea.

The geographic model establishes the location of Nephihah in the Polochic River valley near the present-day town of Panzos. The fortification at this location not only controlled east-west movement from the Caribbean coast inland to Manti via the river corridor, but could block travel north across the mountains to present-day Cahabon or Chahal.

The eastern defensive positions of the Book of Mormon in the east sea region were centered on the sites of Moroni, Lehi, and the city of Bountiful. These positions extended from the present-day Lago de Izabel–Rio Dulce locality north into the Sarstun River drainage in the modern state of Belize. They served to protect the northward coastal route and, as an eastern anchor to the nearly 300-mile-long lateral corridor that parallels the mountain barrier, permitted the Nephites rapid east-west movement from sea to sea.

This lateral route from ancient Manti (modern Coban) to the west sea was used for the last time by the Nephites in A.D. 327 during their withdrawal from Zarahemla. The geographic model indicates that their retreat brought them along this route to Joshua on the Pacific coast, where Mormon, the Nephite leader, fortified the entrance to the narrow coastal corridor that extends northwestward toward the Isthmus of Tehuantepec. This narrow coastal corridor situated between the modern cities of Tapachula and Arriaga thus became the scene of the protracted war between the Nephites and their enemies. That war continued for 48 years, or

11

until the Nephites were driven out of the city of Desolation for the final time.

The narrow Pacific coastal shelf along the Pacific shore of southeastern Mexico has been the primary transportation corridor for overland travel between central Mexico and Central America since the first arrival of man in the Americas. It is a natural transportation corridor and the most expeditious land route in the region. The natural topography makes alternative routes less direct, for flanking this coastal shelf on the north are the rugged mountains that comprise the continental divide. Northward, beyond these ranges and the Grijalva Depression, lie the jungles and extensive river systems of the Gulf lowlands that seriously restrict overland travel.

The geographic model developed in chapters 6 and 7, and correlated with the terrain and geography of Mesoamerica in chapter 8, establishes an important association. The Book of Mormon topography described as the "narrow neck of land" that connected the Nephites' land southward with the Jaredites' land northward was this narrow coastal shelf paralleling the Pacific Ocean.

One of the traditional assumptions of Book of Mormon scholars and casual readers alike has been to equate the "narrow neck of land" with an isthmus. Because this assumption has been widely accepted without careful examination, it has complicated and confused the numerous attempts made to identify the setting of the book, for the identification of the proper isthmus is frequently the primary focus of attempts made to identify the Book of Mormon geography. Careful analyses of all the references in the text to this topographic feature fail to identify the presence of two seas flanking the transportation corridor. The west sea is clearly evident in the descriptions given in the text, but the east sea is never specifically mentioned as being associated with the narrow corridor. Since two bodies of water flanking a narrow strip of land create an isthmus, the "narrow neck of land" as described in the Book of Mormon does not qualify as an isthmus. The description of a transportation corridor narrowly constricted on the west flank by the sea and on the east flank by a possible mountain barrier does, however, qualify as a land bridge.

Throughout Nephite history, this strategic west sea land bridge was critical to their defense of the land northward. Nephite protection of the entrance into this corridor began as early as the first century B.C. based on the information given in Alma 22:32-34. The Nephite defensive strategy repeatedly included the defense of the entrance into this corridor. It was defended from fortifications at Judea and in the land of Bountiful between 67 and 65 B.C. and again from 35 to 31 B.C. This corridor became the Nephite place of refuge during a war with the Gadianton robbers between A.D. 17 and 22. Last of all, it was a pertinent defensive asset to the Nephites in their final war, for it helped them block Lamanite access to their resources and population in the land northward during 48 years of bloody warfare.

The Nephite defeats in the coastal corridor at Desolation in A.D. 375 and at Boaz during the following year resulted in their complete loss of the Pacific coast defensive system. Thereafter their purpose was simply to control the final route of access in the Isthmus of Tehuantepec that led into the land northward. Ancient Jordan and its adjacent fortifications situated at strategic locations in the Isthmus of Tehuantepec became the Nephites' final hope for maintaining a secure homeland in the gulf lowlands to the north.

The destruction of Jordan about A.D. 379 left the Nephites with no other options than to withdraw to the north the remaining 100 miles into the natural defenses afforded by the Tuxtla Mountains. There at Ramah, the same location where the Jaredite culture had been extinguished some 600 to 1,000 years before, Mormon proceeded to gather the remnants of his people.

The traditional four years of gathering was concluded in A.D. 385. Situated on the slopes of the hill that they called Cumorah, 23 Nephite armies, each containing 10,000 men, anxiously awaited the arrival of the Lamanite enemy. That final battle was apparently concluded in short order, for Mormon states that "on the morrow" (Mormon 6:11) the few survivors viewed the battleground where at least 230,000 Nephites had been slaughtered. Coupled with the Lamanite casualties, the total cost of human life on Cumorah during that time of terror probably exceeded a million souls.

## NOTES

1. The term *Mesoamerica* is used to define a cultural area of high development that existed prior to the Spanish conquest. This area began in the Rio Panuco–Sinaloa regions of central Mexico and extended southward to the mouth of the Motagua River in modern Honduras. The Gulf of Nicoya in Costa Rica was the southern boundary of Mesoamerica on the Pacific coast.

# 2

# THE RESEARCH POTENTIAL OF THE BOOK OF MORMON

The value of the Book of Mormon as a research document for reconstructing its internal geography depends on how its data is used. This chapter examines the importance of using appropriate scientific research methods for unlocking sources of knowledge contained in historic manuscripts.

The human race has a fascination for the past. This fascination is a common bond that extends beyond cultural barriers and even beyond time. A person's interest in the past begins to stir at an early age when the concepts of time and change are first grasped. This curiosity is akin to the interest and patience one uses to unravel a cluster of snarled twine. The past is, in a sense, a tangle of culture, environment, and time that the historian and archeologist carefully attempt to unsnarl. Slowly the researcher exposes more of the core. Carefully the elements of time and place are extricated, permitting a more comprehensible view of the human situation. As archeologists, we have a complex snarl of cultural twine to unravel before we will understand in depth the history and prehistory of the Americas.

The scholar's ability to perceive a research problem is very important in solving that problem. Ralph Waldo Emerson once reportedly stated, "People see only what they are prepared to see." Experienced field archeologists understand this. Frequently an archeologist will identify an ancient cultural site that has never before been recognized. The identification of that site and what occurred there is made strictly by association of elements. The archeologist recognizes and mentally orders the patterns that are on that site. Then the archeologist consults his or her intellectual catalog of patterns that have been learned at other locations. Through comparison and thought, the person establishes an understanding of what happened at that location. When the time

14

comes to leave, the archeologist walks away having added the unique characteristics of that site to the storehouse of information. The knowledge acquired at that location increases the archeologist's capacity for solving new problems; the archeologist's level of perception has expanded.

As important as perception is in understanding the past, the archeologist's perspective is even more critical. A scientist's perspective involves his or her view of facts and events — thus, to the scientist, perspective is embodied in the mass of theory that influences the scientist's professional perception of the problem. To the archeologist, perspective is an understanding of the past — the appropriateness of the information the archaeologist used to order the complex cultural information that is perceived in the field and laboratory. An archeologist's perspective is the interaction of training and experience with his or her own unique reasoning capacity. The diversity and quality of this perspective enhances the archeologist's special capacity for understanding and explaining the past.

Here again, the analogy of the tangled string can be usefully applied. Everyone has shared the experience of being unable to extract a difficult knot from a snarled line. However, upon turning the cordage to attack the knot from a different angle or perspective, a relatively easy solution may be found and the knot removed. The knot did not change, but the perception was altered because of a new perspective on the problem.

The history of science furnishes many examples of difficult problems like these tangled knots — problems that were better identified and later solved once the perspective or theoretical base of the science was shifted or restructured (see Kuhn 1962). Unraveling the geographical associations of the Book of Mormon is an identical experience. The perspectives used in the past have not contained the theoretical base for establishing a viable model of the Book of Mormon geography that could be field tested. The systems-theory perspective permits that correlation.

The importance of a well-defined theoretical perspective for unlocking hidden information from the Book of Mormon can be aptly demonstrated by noting three separate research programs. Recently published studies of the Book of Mormon have helped substantiate the book's claim to have been the American product of a number of ancient authors having a Near Eastern background.

One study used computers to identify and evaluate a variety of distinct, individualistic writing patterns incorporated in the text (see Larsen, Rencher, and Layton 1980: 225-251).

In a different study, an analysis of the Book of Mormon's literary style has demonstrated a positive correlation with ancient Near Eastern literary traditions based on the identification of specific literary elements in the book (see Welch 1981: 198-210).

Current research from a third perspective links the book's cultural factors with ancient America. Anthropologist John Sorenson's recent publication (1985) on the ancient setting of the Book of Mormon provides an excellent general correlation of the text's cultural background within southern Mesoamerica. Sorenson's insight into the cultural background of both the region and the Book of Mormon establishes an important anthropological steppingstone.

Thus, three recent and diverse research efforts using different research perspectives to study the cultural and stylistic contexts of the Book of Mormon have provided viable evidence reinforcing its claims of being an ancient record of human activities on a portion of the American continent as recorded by a variety of writers with Near East Asian origins. These important contributions to understanding the Book of Mormon are the result of using sound research methods and theory to retrieve hidden information. The perception and perspective of these researchers produced these valuable results.

This book presents new perspectives for enhancing our perception of the geography or spatial organization in the Book of Mormon. This book is not provided as the final statement on the geography of the Book of Mormon. The complexity of these associations requires the investment of years of field research, an extensive effort that will gradually refine this knowledge. What this present work does provide is a platform from which intensive field work can continue.

The difficult problem concerning the Book of Mormon's internal geographic structure and its setting in the Americas is like the problem of unwinding our complex ball of snarled twine. Researchers have examined the snarl of twine for years and have picked away, trying to find the core and reveal its hidden knowledge. Unfortunately, the ball of twine has been seen from a limited perspective. That limited perspective combining the diverse approaches of a variety of researchers has provided valuable insights into the pros and cons of the book's setting, but unfortunately has not contained the theoretical tools needed to separate the tangled threads. Working from restricted perspective and perception (i.e., experience in solving the problem) the various researchers have created a more complex situation than actually exists.

Frustrated twine twisters can achieve a new perspective of the Book of Mormon, a perspective that permits a steady unraveling of its geography. The analytical-theoretical tools for studying geographical associations have increased dramatically during the past two to three decades. New views of cultural and geographic relationships have been developed. It is now possible to apply a variety of scientific concepts to the geographic analysis of the Book of Mormon. Researchers now have a more comprehensive means of evaluating the interaction of spatial variables such as settlements and routes than has ever before existed. Theories emphasizing order and association in time and space have become viable research tools for studying the cultural system revealed in a historic manuscript like the Book of Mormon. As the following chapters demonstrate, these approaches permit the analysis of previously unevaluated information contained in the book.

Once the model of the Book of Mormon showing its complex weave of settlement and route networks has been revealed, is that the culmination of all efforts to understand the book? Not at all; the work has only begun. That geographic model must be integrated into an archeological perspective in order to test its veracity.

A historic manuscript like the Book of Mormon containing extensive cultural material, including both temporal (time) and spatial (space) information, can be superficially compared with an archeological site. Both the site and the document contain social, topographic, time, and space associations that are both stated and implied. Based on theoretical perspective and experience, the researcher can identify the patterns in either context and prepare a research approach to establish order and extract data. In a sense, an archeologist dealing with a written history temporarily trades trowel and brush for conceptual tools to help "uncover" the form and establish the cultural processes or the human interactions behind the events recorded in the manuscript. Material developed from a history in this way can later be tested in the field using the classic archeological methods to substantiate or refute the original hypotheses.

Historic documents giving explicit references to settlements, environmental factors, and distances have been effectively used by archeologists to conduct field research and thus expand the knowledge of specific cultures beyond the facts provided in the documents.

Modern archeological research in Israel and Palestine based on settlement relationships provided in the Old Testament is a good example. Biblical archeologists using that text have expanded our understanding of numerous sites, including Jericho, Shiloh, Bethel, Gibeah, Jerusalem, Hazor, Megiddo, and Gezer. Archeology is restricted in what it can provide, however, for as G. Ernest Wright in the introduction to his work *Biblical Archaeology* states, "The support archaeology can give to the biblical record is limited. It cannot 'prove the Bible true' but it can illuminate the historical setting."

Consider also Heinrich Schliemann's excavations in the last century at the ancient sites of Troy and Mycenae. His excavations were based on a study of settlements and environments in the Aegean region drawn from Homer's *Iliad*. Schliemann's initial contention, which proved to be correct, was that the *Iliad* contained information of historic value that could be used to locate its ancient settlements.

Since Schliemann's time, historic records have been used to furnish useful information for researching various segments of the past. The important factor is that Schliemann's perspective was unique; archeologists had not previously studied ancient settlements using documents believed to have a mythological origin. Thus, a researcher's perspective based on theory and experience conditions his or her orientation to and perception of the past.

The Book of Mormon furnishes an excellent case for conducting a research strategy similar to those used by biblical archaeologists and Schliemann, for this book also is a historic manuscript translated and printed in the early nineteenth century. The original documents from which the translation was made are not available for scholarly evaluation. Hence, a successful correlation of the Book of Mormon's geographic models with the ancient cultural and topographic factors of the Americas is a research problem that parallels those solved by Schliemann and the biblical archeologists.

It will be demonstrated in the following chapters that a comprehensive and consistent spatial order exists within the Book of Mormon. Previous researchers have identified elements of this spatial structure and have made important contributions to the understanding of the book. Their efforts should not be overlooked; they began the process of correlation by making the initial pertinent probes into the geographical reality of the Book of Mormon. The information in the following chapters is offered as an additional step forward on the long and difficult journey to understanding the cultural and environmental setting of the Book of Mormon.

# 3

# ASSUMPTIONS — THEIR USE AND ABUSE

The Book of Mormon contains only a few geographic references that are easily and universally understood. Most references are given in complex associations that can be easily misinterpreted. Assumptions about these complex descriptions have not always been carefully established. Researchers have tended to construct elaborate geographic models on weak and even false premises. This chapter examines the assumptions used in understanding geographic locations and provides the criteria needed to differentiate between probable and improbable assumptions relative to Book of Mormon geography.

The Book of Mormon was originally prepared to emphasize theology presented in a historical context. Mormon, the primary editor, compiled the work from a variety of records that had been kept by generations of Nephite and Jaredite historians. Mormon was not too concerned that the history should provide a cultural-geographic frame of reference. Rather, he centered his summary on the theological implications of his people's struggle to survive and on his deep concern for the spiritual welfare of their posterity.

Geographic references are therefore generally subtle and woven into the general history in such a way that only through very careful analysis can the intricate geographic framework be identified and analyzed.

Perhaps the most difficult task in researching spatial and temporal associations in the Book of Mormon is to separate facts as clearly stated in the text from unsubstantiated traditional concepts. Traditional assumptions about place associations in the text may or may not be correct. The general acceptance of an assumption does not establish its veracity.

Speculation devoid of critical and logical analysis has frequently been used to establish premises about Book of Mormon geography. Although initiated with the best of intentions, an erroneous assumption will lead only to confusion, for speculation based on a false premise requires additional speculation to reinforce the original distortion. Truth is not often found in elaborate, contrived associations, but rather in simplicity and the consistency of all known factors.

What, then, is the boundary that separates fact from assumption in the complex web of geographic detail in the Book of Mormon? A summary of information provided in the Book of Mormon about its geography and setting is given below. These twelve statements are presented as "facts" because they are clearly stated in the text and are not derived through analysis, nor are they explained by various and diverse interpretations.

Fact 1: The Book of Mormon is an abbreviated history compiled by religious leaders of ancient peoples of Near East Asian origin that settled in the Americas.

Fact 2: Three separate colonies were established on the American continent following sea migrations. Jared and Lehi were the leaders of two colonies, and Mulek, a son of Old Testament King Zedekiah, accompanied the third migration.

Fact 3: The colonization led by Jared and his brother occurred between 3,500 and 2,500 B.C. contrasted with the separate arrivals of Lehi's colony and the group that included Mulek, both latter migrations occurring during the first half of the sixth century B.C.

Fact 4: Shortly after their landing, a segment of Lehi's group under the leadership of Nephi settled inland in the land of Nephi and became known as the Nephites.

Fact 5: A segment of the Nephites abandoned the land of Nephi probably during the third century B.C. and settled at Zarahemla among the people of Zarahemla, who included descendants of the migratory party accompanied by Mulek.

Fact 6: A Nephite colony temporarily reoccupied the settlements of Nephi and Shilom within the Lamanite-controlled land of Nephi between 200 and 120 B.C.

Fact 7: The locality of the total recorded experience is flanked by north, south, east, and west seas.

Fact 8: Both the lands of Zarahemla and Nephi extend from the borders of the east seashore to the borders of the west seashore.

Fact 9: The land southward (incorporating the lands of Nephi and Zarahemla) and the land northward (the homeland colonized earlier by Jared and his migration party) were separated by a narrow neck of land, also referred to as a narrow passage of land.

Fact 10: The destruction of the civilization founded by the descendants of Jared's party occurred between 600 and 100 B.C. in the land northward at the hill the Jaredites named Ramah.

Fact 11: The Nephite-Lamanite conflicts culminated with the destruction of the Nephite political and economic system in A.D. 385 in the land northward at the hill the Nephites named Cumorah.

Fact 12: The Hill Ramah was identical with the Hill Cumorah.

With the identification of these basic facts, it can be concluded that all other geographical associations that may be derived from the Book of Mormon are open to interpretation and therefore can be classified as assumptions until proven to be correct or refuted. Assumptions should never be accepted without careful analysis to establish validity. Once the validity of a geographic assumption has been substantiated, that premise can be considered a hypothesis requiring field evaluation before being accepted as a fact.

Readers can judge the validity and soundness of any stated assumption about Book of Mormon geography by examining the writer's logic using the following criteria:

1. A sound assumption is based on all associated references. An invalid or poorly established assumption is based on the selective use of certain references in support of a premise and the ignoring of other relevant references that are contrary to the writer's purpose.

2. A sound assumption enhances consistency or harmony among diverse data. An invalid assumption is not consistent with other elements of known fact.

3. A sound assumption expands clarity in explanation. An assumption may answer a particular problem, but its value is questionable if it does not further clarify other relevant, more general spatial associations.

4. A sound assumption results in simplification among geographic associations. As assumptions are refined and become closer to truth, their justification becomes simplified rather than more complex. An assumption is doubtful when its justification can be achieved only through greater and more abstract elaboration.

When these four criteria are applied during the formation of any assumption about the geographic reconstruction of the Book of Mormon, the results will be more highly accurate. An example of the analysis of an assumption using these criteria is as follows:

Statement of Assumption: The narrow strip of wilderness, often referred to simply as "wilderness," was a physical barrier that separated the land of Zarahemla from the land of Nephi.

References on the Subject: Alma 22:27-34; 27:14; 43:22-24, 31-35; and 50:7-11.

Analysis of Associations Based on the References:

1. The narrow strip of wilderness extended from the east sea to the west sea (Alma 22:27-29; 50:8-9, 11).

2. Inland, the narrow strip of wilderness was adjacent to both the land of Manti and to the headwaters of the Sidon River (Alma 22:27; 43:22, 24, 32-34; 50:11).

3. The narrow strip of wilderness extended from the east to the west in its orientation to cardinal directions (Alma 22:27-29; 43:22, 35; 50:7-9, 11).

4. The narrow strip of wilderness separated the land of Zarahemla and the Nephites on the north from the land of Nephi and the Lamanite peoples to the south (Alma 22:29, 33-34; 27:14; 43:22-24, 31-35; 50:7-9, 11).

Conclusion: The analyses obtained from the references validate the assumption as stated above. Furthermore, the analyses are also consistent in giving an east-west orientation to the narrow strip and in identifying its inland association with the land of Manti and the headwaters of the Sidon River. The nature of this physical barrier is not explicitly identified; however, its probability of being a topographic barrier such as a mountain chain is implied in the information that the Sidon River originates in its proximity to later drain northward past Zarahemla toward its eventual outlet into an unnamed sea.

Thus, in this example of assumption development, an understanding of the diverse factors relative to the barrier system is clarified and neatly summarized. There is no need to further justify the conclusion through elaborate mechanisms, a technique usually employed to shore up a weak or flawed assumption.

The analyses and conclusion provided above fulfill the criteria outlined for verifying an assumption. All of the references were used to establish consistency in associations that clarify and substantiate the original assumption. If the references should not support the assumption, then the assumption must be altered to correspond most succinctly with all the references. If the references are not consistent, an error is being made in the interpretation of a reference.

All assumptions developed in these chapters are established through the use of these criteria. In the more difficult cases, the analyses of specific assumptions are provided in the discussion. Thus, the development of settlement patterns in the subsequent chapters occurs through this reasoning process coupled with the use of systems concepts as summarized in the addenda. Both processes are interwoven to establish spatial models with the highest possible level of consistency.

The spatial assumptions offered within this work are considered tentative conclusions based on the references that are available and provided in appendix A. These conclusions or hypotheses are not sacred statutes, but rather are a series of consistent explanations that require field testing to establish or refute their validity.

# 4

# TERMS AND PLACE COMPLEXITY IN THE BOOK OF MORMON

The Book of Mormon contains a variety of terms relating to directions and geographic locations that can be interpreted with various meanings. These important geographic terms and their meanings are examined in this chapter.

The historical structure of the Book of Mormon is concerned with the relationships that existed between the Nephite and Lamanite cultures. The incomplete history of their thousand years of peace and conflict is the framework upon which the theological tapestry of the text is woven. As a result, areas where conflicts occurred receive the primary geographic emphasis in the book. Vast interior territories where the populations were concentrated are not described but may only be occasionally noted during journeys or when they become zones of conflict.

The geographic substance of the Book of Mormon is incomplete not only because of this type of partial reporting, but also because the book was never intended to be either a history or a geography. In addition, many fragmentary geographic references are not always readily identifiable but are buried in the elements of the narrative. Ambiguity is the fourth factor that further complicates geographic correlation of the text. Much of the difficulty in understanding the geographic statements in the text stems from the ambiguity of certain terms and concepts.

Ambiguity in the meaning of locational terms occurs when the reader lacks the associations that are required for clarity. Depending on the situation, this lack of clarity may be due to the wording, or it may be the reader's failure to perceive the problem and then to study it through until understanding results.

The term *wilderness* is a good example of apparent ambiguity in the text that can be reconciled by study. Without careful examination of the different uses of the term wilderness, readers of the Book of Mormon will generally consider all wildernesses as inhospitable environments. This conclusion is only partially correct. A wilderness can be an inhospitable barrier, as was the "narrow strip of wilderness" that separated the Nephites from the Lamanites. But the term *wilderness* also is used for an uninhabited but accessible environment, such as the east wilderness, that was colonized by Moroni (see Alma 50:9) after the Lamanites had been driven out of it. Thus, in the former use of the term, a wilderness is an uninhabited zone where the topography and the vegetation preclude easy access or passage, while a wilderness in the latter use of the term is a place that can be inhabited and efficiently used by a population having the appropriate technology.

The frequent difficulty encountered in understanding locational names and terms can be reduced by consulting all the text's references to any given location. Appendix A is a compilation of the settlement and topographic references to geographic locations in the Book of Mormon. This appendix has been provided to facilitate the rapid review of any specific place. Appendix A consists of two parts. Part 1 is a listing of all locations with numerical designation for each location to simplify the geographic models. Part 2 is an alphabetical listing of locations with references provided for each place.

## SETTLEMENT TERMS AND CONCEPTS

Terms for settlements are generally quite clear when applied to cities, towns, and villages. Enviromental loci can also be easily understood in the references to valleys, plains, hills, and rivers.

The difficulty in understanding the text's settlement terminology begins with its references to various lands. *Lands* were those settlement-related territories that were larger than specific settlements and where the environment had some influence on population dispersement. This common term can be best understood by comparing its most divergent uses. On one end of the land spectrum are found the gross distinctions of the greater land northward and the greater land southward. These are clearly large territories encompassing complex topographies and multiple settlements and routes. For consistency and convenience these large-scale lands will be referred to in this volume as "greater" lands.

On the other end of the spectrum are those lands identified by the name of their primary and only referenced settlement — for example, the land of Moroni (Alma 50:13-14; 51:22-24) and the land of Jerusalem (Alma 21:1-2). This latter use of the term involves those zones that can be referred to as "lesser" lands. This category comprises the immediate territory around a given settlement and was probably synonymous for the economic support area used by that settlement's population. Several examples may help clarify these categories of land terminology. In the primary references to the 87 B.C. Amlicite invasion of the city of Zarahemla, as provided in chapter 2 of Alma, initial warfare erupts in the adjacent "lesser" lands of Gideon and Minon to culminate in the "lesser" land of Zarahemla, which name was used synonymously with the city of Zarahemla (c.f., Alma 62:6-7). The land of Nephi is also used in this "lesser" land context in Mosiah 9:6-8; 7:4-7, 21; 20:7-8; 21:1-2, 7-12, meaning those areas immediately about the settlement where the inhabitants of the settlement obtained their subsistence.

Thus, the "greater" and the "lesser" land categories can be readily understood. The intermediate category of "middle" lands will be used to classify those lands referenced in the text that clearly do not fit into either the "greater" or "lesser" lands categories. It is in the "middle" lands within this spectrum where the original authors' perception of territory is not readily apparent in the text. These references pertain specifically to the lands of Zarahemla and Nephi, which are frequently used in a different context from the "lesser" lands category noted above.

The term *Zarahemla* is found in all three contexts — once as a term synonymous with the greater land southward (Ether 9:31); in numerous contexts as the immediate territory or "lesser" land around the Nephite capital city; and yet in other references as an intermediate territory that can only be placed between these two categories. In Alma 22:27-29, 34, for instance, Mormon provides a description of the Nephite and Lamanite territories in the land southward. Nephite holdings on the north of the narrow strip of wilderness are referred to as the land of Zarahemla; Lamanite territory to the south of that barrier zone is called the land of Nephi. Since both lands are (1) situated in the "greater" land southward, (2) involve cultural areas spanning from the east sea to the west sea, and (3) are thus too large to be included as "lesser" lands, this use of Zarahemla and Nephi constitute a "middle" category of lands. Perhaps the "middle" lands can be best understood as separate cultural-political spheres of influence, the "middle" land of Zarahemla being controlled by the Nephite government and the "middle" land of Nephi being dominated by the Lamanite cultures.

The majority of the Book of Mormon consists of Mormon's abridgment of a variety of Nephite records; therefore, the treatment is heavily weighted toward the Nephite culture. Less information is available on Lamanite settlements. This factor is most apparent in examining appendix B, which is an alphabetical listing containing basic information on each settlement cited in the text and incorporated into this study.

Certain interesting factors become apparent in studying the names of Nephite versus Lamanite lands and settlements as shown in appendix B. Of the 27 city-size settlements under Nephite control shown in columns 3, 4, and 7 of this table, 14, or 52%, contained both cities and lands of the same name. In contrast, only seven settlement areas developed by Lamanites can be used in the network analysis. The information on the others is too sparse to permit spatial associations to be developed. Of these seven Lamanite settlements shown in columns 3, 4, and 7, only one site (Jerusalem) contains the same city and lesser land designation. Other than the Lamanite capital of Nephi, which is included as a Nephite settlement in the table because it was originally settled and named by the Nephites, Ani-Anti and Jerusalem are the only Lamanite settlements settled and named by Lamanites. All of the other settlements apparently of Lamanite origin are referred to as lands. This general comparison of the two cultures set forth in appendix B demonstrates the paucity of information available on Lamanite settlements.

The contrasts shown on this table also suggest, as the text states, that the two cultures used different forms of territorial-political jurisdiction, with the Nephites having an established judicial system that brought greater cohesion to their federation. This high incidence of Nephite cities affiliated with settlement territories as shown in appendix B may be a further indication that they established and governed their settlements as autonomous city-states with a centralization of power shared between judicial administrators and priesthood authorities.

The Lamanites, in contrast, had a loosely structured chieftain system of government with the localized rulers sharing common kinship ties. This system existed until 72 B.C., when Nephite rebels gained control of the primary leadership at the Lamanite capital of Nephi (see Alma 47) and probably instituted a more structured system emphasizing central control. Since all the geographic associations among Lamanite settlements are provided before 72 B.C., the basic information given in appendix B suggests their territories were possibly less urbanized than those of the Nephites.

The text further indicates that basic technological differences existed between the two cultures. The Lamanites were evidently farmers and hunters, while the Nephites had a more complex subsistence base possibly oriented not just to agrarian activities, but also to commodity production and long-distance trade (see 3 Nephi 6:11; Helaman 6:11-13). Their extensive commodity production and trade could well explain the curious references that note the rapidity of Nephite economic recovery after periods of intense political stress (cf. Alma 50:17-18; 62:48-51; Helaman 3, 4, 11:20; and 3 Nephi 6:4).

## NORTH AND NORTHWARD

The terms *north* and *northward* are used in a variety of contexts in the Book of Mormon, as are *south* and *southward*, *east* and *eastward*. *Westward* is never used.

A review of the use of these terms is most easily accomplished using *A Complete Concordance of the Book of Mormon*, by George Reynolds (Salt Lake City: Deseret Book Company, 1973).

*North* is most frequently used as a cardinal direction. *North* is also used to describe a portion of the Nephite territory, as the "north country" (Helaman 4:7; Mormon 2:3; Ether 1:1, and 9:35). These references all pertain to the land northward, which was the Jaredite homeland. Thus, *north country* is synonymous with the "greater" land northward.

The term *northward* is used in two basic contexts. It is used in the majority of instances in the descriptive name *land northward*, meaning the area originally inhabited by the Jaredite peoples and later incorporated into the Nephite territory. In the second category, the term *northward* is used as a direction. Seven separate references employ *northward* as a direction (Alma 52:23, 56:22, 36, 63:6; Mormon 2:20; Ether 1:42, 2:1).

*Southward* is used in a manner that parallels the usage of *northward*. In most instances *southward* refers to the land area inhabited by the Nephites and Lamanites that was separated from the "greater" land northward by the narrow neck of land. In two references, however, *southward* is used as a direction (Alma 17:1 and Ether 15:10).

*Eastward* is used only in three places in the text (1 Nephi 17:1; Ether 9:3, 14:26). In all three contexts *eastward* is a direction.

A careful reading of all the references in the text concerning north-northward, south-southward, and east-eastward establishes that all six are never used as interchangeable directions. This means that these six terms are not six ways of defining three cardinal directions, but rather are six different points of the compass. North, south, and east are three of the four cardinal directions. Logic suggests therefore that since northward, southward, and eastward are not identical with the cardinal directions, they must be the intermediate quadrants at 45 degrees between the cardinal points of the compass. But which directions do these three terms represent? In the Book of Mormon does *northward* signify the northeastern or northwestern direction?

The question of which direction northward represents is answered in the text. Mormon clarifies the problem in his account of the final withdrawal of the Nephites from the land southward into the land northward as noted in Mormon 2:3-27. In A.D. 327 the Nephites "began to retreat towards the north countries." Their retreat took them to the land of Joshua, "which was in the borders west by the seashore." At this west sea location, Mormon and his army were able to retain their security until A.D. 345, when they retreated into the "greater" land northward to establish a defense at Jashon. Jashon was in the Jaredite homeland near the hill named Shim that was in the land northward. Withdrawing from Jashon, the Nephite army retreated even deeper into the land northward, for Mormon states "We were driven forth until we had come northward to the land which was called Shem." There is no question that they were fighting in the "greater" land northward because Mormon relates that the Nephites, after obtaining a victory at Shem, mounted an offensive and by A.D. 350 had succeeded in taking "possession of the lands of our inheritance," which means that they had returned into the land southward.

This series of troop movements detailed in the second chapter of Mormon indicate that northward was the northwestern direction. From some unspecified location in the land southward, possibly Zarahemla, the activity progressed in a westerly direction to the west sea where protection was temporarily obtained at the Nephites' traditional refuge in the narrow neck of land. The retreat then continued into the land northward, where the direction of travel from Jashon to Shem was stated as being northward. Since the retreating Nephites were originally intent on finding security in the "greater" land northward, they would have taken the most direct route on departing from Zarahemla. They would not have traveled west to later travel northeast; therefore they were retreating in a general northwestern direction.

This analysis demonstrates that the "greater" land northward was actually northwest of the "greater" land southward and therefore the land southward was southeast of that homeland of the Jaredite peoples. Eastward then, in the Book of Mormon context, meant northeast. Had westward been used, it would have signified the southwestern quadrant.

The Book of Mormon never employs the terms *northwest, northeast, southwest* or *southeast* although these names for the four quadrants were known to at least one of the ancient writers (*south-southeast* is noted as a direction in the Near East as stated in 1 Nephi 16:13). The complete lack of these terms in the text, even though they were known, further substantiates the correlation of northward to northwest, eastward to northeast, and southward to southeast.

The distinction of north from northward is important in understanding spatial associations in the Book of Mormon. The complete consistency found throughout the book in the use of these terms is also important; north and northward as directions were never mixed for any set of locations. This means that these terms can be interpreted as specific directions. The reconstruction of the book's geographic model can proceed in the following chapters using the specific quadrants and cardinal points of the compass as stated in the text with complete confidence in the fidelity of the account.

## THE LANDS OF BOUNTIFUL

The numerous references to the land of Bountiful provided in appendix A demonstrate the existence of two very separate and contemporary entities both given the name Bountiful. References including Alma 22:29-33; 50:11, 32; 63:5; Helaman 4:5-8; and 3 Nephi 3:22-24 all correlate the land Bountiful with the adjacent land Desolation and the west sea. On the other hand, there are references that correlate the land of Bountiful with the adjacent land of Jershon and the east sea (Alma 27:22; 51:26-32; 52:9, 15, 18, 39; 53:3; Helaman 1:28-29; 5:14-16). The spatial associations given in these references are always consistent. The places associated with the east sea Bountiful, including the city of Bountiful, are never mixed with the references and places associated with the west sea Bountiful.

The text contains no reference to an intermediate Bountiful somehow linking the east sea and west sea Bountifuls. These two coastal zones are separate and quite distinct from one another. Thus, the common notion that a single, all-encompassing Bountiful existed spanning the distance between the two seashores is not acceptable, for there are no supporting data for such an assumption.

The answer to this riddle of why two separate lands were identically named Bountiful by the Nephites is contained in the similarities of these places. Both Bountifuls were within the Nephite cultural-political sphere. Environmentally, they were adjacent to seashores in coastal lowland topographies. Both Bountifuls were strategically important to the Nephites, for they each contained narrow passes providing access into separate territories that the Nephites controlled. The west sea narrow pass led into the "greater" land northward via the narrow neck of land (Mormon 2:29; 3:5). The east sea narrow pass[1] beyond the fortified settlement of Bountiful (Alma 52:9) led into the land northward or northwest of that pass and also of the city of Bountiful. It should be noted that the identity of this unnamed northward land has frequently been mistaken for the "greater" land northward, or the Jaredite homeland, because of the ambiguity in the usage of the term *northward*. In reality, the "greater" land northward was accessible only via the land of Bountiful situated on the west seashore. The Book of Mormon contains no references to travel from the "greater" land southward into the "greater" land northward via the east sea land of Bountiful.

The only conclusion concerning the term Bountiful that can be made based on all these references is that two separate Bountifuls existed in the "greater" land southward and that the name *Bountiful* was a descriptive designation probably related to the similar environmental conditions found on those separate coastal lowlands. This supposition is strengthened by the references naming Bountiful as a plentiful wilderness zone "filled with all manner of wild animals of every kind" (Alma 22:31; 3 Nephi 3:24; Ether 10:19-21).

One additional factor further reinforces the premise that two separate Bountifuls existed in the Americas: a third Bountiful is mentioned in the Book of Mormon. Nephi relates in 1 Nephi 17:4-7 that, after leaving Jerusalem in the Eastern Hemisphere, Lehi's party traveled for eight years in the wilderness before arriving on the seashore. This group named the land "Bountiful, because of its much fruit and also wild honey; and all these things were prepared of the Lord that we might not perish. And we beheld the sea, which we called Irreantum, which, being interpreted, is many waters . . . we called the place Bountiful, because of its much fruit."

This reference to an Old World Bountiful contains the identical description as that given to the later Bountifuls of the greater land southward. All three were coastal lands containing a diversity of readily available wild food. Bountiful, therefore, to the peoples of the Book of Mormon, was not a socio-political territory in the same sense as were the "middle" and "lesser" lands of Zarahemla and Nephi. Rather, they evidently used the term *land of Bountiful* as a general description of any specific seashore environment that was naturally abundant in desirable foods.

## THE LAND OF DESOLATION

The land of Desolation is found in two contexts. In several references (Alma 22:30 and Ether 7:6) the land of Desolation is synonymous with the "greater" land northward. In all other contexts, however, it is a more limited area, possibly of "lesser" land status, located in the "greater" land northward (Alma 22:31-34; 46:17; 50:33-34; 63:5; 3 Nephi 3:22-24; Mormon 3:5; 4:1-2, 18-19). These references further establish the city of Desolation in the land of Desolation, both of which were adjacent to the land Bountiful and the west sea. In this limited context, the land of Desolation was a borderland associated with the strategic position referred to as the narrow neck-narrow pass complex that led into the "greater" land southward (Mormon 2:29; 3:5).

The land of Desolation was therefore situated on the northward side of the border in the "greater" land northward, and the land of Bountiful was southward from the narrow pass in the "greater" land southward (Alma 22:31). This border position was referred to by Mormon as the "line Bountiful and the land Desolation" (Alma 22:32; Helaman 4:6-8). These two references indicate that the narrow neck was so restrictive that a line of fortifications was established across the corridor to control Lamanite access into the "greater" land northward. This line of fortifications extended from the east to the west seashore and could be traversed by a Nephite in a day to a day and a half. In Alma 22:33, a similar statement is made that "the Nephites had inhabited the land Bountiful, even from the east unto the west sea."

Note that all three references are consistent in content; all specify that the west sea Bountiful and its "line Bountiful" extended from the east and connected with the west sea. All three comments lack any reference to the east sea. The following section assesses the ramifications of this identification.

## CONCEPTS AND ANALYSES OF THE NARROW NECK

The narrow neck of land separated the "greater" lands northward and southward at the "line Bountiful" border between the lands of Desolation and Bountiful (Alma 22:31-32). The preceding section showed that no reference actually names the east sea in association with either the narrow neck or with the west sea land of Bountiful. Several questions arise. Is it warranted to assume that the east sea is implied in the three references? Is the resulting model consistent with all the other geographic information supplied in the text?

Three options actually exist for the analysis of the narrow neck locality. The first and most traditional concept is that the east sea is implied in these three references (Alma 22:32, 33; Helaman 4:7). This assumption thus identifies the narrow neck–narrow pass/passage as an identical unit, an isthmus connecting two larger land masses flanked by the east sea and the west sea. For clarity, this concept can be called the "isthmus" option.

The second option, referred to as the "modified isthmus"

concept, is based on the assumption that the east sea did not form the eastern terminal of the "line Bountiful." This assumption is consistent with the omission of any direct naming of the east sea in these three references. This concept is based on the assumption that Mormon identified the narrow neck as an isthmus connection between the lands northward and southward (Alma 22:31-34) but that the narrow pass or passage is not identical with that narrow neck or isthmus. Rather, the narrow pass was a strategic complex much smaller than the isthmus and situated within the narrow neck or isthmus adjacent to the west sea.

The third option for explaining the narrow neck topography can be referred to as the "coastal corridor" concept. This assumption is also based on the exclusion of the east sea from the proximity of the narrow neck of land, consistent with the three references noted above. In this concept, the narrow neck of land is identical to the narrow pass/passage strategic complex. The major difference between this concept and the other two is the elimination of an isthmus connecting the greater lands northward and southward. In other words, the narrow neck/passage/pass was identical with the "line Bountiful" defense system and was situated on a narrow coastal plain flanked by the west sea. This fortified complex, which was a day to a day-and-a-half travel in length, could not be flanked by a hostile army attacking northward from the land of Bountiful. The west sea served as the western barrier while an unspecified formidable land barrier lay along the eastern flank of the fortified complex.

The question thus arises: Which of these three options is correct? Veracity lies with the concept that has the greatest clarity and simplicity, is most consistent, and correlates best with all the other supporting geographic information in the text.

Consider the references in Alma 22:27-34. The east sea is mentioned by name only in verses 27 and 29 in the context of the lands of Nephi and Zarahemla. An inference to the east and west seas is also made in the second phrase of verse 32: "And thus the land of Nephi and the land of Zarahemla were nearly surrounded by water." Since Zarahemla and Nephi were "middle" lands in the "greater" land southward, and since both lands were separated by the narrow strip of wilderness barrier zone that extended from the east sea to the west sea, this phrase is not concerned with the coastal condition of the "greater" lands northward and southward and therefore is not relative to an isthmus association. In addition, no information is given establishing any proximity between the east sea and the the west sea.

Alma 50:25-36 relates the rebellion of the Nephites of the settlement of Morianton situated on the borders of the east sea. This people fled Nephite control seeking safety in the "greater" land northward. They left the east sea, taking a course that led to the west seacoast, for Teancum in pursuit "did not head them until they had come to the borders of the land Desolation; and there they did head them, by the narrow pass which led by the sea into the land northward, yea, by the sea, on the west and on the east." This reference is consistent with all others and indicates that movement from the land southward into the greater land northward could be accomplished only through a narrow pass in the borders of the land of Desolation adjacent to the west seashore.

The inhabitants of the land of Morianton left their east sea locality to journey via the west sea land of Desolation into the land northward. Their defeat by the narrow pass is clear. But what is not clear in this reference is whether they were defeated by the Nephite army attacking on the seashore from the east and the west, or whether they were defeated at a place where there was a shoreline on their east and their west. Based on a comment in the book of Ether, there is a good possibility that Morianton was defeated at a place in the narrow neck where coastal lagoons existed on both the east and the west of the battleground. Ether 10:19-21 relates that a city was built during the reign of Lib "by the narrow neck of land, by the place where the sea divides the land." These references examined together suggest that an estuary and lagoon may have existed in the vicinity of the narrow neck, possibly resulting in a very narrow coastal shelf restricting travel northward into Desolation.

The narrow neck is referred to again in Alma 63:5 relative to the shipbuilder Hagoth. To facilitate colony resettlement into the land northward, Hagoth "built him an exceedingly large ship, on the borders of the land Bountiful, by the land Desolation, and launched it forth into the west sea, by the narrow neck which led into the land northward." No indication is given in this reference to the nearby existence of an isthmus or an east sea. The next reference to the border zone between Bountiful and Desolation relates to an incident in A.D. 17 when the Nephites withdrew into that defensive position for protection against the Gadianton robbers (3 Nephi 3:13-26; 4:1-28). Here no references are made to either the east or west seas, nor to the narrow neck or an isthmus. The scripture simply states in 3 Nephi 3:23 that the Nephites gathered in "the land which was between the land Zarahemla and the land Bountiful, yea, to the line which was between the land Bountiful and the land Desolation." The references to the lands Bountiful and Desolation and to the line between these localities, coupled with the later verses (3 Nephi 4:23-26) concerned with the defeated robbers' aborted attempt to flee into the "greater" land northward, all indicate that the scene of this conflict was in the narrow neck by the west sea.

The remaining references to the narrow neck–narrow pass locality relate to the final Nephite war and the Nephites' struggle to retain the city of Desolation in the land of Desolation. With the treaty of A.D. 350, the Nephites and Lamanites divided the lands of their inheritance. "The Lamanites did give unto us the land northward, yea, even to the narrow passage which led into the land southward. And we did give unto the Lamanites all the land southward" (Mormon 2:28-29). The Nephites then consolidated their armies "at the land Desolation, to a city which was in the borders, by the narrow pass which led into the land southward. And there we did place our armies, that we might stop the armies of the Lamanites, that they might not get possession of any of our lands; therefore we did fortify against them with all our force" (Mormon 3:5-6). These references leave no doubt that this site of conflict was in the narrow neck vicinity, even though the west sea is never directly mentioned. Once again no reference is made either to the east sea or to an isthmus condition.

After a review of all the references on the narrow neck/passage/pass, the following statements can be advanced:

1. The references pertaining to this geographic area contain no specific mention of an isthmus condition. That concept stems partially from a misinterpretation of Alma 22:31-33. The problem occurs when the first and second phrases of verse 32 are linked, and the problem is reinforced by the inaccurate linking of the second and third phrases of that verse. Phrase one states: "And now, it was only the distance of a day and a half's journey for a Nephite, on the line Bountiful and the land Desolation, from the

east to the west sea." This phrase explains the distance across the narrow neck or corridor in terms of travel time along the line that separated the lands of Bountiful and Desolation. This line ran from an unstated location on the east to terminate on the west sea.

Phrase two of verse 32 reads: "Thus, the land of Nephi and the land of Zarahemla were nearly surrounded by water." This phrase notes the association of the lands of Zarahemla and Nephi to adjacent seas. Facts 8 and 9 as stated in chapter 3 establish that the "middle" lands of Zarahemla and Nephi were in the "greater" land southward and were flanked on the east and west by those respective seas, consistent with the information given in this second phrase.

Phrase three of this verse states: "There being a small neck of land between the land northward and the land southward." This phrase, when compared with phrase two, is concerned with three entirely different topographic features: (1) the narrow neck of land, (2) the large land areas northward from that narrow neck, and (3) the large land areas southward from that narrow neck.

A careful reading of all three phrases leaves no doubt that each discusses distinctly separate but interrelated subjects. The narrow passage area of the line Bountiful in phrase one is actually related to the description of the narrow neck or passage given in phrase three. These two phrases describe the same subject using two separate associations — distance across and "greater" land relationships. They can be linked. Phrase two is an anomaly; its only common feature with either of the other two phrases is its reference to seas, specifically the west sea association. The line Bountiful is also associated with the west sea, as noted in phrase one, but this commonality hardly justifies any conclusion that phrases one and two are identical or discuss the same topic.[2]

2. The flawed concept that the east sea lies on the opposite side of the narrow neck from the west sea is introduced in the misconception discussed in the preceding paragraph. All three references on this narrow neck geographic area (Alma 22:32, 33; Helaman 4:7) contain no mention of the east sea, but only note a general direction east. Since all three references are identical and none uses the term *east sea,* it is erroneous to assume that an east sea is implied in these references. What is actually related is that the land of Bountiful, incorporating the line Bountiful, was

inhabited from its eastern periphery to the shore of the west sea. The reader is left in doubt as to the type of land-form that actually constituted the eastern periphery of that land. Had the original writer intended to state that Bountiful was inhabited from the east sea to the west sea, he would undoubtedly have made that important distinction in at least one of the references in the text.

The Book of Mormon contains absolutely no information that the narrow neck was an isthmus. Thus, the "isthmus" and "modified isthmus" options discussed above should be discarded. When the criteria for establishing accuracy in assumptions, as discussed in chapter 3, are consulted, the "coastal corridor" option is found to be consistent with all the information provided in the text. In addition, the use of the "coastal corridor" option brings further clarity to the reading of these geographic associations. The general coordination of the "greater" lands northward and southward with their associated seashores is simplified by these basic topographic relationships.

The picture that emerges after discarding the idea that the narrow neck was an isthmus is quite simple. There was a land northward where the Jaredites settled and a land southward where later the Nephites and Mulekites settled. These large areas were separated by a narrow corridor or land bridge that paralleled the west sea. The boundary between the land of Desolation to the north and the west sea land of Bountiful to the south was in this narrow corridor and was more then a day's march from its eastern periphery to the west seashore. The lands of Zarahemla and Nephi, situated in the land southward, were bounded by seas on the east and on the west. No reference is made to the east sea bordering either the narrow corridor or the land northward.

Consider the irony of this situation! By proposing the replacement of the almost sacred "isthmus" theory with the coastal corridor hypothesis, an interesting sequence of associations has transpired. For years the narrow neck of land has been thought of as an isthmus connecting two large land masses. This association has directed some individuals to identify the Isthmus of Tehuantepec in Mexico as the prime candidate for the narrow neck. The faulted Tehuantepec–narrow neck association combined with that area's advanced ancient civilization have justified a general placement of the Book of Mormon geography in its actual setting. But, the inherent inadequacy of the Isthmus of

Tehuantepec–narrow neck correlation has hampered detailed Book of Mormon correlations in the area. Scholars have been so tied to an isthmus explanation that they have not grasped the book's more specific geography.

## NOTES

1. This diversity of narrow passes leading into separate lands that lay northward from the passes could represent an error in the text, and Moroni may have been stating that he would be fortifying the west sea narrow pass while he was in the vicinity of the west sea.

If, on the other hand, the statement in the text is accepted as correct, then in 67 B.C. Moroni's epistle to Teancum was indeed directing Teancum to fortify a pass near the east sea settlement of Bountiful. This conclusion results from the fact that Teancum was at the east sea defensive zone plotting an attack on the Lamanite-controlled city of Mulek (Alma 52:1-18) at the same time that Moroni was in the west sea region strengthening those defenses against their enemy. It is thus inconsistent with the references to assume that Moroni intended Teancum to leave his position on the east sea and journey into west sea lands under Moroni's control to develop a strategic control at the west sea narrow pass.

This assumption of a separate narrow pass near the east sea is also consistent with an occurrence during the later conflict of 51 B.C. when Lamanite forces under the control of the dissident Coriantumr sacked Zarahemla and then initiated an advance on the city of Bountiful near the east sea, "for it was his determination to go forth and cut his way through with the sword, that he might obtain the north parts of the land" (Helaman 1:22-29). This reference clearly indicates the existence of a route from Zarahemla to the city of Bountiful that then led north into an undisclosed portion of the land of Zarahemla adjacent to the east sea.

2. This analysis of the phrases in verse 32 should not be construed as the primary argument justifying the reasoning for a coastal land bridge versus the isthmus theory. Rather, this examination is advanced to demonstrate the disparity of the three phrases that have so long been casually accepted as descriptions of an isthmus condition. The inadequacy of the isthmus interpretation stems from (1) the lack of any specific isthmus description in any Book of Mormon reference, and (2) the fact that spatial analyses of all the book's locations fail to demonstrate an east-west sea proximity that would be associated with an isthmus.

# 5

## SYMBOLS, PATHS, AND ROUTES

Identification of the geography of the Book of Mormon must be based on the analyses of its locations as units in a system. Spatial analysis, or the study of how places interrelate in their terrestrial space, provides the theoretical means for this application. This chapter begins the analyses by discussing the basic elements of a settlement model — symbols, paths, and routes.

Human beings organize the distribution of their activities upon the face of the earth. This distribution is referred to as spatial organization and involves the relationships between people's places of activity and the natural environment. Spatial organization in a settlement system, such as that described in the Book of Mormon, can be understood by studying the structure of the settlement system and examining the processes such as trade, warfare, and resource procurement that influenced the location of settlements.

Commenting on the interaction of structure and process, geographers have stated that these two factors are "a fundamental aspect of any locational problem, so that whether we are trying to explain the distribution of neolithic agricultural sites in Europe or whether we are trying to decide where to locate a number of hospitals to serve a spatial distribution of people, we can break the problem down into terms of process, structure, and their interaction" (Abler et al. 1971:88). This chapter will examine through descriptive means the settlement system in the Book of Mormon to facilitate the later discussions of the processes involved in shaping that structure.

Settlement systems are simply abstractions about human habitations and their spatial layouts. They consist of clusters of habitation and associated activity locations and the interaction in movement of peoples, goods, services, and information within the system. The difference between past and present settlement systems is associated with the environmental diversity and the choices available to each culture in adapting to and using its environment.

The way people use space involves both conscious and unconscious decisions within which operates the basic "law of minimum effort" or *lex parsimoniae*. To quote the geographer Peter Haggett, the concept of *lex parsimoniae* "suggests that natural events reach their goal by the shortest route. It appears first in physics in the eighteenth century with the work of Lagrange as the 'principle of least effort' and reappears in systems analysis as the concept of 'minimum potential energy,' in operations research as 'geodesics' (or optimal movement paths), and in the social sciences as the 'principle of least effort' " (1966:32).

This concept is important in an analysis of the settlement networks in the Book of Mormon, for it enables the identification of the least-effort routes between places based on references in the text. The corollary assumption is that other potential routes were not mentioned in the text probably because terrain features or distance did not accommodate minimum effort travel between the locations. Since mountain, wilderness, and river barriers are explicit factors in settlement distribution and route development, as stated in the Book of Mormon, then the "law of minimum effort" provides a practical means of understanding and explaining route relationships.

## RESEARCH PHASES AND NETWORKS

Before proceeding with a spatial analysis of the Book of Mormon, a discussion of the method and symbols used to conduct the investigations is pertinent. An examination of the procedures that are used in the following chapters will greatly facilitate an understanding of the settlement systems being studied. The research begins with the most simple associations and moves toward the identification and analyses of the more complex networks, progressing through a series of research phases into a definition of the comprehensive model of the entire system.

The reference information correlated in appendix A pertains to each settlement or place mentioned in the text that can be integrated into the final model. These basic references are established on the locale level, and that is where the networks analyzed in chapters 6, 7, and 8 originate as basic localities.

A localized system of places or vertices in specific areas of Book of Mormon territory is identified in this study as a district. Districts are postulated using network analysis of connected localities as demonstrated from the references correlated in appendix A. Five districts have been established in this study. These districts include the Moroni, Cumeni, Nephi, Joshua, and Moron districts and are presented in chapters 6 and 7 in their initial series as preliminary network graphs.

After the analysis of districts, these units are consolidated into regions in this study. The first three districts noted above are in the greater land southward complex and are thus consolidated into the preliminary Manti regional network in chapter 6. The other two districts, Joshua and Moron, are primarily situated in the greater land northward and are combined in chapter 7 into the preliminary Desolation regional network system.

The final consolidation of both regions into an area network showing the comprehensive coordination among all the individual localities within one single system occurs in chapter 8. The area model is not as advanced as the final comprehensive network, for it too is a part of the initial series of models developed in this first phase of spatial system reconstruction. This initial series of models on the district, region, and area level of complexity experiences further refinement in chapter 9 during their correlation with the topography of southern Mesoamerica.

As the analyses of districts, regions, and area systems progress in chapters 6 through 9, using graph networks, all the settlement and topographic localities are incorporated, resulting in these basic comprehensive models or base models as they will be referred to throughout this volume.[1]

## SYMBOLS FOR PLACES

Settlement models are best displayed using the most simple arrangements. This is why model locations in this study are given numerical designations and why symbols are used to show topographic places such as plains, hills, and river crossings. Adding names to these symbols only makes the associations more complex, obscuring the geometric relationships. Therefore, proper names are given only in the legends.

A system is shown using two-dimensional graphs. A settlement system has a geometric quality consisting of places (vertices) and interconnecting routes (edges). If the system is linear, demonstrating a series of connected places, that system is referred to as a path.

Figure 2 presents the symbols used to represent the places and routes in this study.

Some lesser lands (see appendix B and the discussion in chapter 4 on "lesser" lands) do not have identified settlements (i.e., city, town, or hamlet) within the land. Therefore, the symbols include both settlement-specific positions and lesser land positions as shown in figure 2A. All squares are symbols for specific cities, towns, or villages referenced in the text, while all numbered circles symbolize lesser lands that may or may not have a referenced habitation zone (i.e., city, town, or hamlet). The reason for this difference is shown in appendix B, where a number of lesser lands are given that have no reference to a primary settlement (e.g., Amulon, Antionum, Antum, etc.). In contrast, other references in appendix B are to specific settlements where no information is given concerning the lesser land where they were situated (e.g., Angola, Ani-Anti, Antiparah, etc.).

Figure 2B is a complex graph where three places are all in association, two as specific settlements and the third as a lesser land. The difference in the edges between these places is shown as either dashes or lines. The line indicates a close and direct relationship between two places as indicated in the text. Dashes show a relationship that may be distant and could involve the intermediate positioning of settlements and even lesser lands that are not referenced in the book.

Figure 2C shows a segment taken from the Moroni Network described in chapter 6. Here four lesser lands and their relationships to the east sea are demonstrated. All four lands have direct associations with at least one other place. To travel from Aaron (8) to Moroni (5), one must go through Nephihah (3) or via Lehi (9) if the longer route is taken. In Alma 50:13-15, 25 and 62:30-32 the associations of these lesser lands are provided. Note that, although all are referred to as cities in the text, their status as lesser lands is signaled in the statement that Nephihah joined both the borders of Aaron and Moroni. Thus, lesser-land symbols have been used in this graph, rather than the town or city symbols,

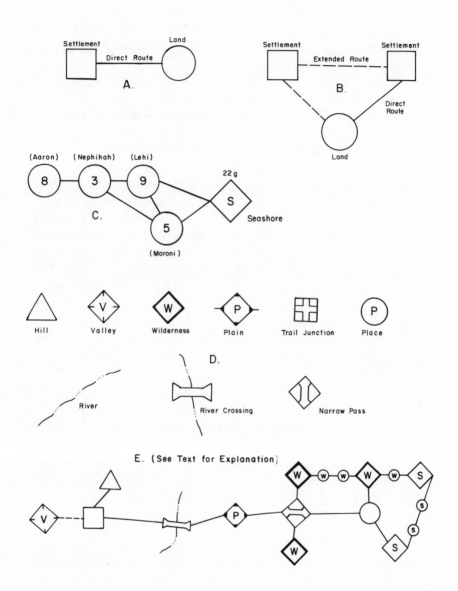

FIGURE 2:     Explanation of Graph Network Symbols Used in This Volume

because other unnamed cities may have existed in these lands as implied in Alma 62:32. The use of additional symbols to convey nonsettlement environmental locations is conveyed with the seashore symbol in figure 2C.

The seven environmental symbols used in this study are presented in figure 2D.

Figure 2E is a hypothetical graph that demonstrates symbolic associations used in the network models. It is not a model that correlates with the Book of Mormon settlements and terrain, but has been prepared to explain network associations using the variety of symbols developed in figures 2A through 2D. North in figure 2E is associated with the top of the page, and east and west are to the right and left respectively. Reading this graph from left to right indicates that a valley has an extended route association eastward to an urbanized settlement that is directly associated with a hill to its northeast and a river crossing to the east. The river crossing is directly connected to a plain that ultimately leads east to a narrow pass in a wilderness complex to the north and south. To the east of the narrow passage, the route is directly linked to a minor land that is adjacent to a seashore on the southeast. The wilderness area to the north of the minor land also connects with the wilderness to the west and to the seashore to the east as shown by the circled W links. The circled S links between the two seashore symbols demonstrate a constant expanse of sea along the southeastern, eastern, and northeastern flanks of the minor land.

The variety of symbols shown in figures 2A through 2E will be used to diagram the networks of the Book of Mormon, beginning with an explanation of paths and routes.

## PATHS AND PLACES

The use of connected paths presents the most practical means of beginning an assessment of the spatial organizations of the Book of Mormon. A path consists of two or more direct and/or extended routes. In spatial terminology, a path is a "collection of routes linking a series of different places" (Abler et al. 1971:256) — for example, a path connects New York City and Los Angeles via Baltimore, Knoxville, Little Rock, and Albuquerque. Another path includes a series of intermediate routes between

New York and San Francisco via Philadelphia, Indianapolis, Cheyenne, and Salt Lake City. A third path links New York and Seattle via Cleveland, Chicago, and Billings. These three paths have only one place in common, New York; hence they are relatively simple geographical associations. By adding the connecting paths between Seattle–Los Angeles, Billings-Albuquerque, and Chicago-Knoxville, the system becomes much more complex and efficient for transportation.

A similar condition exists in the Book of Mormon. An analysis of its settlements results in the identification of four important paths situated in the land southward. These consist of the Zarahemla-Nephi path, the Zarahemla–City Bountiful path, the Moroni–City Bountiful path, and the Manti-Judea path. All four paths share common locations; thus, by connecting these various paths, a complex transportation system can be demonstrated.

## THE ZARAHEMLA-NEPHI PATH.

The connecting routes between Nephi and Zarahemla are shown in figure 3. This figure contains two separate graphs of the Nephi-Zarahemla path with the first (A) demonstrating the network with its variety of localities and routes.

The path shown as figure 3A is the most referenced series of routes identified in the text. It was first used about 200 B.C. during the initial withdrawal by Mosiah and his followers from Nephi when they journeyed north to Zarahemla. Numerous references exist that indicate that the multiple routes on this path were generally in a north-south orientation. Settlements along the path include from north to south, Zarahemla (1), Gideon (7), Minon (6), Manti (4), Shilom (41), and Nephi (43).[2]

This path contained topographic features in addition to settlements. The wilderness zone between Manti and Shilom was actually a segment of the narrow strip of wilderness (50a and b) that extended east to west from the borders of the east sea to the west sea, serving as a formidable barrier to north-south movement (Alma 22:27-29; 50:6-11). From about 200 to 35 B.C., the lands of the Nephites occupied the areas north of this barrier, while the lands of their enemies, the Lamanites, occupied the area to the south of this "narrow strip of wilderness" (see the discussion in chapter 3 for an analysis of this mountainous bar-

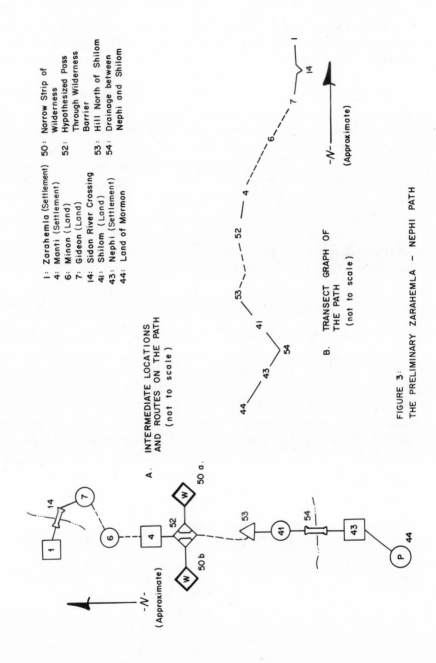

1: Zarahemla (Settlement)
4: Manti (Settlement)
6: Minon (Land)
7: Gideon (Land)
14: Sidon River Crossing
41: Shilom (Land)
43: Nephi (Settlement)
44: Land of Mormon

50: Narrow Strip of Wilderness
52: Hypothesized Pass Through Wilderness Barrier
53: Hill North of Shilom
54: Drainage between Nephi and Shilom

A. INTERMEDIATE LOCATIONS AND ROUTES ON THE PATH
(not to scale)

B. TRANSECT GRAPH OF THE PATH
(not to scale)

-N-
(Approximate)

-N-
(Approximate)

FIGURE 3:
THE PRELIMINARY ZARAHEMLA – NEPHI PATH

rier). The most descriptive geography of the text comes from the 72-60 B.C. war, when the Nephites used this narrow barrier zone as part of their defensive system against Lamanite invasions into their territories.

Several other topographic features are shown on the Nephi-Zarahemla path. These include the corridor through the wilderness (50) south of Manti, which for convenience is symbolized as a narrow passage (52) in figure 3A. Other features on the path include the river crossing (14) between Zarahemla and the land of Gideon, the hill (53) north of Shilom, a natural drainage channel (54) between Nephi and Shilom, and the extensive area known to the Nephites as the land of Mormon (44).

Figure 3B is a transect of the same graph without the site symbolism. A transect is different from a path or series of transportation routes as it represents a vertical view of the earth as though the terrain had been bisected from Zarahemla to Mormon. Here the lower river crossing on the Sidon River (14) and the drainage (54) between Nephi (43) and Shilom (41) are shown as the lowest elevations, contrasted with the higher elevations associated with the hill north of Shilom (53) and the pass through the narrow strip of wilderness (52) adjacent to but above and south of Manti (4). The land of Mormon (44) is to the south or southwest of Nephi since it was adjacent to Jerusalem, which was to the south or southeast. Mormon was also above Nephi, for it is the area where Alma, while in hiding, could observe the activities of Noah's forces at Nephi.

Figure 3 provides two different ways of viewing a segment of a network, either as a path (3A) or as a transect (3B) through the terrain. Both graphs are consistent with the information given in the text—Zarahemla was north of Nephi, and movement between these two places always went down to Zarahemla from Nephi or up to Nephi from Zarahemla.

## THE ZARAHEMLA–CITY BOUNTIFUL PATH

The second path to be introduced is the Zarahemla–City Bountiful path demonstrated in figure 4. This path consists of a series of routes extending eastward from Zarahemala (1) to the land of Bountiful (2) in the borders of the east sea (22a). This path includes the river crossing (14) east of Zarahemla and the inter-

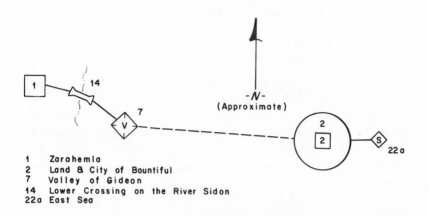

1   Zarahemla
2   Land & City of Bountiful
7   Valley of Gideon
14  Lower Crossing on the River Sidon
22a East Sea

FIGURE 4:   The Preliminary Zarahemla –
            City Bountiful Path

mediate valley of Gideon, where the land of Gideon (7) lay. An extended route from the Zarahemla-Gideon complex connects with the City of Bountiful in the east sea land of Bountiful (2).

The east-west orientation of this path is based on the fact that the east sea was east of Zarahemla, as stated in Alma 22:29, 27:22, and 50:7-11. This route therefore lay to the north of, and was parallel to, the narrow strip of wilderness barrier zone that extended in an east-west direction between the shores of the east and west seas (not shown in figure 4).

This path is first noted relative to Chief Captain Moroni's troop movements in the 72-60 B.C. war. In 62 B.C., Nephites at Zarahemla rebelled against their government and forced the chief judge, Pahoran, to flee to the land of Gideon for safety. This insurrection came at a very difficult time for the Nephites during the major Nephite-Lamanite war. In his letter to Moroni, Pahoran requested that Teancum and Lehi, Moroni's lieutenants, be left in charge of the Nephite forces in that sector while Moroni came to the aid of the tottering government (Alma 61). Moroni, Lehi, and Teancum at that time were defending the Nephite fortifications in the east sea area, specifically the recently recaptured fortifications at

Mulek and Gid. Their base of command at the nearby fortified city of Bountiful was probably Moroni's residence when he received Pahoran's letter. Thus, to respond to Pahoran's request, Moroni departed from the east sea defensive complex and traveled westward to the land of Gideon.

The existence of the Zarahemla–City Bountiful path is further confirmed during the troop movements relative to the Lamanite invasion of Zarahemla in 51 B.C. After sacking Zarahemla, Coriantumr, a Nephite dissenter, rapidly moved his troops eastward to capture the city of Bountiful. His march through the "center of the Land" was not successful, and he was subsequently defeated by Moronihah's forces (Helaman 1:14-33).

## THE MORONI–CITY BOUNTIFUL PATH

The third path, as shown in figure 5, is more complex, for it involves the series of routes and settlements near the east sea that linked Moroni (5) with the fortified site of Bountiful (2). This path includes the east seashore and the lands of Lehi (9) and Morianton (10) and the settlements of Omner (11), Gid (12), and Mulek (13). All of these places are directly connected, as the routes in figure 5 indicate, with the exception of the route between Mulek and Bountiful, which passed through a plain that was situated between these settlements. These direct routes, plus the fact that all seven settlements were adjacent to the east sea (cf. Alma 50:13, 15, 25; 51:22, 25-26, 28, 32), indicate that the Moroni-Bountiful path was situated within a relatively small area flanked by a single shoreline.

This path, as shown in figure 5, is not oriented to the cardinal directions; directions will be identified as this complex is further analyzed in the following chapter.

The close proximity of Bountiful, Mulek, and Gid is further indicated in the missionary journeys of Lehi and Nephi about 30 B.C., when they traveled from the city of Bountiful to Gid and then to Mulek (cf. Helaman 5), as shown by the routes in the diagram. Figure 5 also includes a route directly between Gid (12) and Morianton (10) based on the information in Alma 55:25-26 and 33 concerning Moroni's preparations for an attack on Morianton after the recapture of Gid. No reference is made to Omner (11), which may have been in a position that it could be bypassed by the Nephite army.

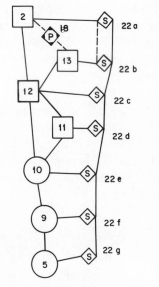

2: Bountiful
5: Moroni
9: Lehi
10: Morianton
11: Omner
12: Gid
13: Mulek
18: Plain
22: East Seashore

Note: direction not
specified on
this graph

FIGURE 5: The Preliminary Moroni -
City Bountiful Path

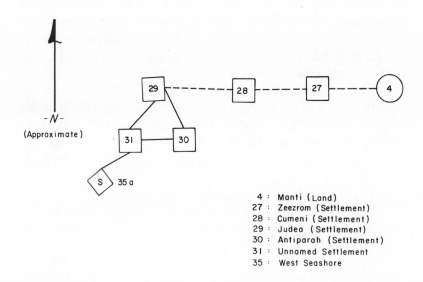

- N -
(Approximate)

4 : Manti (Land)
27 : Zeezrom (Settlement)
28 : Cumeni (Settlement)
29 : Judea (Settlement)
30 : Antiparah (Settlement)
31 : Unnamed Settlement
35 : West Seashore

FIGURE 6: The Preliminary Manti - Judea Path

The east sea, as shown in figure 5, consists of a series of direct routes linked to a variety of seashore vertices. Any location on a body of water is theoretically directly accessible by boat to any other position on that same body; thus, this sea path represents the connectivity among adjacent seashores via waterborne travel. Since coastal shipping was used by the Nephites (Alma 63), it is appropriate to demonstrate that any coastal settlement adjacent to the seashore was theoretically accessible by sea from any other settlement located on that same coast.

Land travel along the seashore from the city of Bountiful (2/22a) to Mulek (13/22b) is indicated by the broken line of the indirect route that connects these two shoreline locations. Alma 52:22-27 details the ploy used by Moroni to decoy the Lamanite defenders away from the captured fortifications at Mulek. In this instance, a small Nephite force marching by the seashore was pursued northward along the coastline to the land of Bountiful, where they subsequently lured their enemy into a trap and thus defeated the Lamanite forces from Mulek. The shoreline route between Mulek and Bountiful is thus represented by the extended route shown in figure 5.

## THE MANTI-JUDEA PATH

The fourth path, as shown in figure 6, links the land of Manti (4) with the settlement of Judea (29), which was near the west sea. This path ran generally east to west, extending from Manti through the settlements of Zeezrom (27), Cumeni (28), and Judea (29) to an unnamed city (31) which, like Judea, was located near the west seashore. Mentioned only during the 72 B.C. war, this path roughly paralleled the western half of the narrow strip of wilderness barrier zone as described in Alma 50:8-11.

Antiparah (30) was probably the Nephite forward-fortified position in the west sea locality as noted in verse 11. Thus, with its fall and the subsequent Lamanite capture of Cumeni, Zeezrom, and Manti by 66 B.C., the need was apparent to the Nephites that Judea would have to be strengthened and the Antiparah and Cumeni localities recovered before they could mount a successful attack on fortified Manti in its central position. For this reason, the Nephites began the counterattack on the west sea, where the Lamanites probably least expected an offensive to develop. From that point, the Nephite armies moved eastward, capturing Anti-parah and Cumeni through the use of strategy to minimize casualties. No comment is made in the record of the recovery of Zeezrom; perhaps this settlement was in such a position that it could be bypassed by the Nephites without fear of flanking attacks severing the communication link between Cumeni and Manti.

The four paths discussed above and demonstrated in figures 3 through 6 form the basic framework of the spatial system of the land southward. These paths demonstrate how the two-way flow of armies, travelers, information, goods, and services occurred among the various places situated on these interrelated paths. Interconnectivity of these places is lacking, however, and can best be established by dividing the land southward into three districts to be individually reconstructed using these paths.

## NOTES

1. The base model incorporating both environmental and settlement locations has also been simplified into strictly a settlement model for use in conducting the systems analyses that are addressed in addendum 2. The base model of the Book of Mormon area developed in chapter 8 is further refined in chapter 9 and addendum 2 into the Secondary Area Network used by the author to study and identify the Mesoamerican localities of the Book of Mormon peoples.

2. The numbers following the place names are the designations for those places and are consistently associated with the adjacent name to aid the review of the network graphs. These numbers are identical with the designations provided in appendix A.

# 6

# SPATIAL STRUCTURE OF THE MANTI
# REGION IN THE LAND SOUTHWARD

The Nephite-Lamanite period of occupation in the land
southward provides the most detailed geographic information found in the Book of Mormon. This chapter establishes the network of places and routes in the land southward by linking the various paths identified in the preceding
chapter.

The analysis of the spatial system that was in the land southward of the Book of Mormon involves the important settlements
of Zarahemla and Nephi and the peripheral east sea and west sea
settlements—all coupled by the diverse paths identified in the
preceding chapter.

Three separate districts, entitled the Moroni, Cumeni, and
Nephi networks, are developed as base models of the spatial
associations of the land southward. These three systems are then
integrated into the Manti Regional Network, a base model of the
land southward.

## THE MORONI DISTRICT NETWORK

The Moroni Network is the first to be discussed among the
three networks that make up the greater land southward. Figures
7 and 8 are demonstrations of the development of this base model.
Shown in two parts for reader convenience, figure 7 is a preliminary organizational outline of the network to be compared with
figure 8, a graph of the base model for this district. The following
discussions on the Moroni Network involve all the identifiable
locations found in this vicinity, whether settlement or topographic
features, and incorporate those loci drawn from appendix A into
figures 7 and 8.

This network incorporates a part of the Zarahemla-Nephi path

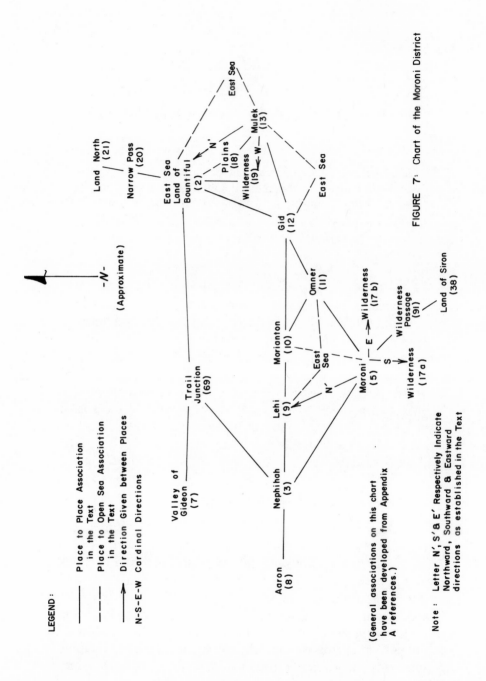

Land North (21)
Narrow Pass (20)

East Sea
East Sea
Land of Bountiful (2)
N'
Plains (18)
Mulek (13)
Wilderness (19) W
East Sea
Gid (12)

Valley of Gideon (7)
Trail Junction (69)
Omner (11)
E ——▶ Wilderness (17 b)
Wilderness Passage (91)
Land of Siron (38)

Morianton (10)
Lehi (9)
East Sea
N'
Moroni (5)
S
Wilderness (17a)

Aaron (8)
Nephihah (3)

FIGURE 7: Chart of the Moroni District

(General associations on this chart
have been developed from Appendix
A references.)

Note: Letter N', S'& E' Respectively Indicate
        Northward, Southward & Eastward
        directions as established in the Text

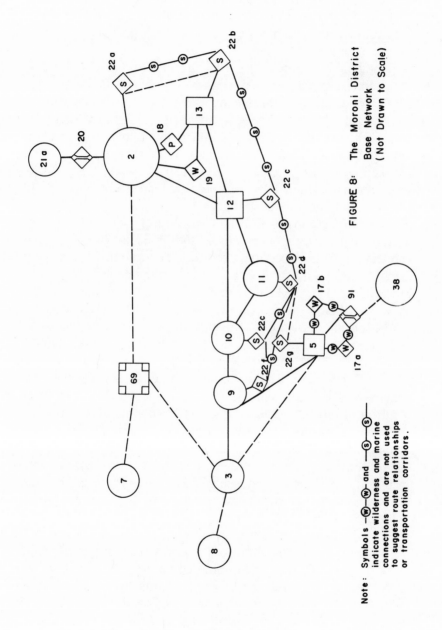

FIGURE 8: The Moroni District
Base Network
(Not Drawn to Scale)

Note: Symbols —Ⓦ—Ⓦ— and —Ⓢ—Ⓢ—Ⓢ—
indicate wilderness and marine
connections and are not used
to suggest route relationships
or transportation corridors.

and all of the Zarahemla–City Bountiful and Moroni–City Bountiful paths discussed in the preceding chapter. It also contains connections between certain places that were prominent in these separate paths.

The land of Moroni (5) is a key position in the identification of the spatial association of the east sea Nephite settlements. Four important routes linking Moroni with other locations can be established in the text. These routes include Moroni's link to the south with the land of Siron (38), in the Lamanite controlled "middle" land of Nephi, and connections to the lands of Nephihah (3), Lehi (9), and possibly Omner (11). Thus, the Moroni–City Bountiful association is more complex than is apparent in the initial path demonstrated in figure 5.

Moroni was constructed in the east sea region by chief captain Moroni at the commencement of the 72-60 B.C. war with the Lamanites. It was placed in a very strategic location, blocking the Lamanite army's most direct entrance into the eastern portion of the "middle" land of Zarahemla. In Alma 50:13 reference is made to Moroni being located on the "south by the line of the possessions of the Lamanites." This information, correlated with the description of the Lamanite lands given in preceding verses 7-11 and in Alma 22:27 and 29, demonstrates the strategic nature of this fortified settlement. Furthermore, Alma 62:34 states that wilderness zones were situated on the settlement's eastern and southern flanks, as shown in figure 8. This comment is consistent with the placement of Moroni to the north and adjacent to the Lamanite lands. The route southward, through a passage (91) in the wilderness and on to the Lamanite land of Siron (38), is shown in figure 8 using direct and extended routes. These wilderness areas adjacent to Moroni were segments of the narrow strip of wilderness that separated the "middle" lands of Nephi from Zarahemla, as noted in these references.

Moroni was on the shore of the east sea, for it was "sunk in the depths of the sea" at the time of the tectonic disturbances associated with Christ's crucifixion at Jerusalem (3 Nephi 8:9; 9:4). Since wilderness areas lay to the east and to the south of Moroni, the east seashore was situated to the north of the settlement. Moroni's route inland to the land of Nephihah would have extended to the west or northwest, eliminating the possibility of the seashore being in that quadrant.

Nephihah (3) was constructed contemporaneously with Moroni, being adjacent to the latter's border and positioned between the lands of Aaron (8) and Moroni (5) (Alma 50:14). Nephihah's direct route to Lehi (9) demonstrates its location to the west of both Lehi and Moroni, for Nephihah was not on the seashore as were these two fortifications (Alma 51:25). Additionally, Lehi had been constructed "in the north by the borders of the seashore" (Alma 50:15). Lehi's direct access to both Moroni and Nephihah indicates not only its proximity to those settlements, but also that its position was to the north of Moroni, as stated in the reference. These data further refine the relationship of Moroni to the east sea, placing the seashore to the northeast of Moroni.

The existence of the sea adjacent to both Moroni and Lehi is not a contradiction. Lehi and its adjacent neighbor, Morianton (10), were apparently situated on the north shore of the sea, while Moroni was on the south shore. The western shoreline, which provided access from Moroni to Lehi, must have existed to the north or northwest of Moroni and to the east of Nephihah, as shown in figure 8.

Lehi's accessibility to Lamanite attack from Moroni is noted in Alma 51:24. This reference states that, with the fall of Moroni, the refugees from that settlement traveled to Nephihah for safety, while the Nephite defenders at Lehi "gathered themselves together, and made preparations and were ready to receive the Lamanites to battle."

The Nephites, anticipating a direct assault from the area of Moroni (5) on either Lehi (9) or Nephihah (3), established depth in their defensive system. Both Lehi and Nephihah were positioned to flank a major assault along the west shore of the sea against either fortification. Had the Lamanites struck against Lehi, then the Nephite forces at Nephihah could have launched an effective counterattack against the enemy's exposed flank. In addition, had Lehi fallen, the fortifications at Morianton would have been the next line of Nephite defense and a secure position for the retreating people of Lehi.

Chief captain Moroni's planning for the defense of the east sea settlements was very thorough. His placement of these fortified settlements around the shoreline from Moroni to Mulek afforded maximum protection against a Lamanite invasion into the Nephite heartland. The north shore of this portion of the east sea was too narrow to afford the Lamanites the option of flanking these Nephite positions, as is evident in the Nephites' effective use of a pincer movement to recapture these settlements in 60 B.C. (Alma 62:30-32).

The Lamanite victors at the captured fortification of Moroni evidently had a different strategy prepared for the capture of the north shore Nephite settlements as evidenced by their success. In short order they captured all of the Nephite possessions along the east sea with the exception of the land of Bountiful. The text in Alma 51:26 only notes that this major defeat included Nephihah (this is probably a reference to the loss of the lands of Nephihah and not the loss of the city of Nephihah, which continued to be defended by the Nephites until its fall in 62 B.C.). The Nephites were also defeated at Lehi (9), Morianton (10), Omner (11), Gid (12) and Mulek (13). The Lamanite army was finally stopped by a determined Teancum and his army at the border of the land Bountiful.

Several clues are given as to why the Lamanites were so successful in this series of conquests despite the Nephites' best planning and preparations. The Lamanites evidently mounted a surprise offensive—not against Lehi or Nephihah, where they were expected, but against the center of the north shore fortifications, attacking probably in the vicinity of Omner (11). The evidence for this assumption is found in Alma 59:5, which states that the Nephite defenders at the fortifications of Moroni, Lehi, and Morianton took refuge at Nephihah and augmented the forces at that site. Had the cities of Lehi and Morianton been taken by a direct assault coming from the fortifications at Moroni, as was envisioned by the Nephite leaders (cf. Alma 51:24), their refugees would have fled eastward away from the enemy and away from Nephihah. The narrow seashore would have been too confining for the defeated Nephites from both settlements to retreat around the Lamanite flank, pass by the enemy, and find refuge at Nephihah to the west in the Lamanite rear.

The Lamanite forces succeeded in capturing the east sea defenses by crossing the east sea water barrier, perhaps at a narrow configuration in that waterway, and then striking the center of the Nephite line, where they were least expected. Their attack then split into two offensives. One force drove to the west against the rear defenses of Morianton (10) and later Lehi (9). The vanquished Nephites at those sites were compelled to withdraw westward through each fortification, eventually to find refuge at Nephihah, as stated in Alma 59:5.

The right prong in the Lamanite offensive turned east against Gid (12) and then Mulek (13) before being halted by Teancum at the entrance into the east sea land of Bountiful. Nephite defenders and their families captured during the fighting at these fortifications were confined at Gid for about four years until the recapture of that site in ca. 63 B.C. (see Alma 55).

The large concentration of Nephite prisoners held at the captured site of Gid (12) is consistent with the assumption that the Lamanites split the Nephite defensive line by staging a surprise attack in the vicinity of Omner (11). Their drive eastward was so rapid that the Nephites at Gid (12) and Mulek (13) had no time to evacuate their families to safety in the land of Bountiful—hence, the large numbers of captured Nephite men, women, and children imprisoned at Gid.

The Lamanite route from Moroni (5), along the south seashore directly across the narrows of the east sea, to the vicinity of Omner (11) on the north shore is shown in Figure 8. Its existence is further verified by the strategy used by the Lamanites to avoid their enemies late in the war. In 61 B.C., the Nephites recaptured Nephihah (3), and the defeated Lamanites fled that settlement going directly to their defenses at Moroni. The Nephites then turned their attention on the recovery of Lehi (9), Morianton (10), and probably Omner (11). To capture these fortifications, Moroni mounted an offensive directly against Lehi (9), while the Nephite forces at Gid (12) and Mulek (13) initiated a second front against the Lamanite defenses on the east. Thus, the Lamanite defenders of these fortifications were caught in a pincer movement between Nephite armies advancing from both the east and the west. The north shore was too restricted to allow the defenders any maneuverability around either assault force. Alma 62:30-33 indicates that the Lamanites at Lehi, under attack from Moroni's forces, fled "from city to city, until they were met by Lehi and Teancum; and the Lamanites fled from Lehi and Teancum, even down upon the borders by the seashore, until they came to the land of Moroni." The Nephites would not have allowed the Lamanites safe passage along their flanks on the north seashore. This reference, therefore, demonstrates the existence of a linking route from the vicinity

61

of Omner across the waterway and then along the south shore to Moroni.

The Moroni-Omner route was more than a safe corridor for the retreating Lamanite armies in the east sea region. It initially provided them with accessibility and the element of surprise needed in capturing the north shore settlements. In addition, during their occupation of the north shore, this route facilitated their needs for rapid supply and reinforcement from their rear areas. The Moroni-Omner connection provided the Lamanites with a much safer and more rapid means of communication than would have been possible using the Moroni-Lehi route, a link that was accessible to interdiction by the Nephite forces at Nephihah.

The fortified settlement at Nephihah was the last Nephite settlement in the 72-60 B.C. war to fall to the enemy. Its inland position from the east sea made it an effective blocking position against Lamanite invasion from Moroni and Lehi as long as a sufficient Nephite force could maintain the fortification.

The large Lamanite force that had been displaced at Manti by Helaman in 63 B.C. became an added danger to the Nephite garrison at Nephihah. By combining with the Lamanite forces in the Nephihah locality, they tipped the balance and Nephihah fell (Alma 59:5-9). The retreating defenders fled the city by evidently taking a secure route north as shown in figure 8. Eventually these refugees, which included remnants of the original defenders of the fortifications at Moroni, Lehi, and Morianton, joined Moroni's army headquartered at the Bountiful (2), Gid (12), and Mulek (13) complex. This route north from Nephihah to the Gideon-Bountiful path at junction 69 was the supply and reinforcement corridor for the defenders of Nephihah, and it was their route of retreat when they could no longer defend the fortification. Accessibility northward into the Nephite heartland, as shown in figure 8, demonstrates why this settlement could remain a Nephite bastion for five years while being surrounded on the east, west, and south by Lamanite forces.

To recover Nephihah and also terminate the insurrection in Zarahemla, Moroni gathered forces while traveling from Bountiful to Zarahemla via the land of Gideon (7). Later, after taking control at Zarahemla, Moroni traveled to Nephihah on an undisclosed route and successfully attacked that walled city. The Lamanite defenders at Nephihah were forced to withdraw through the narrow pass in the east entrance of the fortified settlement and to flee into the land of Moroni (5), as noted in Alma 62.

The fortified city of Bountiful on the east sea was also connected by a variety of routes to a number of locations, as noted in the text. It had a series of direct connections to the fortified settlements of Mulek (13) and Gid (12). One route from Bountiful passed through a plain (18) before reaching Mulek (Alma 52:20). Another route passed through a wilderness (19) on the west of Mulek before linking with that site (Alma 52:22). As shown in figure 8, travel from Bountiful to Mulek could also be along the seashore (22a-22b) near Bountiful (Alma 51:28-32; 52:2) and then southward along the coast to the shoreline near Mulek (Alma 52:22-23).

The city of Bountiful was also near a narrow pass (20) that led into a land northward from Bountiful (21) as stated in Alma 52:9. This reference has prompted speculation that this settlement was near the narrow neck of land that linked the greater lands northward and southward and that this is the passage that led into the greater land northward. Such is not the case. Spatial analysis of the city of Bountiful establishes its proximity to Moroni and the east sea. Although the references note that separate lands named Bountiful were on both the east and the west seas, the city of Bountiful is related strictly to the east sea locality. In addition, no connecting routes are mentioned between this settlement and any settlements or lands known to have been adjacent to either the narrow neck or within the Jaredite homeland of the greater land northward.

Evidently a vast territory existed to the north of the "middle" land of Zarahemla, a territory that is referenced in this instance as the land northward of the city of Bountiful. This is the territory that Teancum was protecting from the Lamanites during their major offensive in the east sea locality, as noted in Alma 51:28-30. It is this narrow pass entrance into the northern territory that Moroni was concerned with protecting; hence, his directive (Alma 52:9) to Teancum, based at the east sea city of Bountiful, to establish defenses around that pass.

The Nephite concern for the protection of this northern territory is also noted later in their history. In 51 B.C. a Lamanite attack on Zarahemla in the "center of the land" was successful, and the Lamanite army under Coriantumr's command redirected its offensive eastward toward the city of Bountiful, as recorded in Helaman 1:23-31:

> For it was his [Coriantumr's] determination to go forth and cut his way through with the sword, that he might obtain the north parts of the land. . . .
>
> But when Moronihah had discovered this, he immediately sent forth Lehi with an army round about to head them before they should come to the land Bountiful.
>
> And thus he did; . . . before they came to the land Bountiful, and gave unto them battle, insomuch that they began to retreat back towards the land of Zarahemla. . . .
>
> And now behold, the Lamanites could not retreat either way, neither on the north, nor on the south, nor on the east, nor on the west, for they were surrounded on every hand by the Nephites.

Coriantumr's route of march indicates that the "north parts of the land" were therefore more accessible via the east coast land of Bountiful than they were by traveling directly north from Zarahemla. Coriantumr would have taken a more direct route from Zarahemla had one been available.

## THE CUMENI DISTRICT NETWORK

The second of the three networks in the land southward consists of the Cumeni Network, as shown in figures 9 and 10. This system incorporates aspects of the Zarahemla-Nephi and the Manti-Judea paths discussed in chapter 5. The central aspect of this graph involves the associations of the Ammonihah complex with these paths.

The Manti-Judea path, as developed in its preliminary format in figure 6, can now be expanded to include other routes and locations. Two routes appear to have existed linking Manti (4) with Cumeni (28). The primary route evidently did not include Zeezrom (27), for this settlement appears to have been bypassed by Helaman during the recapture of Cumeni and Manti. The inclusion of Zeezrom in the list of captured Nephite settlements (see Alma 56:14) and the subsequent lack of any reference to its recapture later in the war indicate that it was situated outside the direct corridor. Possibly Zeezrom was located on a secondary path that was more accessible to the Lamanites.

Information on the primary Manti-Cumeni path is provided in Helaman's commentary on troop movements during the 72-60 B.C. war. In Alma 57:22, 30-31, a Lamanite force sent from Manti to reinforce their besieged garrison at Cumeni was defeated by Helaman and "driven back to the city of Manti." This reference establishes Manti's important connection in the path to Judea and is consistent with the direction and tactics used by Helaman in recovering this series of captured Nephite strongholds. He began on the borders of the west sea with the recapture of Antiparah (30) and then proceeded to Cumeni (28), which he secured before advancing along the primary route to attack the heavily fortified city of Manti (4).

Two important locations existed on the main path between Manti and Cumeni, a trail junction (88) and the settlement of Melek (26). Trail junction (88) is the point where the primary east-west Manti-Cumeni path crossed a north-south path that connected the Nephite settlement of Ammonihah (23) with the Lamanite capital of Nephi (43), as shown in figure 10. This junction is not mentioned in the Book of Mormon. Spatial analysis of these two paths, which extend in different directions, suggests that they junctioned in this general location, hence the designation of this junction as locus 88.

The Nephite land of Melek (26) was situated three days' travel to the south of Ammonihah (23) and was "on the west of the river Sidon, on the west by the borders of the wilderness" (Alma 8:3, 6). Melek was one of the places where Alma the younger conducted missionary work among the Nephites in 82 B.C. Later the converted people of Ammon were resettled from the east sea land of Jershon to Melek to protect them from Lamanite reprisals (Alma 35:13). Since the land of Melek was in the "middle" land of Zarahemla, to the southwest of Zarahemla and west of the Sidon River, the wilderness (33) that is noted on its borders may have been associated with the narrow strip of wilderness that served as a barrier to Lamanite aggression from the south (see discussion on that barrier in chapter 3). Certainly the Nephite desire to move the converted Lamanites from Jershon to a more protected area indicates that the land of Melek, although near the southern borders of the Nephite territory, was not easily acces-

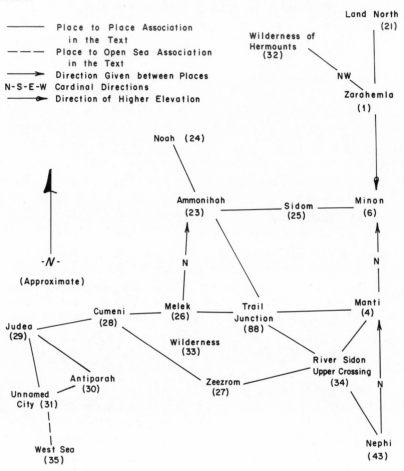

FIGURE 9: Chart of the Cumeni District

(General associations on this chart have been
developed from Appendix A references.)

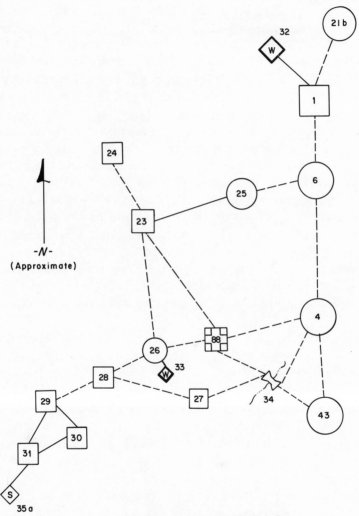

FIGURE IO: The Cumeni District Base
Network (not drawn to scale)

sible to their enemies on the south—hence it was not on the Nephi-Ammonihah path nor on the southern route leading to the more vulnerable Zeezrom.

The secondary Manti-Cumeni path included Zeezrom (27) and the upper crossing of the Sidon (34). This river crossing, a junction of the Nephi-Ammonihah path, marks the location where Nephites ambushed a Lamanite force in 81 B.C. A Lamanite army invaded Nephite territory by traveling the routes symbolized by the Nephi-Ammonihah path. After destroying Ammonihah and taking captives from both Ammonihah and the land of Noah (24), the Lamanite raiders traveled southward on this trail returning to Nephi. A Nephite army, led by chief captain Zoram, left Zarahemla to intercept the raiders. Zoram had learned from Alma that the Lamanites would "cross the river Sidon in the south wilderness, away up beyond the borders of the land Manti. And behold there shall ye meet them, on the east of the river Sidon. . . . And it came to pass that Zoram and his sons crossed over the river Sidon, with their armies, and marched away beyond the borders of Manti into the south wilderness, which was on the east side of the river Sidon" (Alma 16:6-7).

This reference indicates that the Nephites traveled from Manti to arrive on the east bank of the crossing, as shown in figure 10. In addition, the ford was beyond Manti within the south wilderness or the narrow strip of wilderness that separated the Nephite and Lamanite territories.

The extended route placed for convenience to the north of Ammonihah marks the trail that led to the fortified settlement of Noah (24). In 72 B.C., at the beginning of that major war, a second Lamanite invasion from the land of Nephi, probably traveling this same Nephi-Ammonihah path via the upper crossing of the Sidon River (34), attempted an assault on the rebuilt Ammonihah. Alma 49:1-25 relates that the attacking force found Ammonihah heavily fortified and so moved on to the land of Noah to unsuccessfully attack that position. The frustrated Lamanite army eventually withdrew from Noah into the wilderness and returned to the land of Nephi.

The land of Sidom (25) was the refuge for Nephites driven out of Ammonihah (23) during Alma the younger's missionary experiences in that settlement. As indicated in Alma 15:18 and shown in figure 10, Sidom was accessible to Zarahemla and may have been a small settlement on the bank of the river. The names of the river and the settlement are so similar that an editorial error on page 226 of the 1830 edition of the Book of Mormon misspelled as Sidom the name of the River Sidon (cf. Alma 2:17).

Zarahemla (1), the Nephite capital, was linked with several areas to its north, as demonstrated in figure 10. This settlement had direct access to the north and to the west with the Hermounts wilderness zone (32). This is the area where the defeated Amlicites and Lamanites fled in 87 B.C. after their invasion of Zarahemla and subsequent defeat by Alma at the lower River Sidon crossing (14), as related in Alma 2.

Zarahemla also had access via the Sidon River into the unnamed land to its north (21). The general south-to-north flow of the River Sidon through the "middle" land of Zarahemla is indicated by references in the text on terrain (see also figure 3B). The headwaters of the river Sidon were situated above Manti and adjacent to the south wilderness or the narrow strip of wilderness mountain chain (Alma 16:6-7; 22:27, 29; 50:11). Since Manti was south of Zarahemla and Gideon (Alma 17:1) and at a higher elevation than these settlements, the Sidon flowed down from Manti past Zarahemla. This river therefore had a northward flow through the Nephite territory. The text provides no information on the land mass traversed by the river beyond Zarahemla, nor are there references to this river crossing the known lands that bordered either the east sea or the west sea.

The mouth of the River Sidon emptied into the sea (Alma 3:3; 44:22) but which sea? The identity of that sea may be partially revealed by Mormon's statement in Helaman 3:8 that the Nephite population covered "the face of the whole earth, from the sea south to the sea north, from the sea west to the sea east." This statement is consistent with the comment in Alma 22:32 that "the land of Nephi and the land of Zarahemla were nearly surrounded by water." Since the River Sidon flowed to the north through the land of Zarahemla, draining the northern slopes of the narrow strip of wilderness mountain barrier, and since no further reference to this river is made relative to the east and the west seas, it can be postulated that the Sidon flowed into the north sea.

The probable association of the Sidon with the north sea may explain the route to Zarahemla used by the people of Zarahemla in the first half of the sixth century B.C. The record states that this company, which included Mulek the son of King Zedekiah, arrived by ship in the "land north" (Helaman 6:10), meaning the greater land northward. Either at the time of their arrival or at some later time in their history they met and buried the last Jaredite leader, Coriantumr (Omni 1:21; Ether 13:21). Eventually these people "came from there up into the south wilderness" (Alma 22:30-31) to establish a colony at Zarahemla, which was in the center of the land southward (Helaman 1:24-25). Their travel was probably by boat along the shore of a sea, which is assumed to be the north sea, and then up the river to Zarahemla. It was at Zarahemla in the third century B.C. that they were joined by King Mosiah and the Nephites who had traveled north on the Zarahemla-Nephi trail from their abandoned homeland at Nephi.

## THE NEPHI DISTRICT NETWORK

The final localized network to be considered in the spatial analysis of the land southward system consists of the Nephi District Network as developed in figures 11 and 12. This network contains the southern portion of the Zarahemla-Nephi path, the Mormon-Middoni circuit, and the Antionum complex near the east sea.

The Antionum complex in the east sea locality, east of Zarahemla, is where Nephite colonies were established prior to 74 B.C. (Alma 27:22, 26; 30:59; 31:3). Nephite expansion into the east sea zone after 74 B.C. was a result of the Lamanite-Zoramite threat and led to the development of the fortified settlements noted in Alma 50:13-15 and described above in the Moroni Network. However, prior to that period of expansion, the Nephite and Lamanite lands adjacent to the east sea were less populated and, for simplicity, can be best examined as aspects of the Nephi District Network.

A description of the Antionum complex, as shown in figure 12, is centered on the association of Jershon (36), Antionum (37), and Bountiful (2). Jershon, the initial land where the people of Ammon settled around 78 B.C. (Alma 16:12), was near the east seashore and south of the east sea land of Bountiful. This Bountiful was also on the east of Zarahemla and bordered the east sea, as shown by vertex 22h (Alma 27:22).

The land of Antionum was settled by a colony of Nephites known as Zoramites. It was situated near the east sea, east of

Zarahemla, south of Jershon, and near the wilderness south, or the narrow strip of wilderness (Alma 31:3). In addition, Antionum was situated adjacent to and probably north of the Lamanite land of Siron (38), as noted in Alma 39:3.

The defection of the Zoramites from the Nephite cultural sphere was cause for concern to the Nephites. This problem resulted in the missionary efforts of Alma, two of his sons, and his associates attempting to reconvert the Zoramites (Alma 31-35). Their mission further exacerbated the division between the Nephites and the Zoramites, forcing the Zoramite converts to flee for the safety of Jershon. The remaining Zoramites became even more radically opposed to the Nephites; they eventually united with the Lamanites in preparing for war against both the people of Ammon and the Nephites at Jershon (Alma 35:1-11). This instability in the east coast region resulted in a variety of occurrences pertinent to the geography of the Nephi Network. First of all, the people of Ammon were removed inland to Melek, which is demonstrated in figure 12 by the extended route going westward from Jershon (36) to the narrow passage (52) on the borders of the land of Manti (4). In preparation for war, Antionum and Jershon were garrisoned by the opposing armies. At that time, Moroni was appointed chief captain over the Nephite forces and initiated fortifications in the Jershon area (Alma 35:13; 43:3-16; 50:7-10, 13-15).

The resulting conflict between the two cultures expanded into the major 72-60 B.C. war, which did not, however, begin in the Antionum complex. Rather, the Lamanite forces withdrew from Antionum and journeyed westward, traveling south of the narrow strip of wilderness barrier zone to commence an attack on the land of Manti (Alma 43:22). The extended routes shown in figure 12, leading from Siron (38) back into the land of Nephi (43) and then northward to the highland entrance (52) in the wilderness (50) leading into the land of Manti (4), demonstrate the route taken by the Lamanites in their attempt to invade Manti.

Moroni, alerted of the enemy's plans, traveled from the land of Jershon (36) into the land of Manti (4) to ambush and defeat the Lamanites at the third Sidon crossing (Alma 43 and 44). His route was identical with that taken by the people of Ammon earlier when they had departed from Jershon and had traveled through the land of Manti to resettle at Melek. Moroni's early arrival in

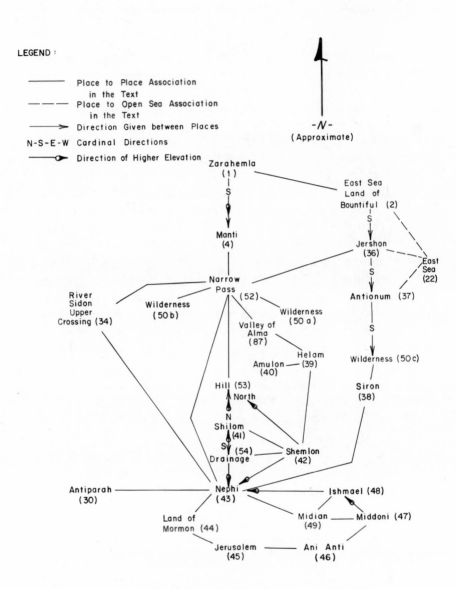

LEGEND :

———————— Place to Place Association
           in the Text
– – – – – Place to Open Sea Association
           in the Text
————————➤ Direction Given between Places
N-S-E-W  Cardinal Directions
————————◗ Direction of Higher Elevation

-N-
(Approximate)

Zarahemla
(1)
S

East Sea
Land of
Bountiful (2)
S

Manti
(4)

Jershon
(36)
S

East
Sea
(22)

Narrow
Pass
(52)

Antionum (37)

River
Sidon
Upper
Crossing (34)

Wilderness
(50 b)

Wilderness
(50 a)

Valley of
Alma
(87)

S

Helam
(39)

Wilderness (50 c)

Amulon
(40)

Siron
(38)

Hill (53)
North
N

Shilom
(41)
S (54)
Drainage

Shemlon
(42)

Antiparah
(30)

Nephi
(43)

Ishmael (48)

Midian
(49)

Middoni (47)

Land of
Mormon (44)

Jerusalem
(45)

Ani Anti
(46)

FIGURE 11: Chart of the Nephi District

(General associations on this chart have been
developed from Appendix A references.)

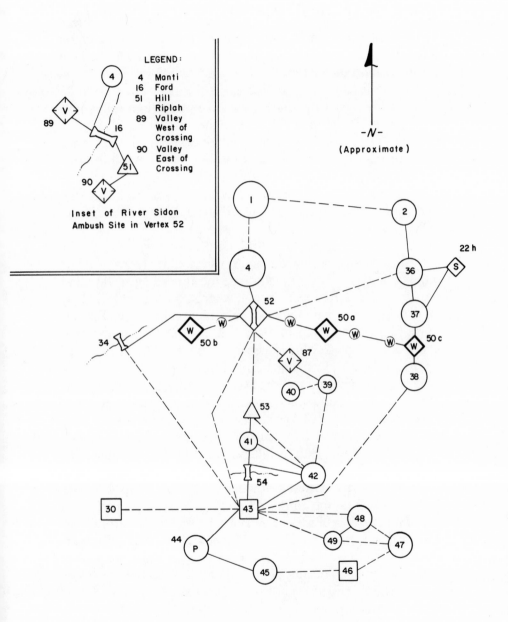

FIGURE 12: The Nephi District Base Network
(not drawn to scale)

the borders of the land Manti (see inset in figure 12 for a graph of the ambush site) permitted him the time necessary for making the ambush arrangements.

Moroni established the ambush at the river crossing in 73 B.C. by placing an army under Lehi's command in a valley (90) to the south of the hill Riplah (51) on the east bank of the Sidon. He did this to cut off the Lamanite withdrawal from the ford once they had passed on the north of the hill Riplah. Another army was placed in the valley (89) on the west bank of the river. A third force was placed northward along the west bank blocking a Lamanite movement toward Manti (Alma 43:32, 42), as shown in figure 12.

This river crossing should not be confused with the earlier ambush site at the river crossing (34) situated to the west of this entrance into the land of Manti (see the preceding section and figure 10). The ford at position 34, where Zoram established his ambush in 81 B.C., was "in the south wilderness, away up beyond the borders of the land of Manti" (Alma 16:6-7). The crossing where Moroni placed his forces in 73 B.C. was "by the head of the river Sidon, . . . down into the borders of the land Manti" (Alma 43:22, 32). This first ambush site in 81 B.C. was on the path between Nephi and Ammonihah and contrasts with the later movement of the Lamanite army of 73 B.C. That army was intent on attacking the Nephites in the land of Manti. Thus, the two ambush sites were located on two entirely different routes at two separate river crossing locations.

Further warfare could have been averted with this Lamanite defeat in 73 B.C. at the entrance into the land of Manti had it not been for a Nephite dissenter. Amalickiah, seeking control of the Nephite government, rebelled against the authorities and fled with a small force to Nephi (43). There, through intrigue, he gained control over the Lamanite peoples in the following year (Alma 46, 47). The extended route from Nephi to the river crossing at point 34 demonstrates the probable path in 72 B.C. followed by Amalickiah's forces to besiege the Nephite fortifications at Ammonihah and Noah as discussed in the preceding section (Alma 48:4-6; 49:1-25).

An extended route is shown from Nephi (43) to Antiparah (30) in figure 12. This transportation link represents the general route used by the Lamanites in the 72 B.C. war to reinforce their garrison at that captured Nephite fortification near the west sea. A similar extended route on the east shows the general connection, probably via the land of Siron (38), that the Lamanites used in their attacks on the east sea. By this date the lands of Jershon and probably Antionum had been recolonized by Nephites who, under Moroni's direction, had established a series of fortified settlements to increase their protection (Alma 50:7-15).

Closer to the settlement of Nephi, several minor complexes can be identified. To the north of Nephi and incorporating a segment of the Zarahemla-Nephi path lay the complex that included the hill north of Shilom (53), Shilom (41), the valley of Alma (87), the minor settlements of Helam (39) and Amulon (40), and the troublesome Lamanite settlement at Shemlon (42). The path from Nephi (43) to the hill north (53) of Shilom and then northward to the narrow passage (52) through the narrow strip of wilderness (50) represents the basic routes followed by Mosiah during his withdrawal from Nephi as reported in Mosiah 11:13. This was probably the same primary route used by the Zeniff colony going to Nephi (Mosiah 9), the Ammon party from Zarahemla searching for the remnants of the Zeniff colony (Mosiah 7), and the sons of Mosiah in their missionary journey to the Lamanites (Alma 17).

An extended route also ran northward from Nephi to the passage through the narrow strip of wilderness zone, bypassing Shilom (41) and the hill north (53). This route represents the trail taken by the people of Limhi when, for the second time, the Nephites abandoned the land of Nephi. The remnants of that Nephite colony, escaping from the land of Nephi with Ammon's search party, traveled to the west around the land of Shilom (Mosiah 22:6-13) and the hill north of Shilom because those localities had evidently been occupied by the hostile Lamanites. Earlier, following the death of King Noah and the subjugation of the people of Limhi at Nephi, the Lamanite ruler had established guards "round about the land, that he might keep the people of Limhi in the land, that they might not depart into the wilderness" (Mosiah 19:28). Ammon's arrival at Nephi led to the Nephite escape by departing at night out of the city of Nephi via the back pass. To avoid detection, they followed this circuitous route around the land of Shilom to return eventually to the main route and travel through Manti and down into Zarahemla.

Several factors suggest that this extended route followed by the people of Limhi to avoid Shilom (41) lay to the west of the main Zarahemla-Nephi path. Limhi and his party would have taken the most distant route from the Lamanite stronghold at Shemlon (42) in order to avoid detection. The main entrance of the city of Nephi was probably on the east, similar to the layout of Nephihah (Alma 62:18-25). An eastern orientation of these settlements for the sunrise observance and morning sacrifice rituals would have been similar to the temple complex orientation at Jerusalem and in keeping with the Israelite tradition claimed in the Book of Mormon. Thus, on the assumption that the entrance of Nephi was in the eastern wall, then the back pass was probably in the western wall of the settlement.

Should this assumption of the orientation of Nephi be correct, then the Lamanite center at Shemlon (42) was situated to the east or northeast of Nephi adjacent to and below the settlement of Shilom (41). This assessment is based on the statement that the tower near the Nephite temple at Nephi overlooked both the lands of Shilom and Shemlon (Mosiah 11:12). Shemlon was also situated at a lower elevation than Nephi, since the references consistently state that the Lamanites at that settlement always went up to attack Nephi, but travel from Nephi was always down to Shemlon. Shemlon also had access up to Nephi, probably via the drainage system (54) that lay between Nephi and Shilom (Mosiah 9:14-15). And, as also demonstrated in figure 12, travel north from Shemlon was up to the hill north (53) of Shilom (Mosiah 10:6-10).

The connectivity of the valley of Alma (87) and lands of Helam (39) and Amulon (40) within the Nephi Network is demonstrated by the direct and extended routes linking Shemlon (42) on the east with the passage through the narrow strip of wilderness (52). This path is identified in Mosiah 23 and 24. Its probable location to the east of the main Zarahemla-Nephi path is based on the assumptions that Shemlon was eastward from Nephi and that, had the Helam-Amulon (39-40) complex been to the west, either the Ammon search party or the people of Limhi during their travels would have made contact with Alma and his followers at Helam (39) or with Noah's priests at Amulon (40). Instead of Alma's colony at Helam being discovered by friendly Nephites, they were found by the Lamanite search party seeking the route taken by Limhi's people. The fact that the Lamanites were disoriented and required Alma's direction in order to find the most direct route back to Shemlon and Nephi (Mosiah 23:35-37) indicates the complexity of the terrain. The extended route in figure 12 between Helam (39) and Shemlon (42) indicates the trail that the Lamanites followed after placing Alma's colony under subjugation.

Alma and the small colony of Nephites at Helam, finding life intolerable under the domination of the Lamanites and Noah's priests from Amulon, eventually escaped to the valley of Alma (87). From there they traveled northward for 12 days, probably via the main route through Manti, before finally finding safety at Zarahemla (Mosiah 24:20-25).

The extended route from Nephi (43) to the upper crossing of the Sidon (34) represents the trail used by the Lamanite armies during their several campaigns against Ammonihah, as discussed in the preceding section.

The final complex of the Nephi Network involves the Mormon-Middoni circuit, which contained the settlements of Nephi (43) and Ani-Anti (46) and the lesser lands of Mormon (44), Jerusalem (45), Middoni (47), Ishmael (48), and Midian (49). A direct route connected Nephi to the land of Mormon (Mosiah 18:4-5, 30-31; Alma 5:3), which possibly was higher in elevation and to the south or southwest of Nephi, being Alma's place of retreat where he hid from Noah's forces at Nephi. The land of Mormon was between Nephi and the land of Jerusalem, for Mormon and Jerusalem shared a common border (Alma 21:1) as reflected in the direct route between the two shown in figure 12.

Nephite missionary journeys from Jerusalem to the village of Ani-Anti (46) and from there into the lands of Middoni (47), Ishmael (48), and the connecting land of Midian (49) are noted in Alma 21:11-12 and 24:5 and are demonstrated as extended routes on figure 12. In addition, two extended routes show Middoni's links with the settlements of Nephi (43) and Ishmael (48), both of which were uphill from Middoni (Alma 20:1-8; 22:1, 3-4). Since Ishmael was at a lower elevation than Nephi (Alma 20:2), as were the Lamanite lands of Shemlon and Middoni, all four settlements may have shared a common drainage system that evidently flowed toward the east, based on the assumption that Shemlon and the Ishmael-Middoni routes were to the east of the city of Nephi. The drainage shown as locus 54 in figure 12 and situated between Nephi and Shilom may have been a tributary of that hypothetical river system, based on Zeniff's statement:

> For, in the thirteenth year of my reign in the land of Nephi, away on the south of the land of Shilom when my people were watering and feeding their flocks, and tilling their lands, a numerous host of Lamanites came upon them and began to slay them, and to take off their flocks, and the corn of their fields.
>
> Yea, and it came to pass that they fled, all that were not overtaken, even into the city of Nephi, and did call upon me for protection (Mosiah 9:14-15).

This reference states that an agricultural area containing water for the herds was situated to the south of Shilom. That area, which may have been a river bottom, was more accessible to the city of Nephi than to the adjacent settlement at Shilom. The city of Nephi's position was therefore to the south, southeast or southwest of Shilom. This assumption is consistent with the references indicating that a hill and higher elevations existed to the north of Shilom (Mosiah 7:5-6; 10:8-10; 11:13).

## THE MANTI REGIONAL NETWORK

The Manti Regional Network of the greater land southward is a compilation of the paths and networks discussed in the three preceding sections of this chapter. The Moroni, Cumeni, and Nephi District Networks can be combined into a single network for the greater land southward since all three models share some specific associations.

Figure 13 portrays the correlation of these various vertices and routes as they can be defined in this, the basic series of network analyses. It should be understood that the base or preliminary systems are only the first stage of network analysis. In chapter 9, by correlating the topography of the models with the topography of the Americas, a setting of these models can be identified. In addition, various aspects of the base networks can be further refined or enhanced into the secondary series of networks. This process is especially apparent relative to the east sea settlements of Jershon (36) and Antionum (37). These settlements

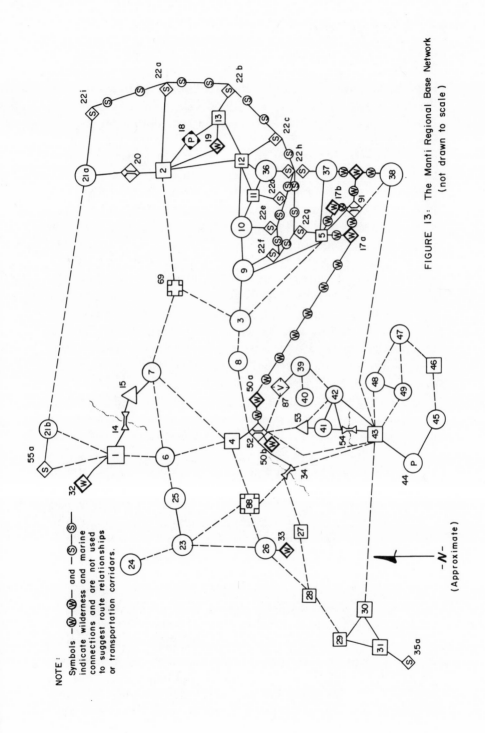

NOTE:

Symbols —Ⓦ—Ⓦ— and —Ⓢ—Ⓢ— indicate wilderness and marine connections and are not used to suggest route relationships or transportation corridors.

FIGURE 13: The Manti Regional Base Network (not drawn to scale)

-N-
(Approximate)

cannot be associated with the settlements developed in the Moroni Network (see figure 8) due to the complexity of the settlement associations and a gap that exists in the record. As a result, these two settlements are first identified in the Nephi District Network (see figure 12), where their associations with the east sea land of Bountiful (2) and the Lamanites' land of Siron (38) can be initially portrayed. The complexity of these settlement associations is apparent in the incorporation of Jershon and Antionum into the preliminary graph of the Manti Region, as shown in figure 13. Thus, a complete configuration of all the east sea settlements can be developed in the basic stages of analyses as provided in this section.

The Manti Regional Network extends from the east seashore (22) to the west sea (35), consistent with the references establishing both the "middle" lands of Nephi and Zarahemla as bordering both seas (Alma 22:27; 50:7-11). Mormon's statements that the city of Zarahemla was situated in the center of the land southward (Helaman 1:24-27) indicate that the network shown in figure 13 is only a partial representation of the settlement lands actually occupied by the descendants of Lehi in the land southward. As discussed at the beginning of chapter 4, the emphasis of the record on locations and routes associated with the intermediate zone of conflict between the Nephite and Lamanite cultures becomes quite apparent at this level of network identification.

By integrating the three district networks discussed above, the regional network can be developed as shown in figure 13. A variety of refinements not possible on the district models can now be made. These adjustments include the connection of the unnamed territories to the north of the "middle" land of Zarahemla and the city of Bountiful (2) as demonstrated by the extended route linking loci 21a and 21b.

The path from the Jershon complex to Manti, as developed in the Nephi Network, can be integrated with the Moroni Network since both districts are situated in the same geographic area. Thus, one primary and direct path can be identified linking the east sea settlements via Nephihah (3) and Aaron (8) with Manti (4). This important corridor had a general east-west orientation extending from Lehi (9) to the narrow passage entrance (52) into the land of Manti adjacent to the north slope of the narrow strip of wilderness (50). This is apparently the route traveled by the people of Ammon in 74 B.C. when they withdrew from their exposed position at Jershon (36) and relocated at Melek (26).

This route was also followed within the year by Moroni's forces when they were apprised of the Lamanite withdrawal from Antionum. Moroni learned that the Lamanites had departed "into the wilderness, . . . round about in the wilderness, away by the head of the river Sidon, that they might come into the land of Manti and take possession of the land." (Alma 43:22). That Lamanite route is shown in a preliminary fashion in figure 12 as the connecting route from Siron (38) via Nephi (43) to the southern entrance to Manti through the narrow strip of wilderness (50a-b and 52). Note that the routes of the Lamanites and Moroni were parallel, both flanking the narrow strip of wilderness. Moroni, learning of the Lamanite intentions, departed from an unnamed city in Jershon and "marched over into the land of Manti" (Alma 43:25), probably passing through the shoreline area, where he would shortly establish the fortified settlements of Omner (11), Morianton (10), Lehi (9), and Nephihah (3).

The path through Lehi (9) to the southern entrance into Manti (52) was evidently used for a third time in 68 B.C. by Nephites fleeing to the west sea in their attempt to migrate into the greater land northward. A land dispute arose at that time between the people of Morianton (10) and the Nephite colony at the fortified settlement of Lehi (9). The people at Lehi fled to chief captain Moroni (5) for safety (Alma 50:27), prompting the departure of the Morianton colony for the security of the greater land northward. Teancum was sent by Moroni to stop that migration. So rapid was the movement of the people of Morianton that they were not halted until they had arrived on the west sea at the borders of the land of Desolation. Teancum subsequently defeated Morianton at the narrow pass that was adjacent to the west seashore (Alma 50:34) and returned the remnants of the colony to the site of Morianton (Alma 50:29-36).

The Morianton incident detailed above establishes the existence of a corridor or system of corridors that extended from the east sea locality to the west sea paralleling the narrow strip of wilderness. This system is the only way that rapid movement of troops could be accomplished from the east sea Jershon/Morianton complex into the interior complex involving Manti (4) and its passage through the south wilderness. The extension of this corridor system to the west, ultimately to connect with the west seacoast, is the only explanation for the ease of movement experienced by the people of Morianton. The western extension of this readily traveled avenue is apparent in the path that connected Manti (4) with Judea (29) as developed in figures 9 and 10. What figure 13 does not show is the connection between the land southward and the land northward, including the borders of Desolation where Morianton was halted. That locality is the topic of the Joshua District Network that is developed in the following chapter.

# 7

# SPATIAL STRUCTURE OF THE DESOLATION REGION IN THE GREATER LAND NORTHWARD

The geographic references of the Jaredite occupation in the land northward can be correlated with the final withdrawal of the Nephites into that same region prior to their annihilation in A.D. 385. This chapter reconstructs the network of places and routes in the land northward using the paths identified in these two separate histories.

The preceding chapter incorporated three separate networks and their associated paths into a spatial organization of the land southward, which has been termed the Manti Regional Network. That network represents all definable associations established by the Nephites and Lamanites from the date of their arrival in the land southward in the early sixth century B.C. until A.D. 327 when the final Nephite withdrawal from Zarahemla began.

The terminal period of the Nephite history between A.D. 327 and 385 is contained in the writings of Mormon, who, as the chief captain of the Nephite forces, experienced and recorded the final destruction of that culture at Cumorah. The path of the Nephites' final withdrawal to Cumorah evidently began in the "lesser" land of Zarahemla and led through a series of lands ultimately into the greater land northward. A graph of those localities has been incorporated into the Joshua District Network, as described in the following section.

The Nephite demise occurred in the land of Cumorah, which was situated in the greater land northward. The land Desolation, also in the land northward, was aptly named by the Nephites, for it contained the ruins of the earlier Jaredite civilization. It was more tradition than coincidence that brought the Nephites' final battle to Cumorah; it was staged on the same ground where the

Jaredite culture had previously been destroyed in the early sixth century B.C.

The earlier history of the Jaredite peoples as abridged by Moroni, the son of Mormon, is found in the book of Ether. The Moron District Network examined later in this chapter provides an analysis of the Jaredite settlements and lands beginning as early as 2,500 B.C. and extending until their collapse through internal warfare. Since both the Joshua and Moron District Networks have some overlap, both systems through spatial analysis can be combined to form the preliminary graph of the Desolation Regional Network.

## THE JOSHUA DISTRICT NETWORK

The Joshua Network consists of several paths and a variety of interconnections. As demonstrated in figures 14, 15, and 16, this district model is shown in three stages of development. Figures 14 and 15 show the Joshua associations both before and after A.D. 350. These two phases of model development are then integrated in the latter part of this section into the Joshua District Network given in figure 16.

Prior to A.D. 350, during the preliminary phase of the Nephite withdrawal from the land southward, a series of retreats led the Nephites from Zarahemla (1) to the settlement of Angola (56)[1] and on through the land of David (57) to the land of Joshua (58), as shown in figure 14.

The text refers only once to Angola (56) and David (57), providing no associations for these localities other than their links to the lands of Zarahemla and Joshua as noted in Mormon 2:3-6.

Joshua was "in the borders west by the seashore," which can be interpreted as the west seashore, for Mormon's retreat was "towards the north countries" (Mormon 2:3-6). Since the term *north countries* is used by both Mormon and Moroni synonymously for the greater land northward (cf. Helaman 4:7; Ether 1:1; 9:35), the route of retreat to Joshua brought them into the vicinity of the west sea, as shown in figure 14, by the direct route linking Joshua (58) with the shoreline at locus 35b. The west sea coastal shelf is the only corridor mentioned in the text that was used by the Nephites for travel into the greater land northward.

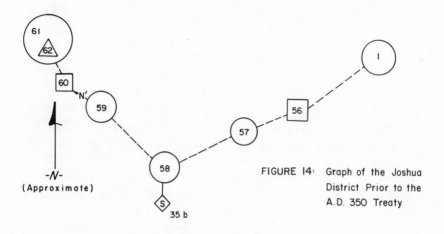

FIGURE 14: Graph of the Joshua District Prior to the A.D. 350 Treaty

LEGEND:

| | | | |
|---|---|---|---|
| 1 | Zarahemla (Lesser Land) | 64 | Teancum |
| 35 | Seashore | 65 | Boaz |
| 56 | Angola | 66 | Jordan |
| 57 | Land of David | 67 | Narrow Passage in the Narrow Neck that marked the boundary between the Land Southward and the Greater Land Northward |
| 58 | Land of Joshua & Land of First Inheritance | | |
| 59 | Land of Jashon | | |
| 60 | Land of Shem | 68 | Unnamed Land above the City Desolation, under Lamanite control |
| 61 | Land of Antum | | |
| 62 | Hill Shim | | |
| 63 | City Desolation | | |

⟶ Direction Given between Places

N-S-E-W Cardinal Directions

⟶● Direction of Higher Elevation

Note: Letter N´, S´ & E´ Respectively Indicate Northward, Southward & Eastward directions as established in the Text

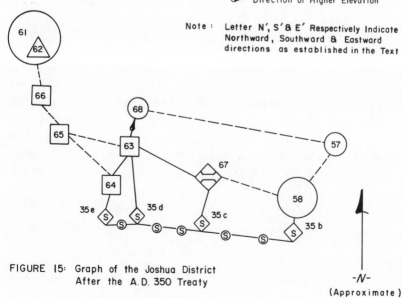

FIGURE 15: Graph of the Joshua District After the A.D. 350 Treaty

Therefore, because of its apparent accessibility into the greater land northward, Joshua was situated on this west sea coastal corridor.

Mormon's description of the land of Joshua does not readily permit an identification of its position on the borders of the west sea. Joshua was a land "filled with robbers and with Lamanites" (Mormon 2:6-8), which indicates that the Nephites were not in complete control of the area. In spite of this political instability resulting from the intense conflicts generated by the combined presence of Nephites, Gadianton robbers, and Lamanites, the Nephites were able to maintain some control of the locality for about fifteen years. They were ultimately driven out of Joshua by a Lamanite offensive initiated in A.D. 345.

It can be assumed that Joshua was not in the vicinity of the narrow neck–land of Desolation complex discussed in the preceding chapters, for its description does not include any reference to the features of that locality. Indeed, no previous references to Joshua are found in the text, nor is this land referred to during the subsequent period of warfare conducted from the city of Desolation.

The correlation of a number of references demonstrates that the west seashore location of the land of Joshua existed in the Nephite territories of the land southward and was in, or adjacent to, the land where the Nephites originally landed when they arrived in the "promised land." These references deal with a common theme — the Nephite-Lamanite lands of inheritance.

The "lands of inheritance" concept has extensive use in the Book of Mormon. In its general meaning, it is associated with the ancient covenant concept of the righteous being awarded lands where they and their posterity could reside and be preserved as long as they honored their contracts with Deity. This concept was brought with the Nephites from Jerusalem. It was used to explain their presence and identity in the "promised land" (cf. 2 Nephi 10:7-19).

An examination of the various contexts and uses of the term *lands of inheritance* provides a confirmation of this assumption that the land of Joshua was included among the lands of the Nephite inheritance.

The most common use of the term *lands of inheritance* is found in reference to the Nephite political territory or the "middle" land of Zarahemla. In A.D. 346, after the Nephites had been driven into the greater land northward, they successfully defended the land of Shem (60) against a superior Lamanite force. The Nephite army then mounted a major offensive that resulted in the recovery of lost territory. Mormon states in Mormon 2:27: "We did go forth against the Lamanites and the robbers of Gadianton, until we had again taken possession of the lands of our inheritance." Mormon's statement should not be interpreted to mean the Nephites had recovered all of their traditional lands in the land southward. Rather, they had "again" taken control of an area now referred to as the land of their inheritance, a land where they "again" had to struggle against Gadianton opposition. This description suggests that the land of Joshua was within the Nephites' lands of inheritance, further indicating that the Nephites had returned to the locality in the land southward that they had lost during the preceding year.

The terms *lands of inheritance, land of our fathers' first inheritance*, and *land of first inheritance* were also used to specify particular localities in the land southward. The land of Nephi, situated around the city of Nephi, is referred to in this context (cf. Mosiah 7:9, 21; 9:1, 3; 10:3; Alma 54:12-13) as are the land of Zarahemla (Words of Mormon 1:14) and the land of Moron (Ether 7:16). Thus, Mormon is referring to Zarahemla in the context of its being the Nephite "middle" land, or Nephite political territory, in his statement in Mormon 2:27 relative to the Nephite return into their lands of inheritance in A.D. 349.

Another land in the vicinity of the west sea is not specifically named but is also referred to in a slightly different "land of inheritance" context. In Mosiah 10:13, Mormon states that the Lamanites taught themselves that they had been wronged by Nephi "while in the land of their first inheritance, after they had crossed the sea." In another reference Mormon describes the areas of the land southward that were inhabited by the Lamanites before the 72-60 B.C. war. He states that the Lamanites were "on the west of the land of Zarahemla, in the borders by the seashore, and on the west in the land of Nephi, in the place of their fathers' first inheritance, and thus bordering along by the seashore" (Alma 22:28).

These two quotations (Mosiah 10:13 and Alma 22:28) establish two important factors — (1) the landing place of Lehi's party is identified by Mormon as the land of the first inheritance of the Nephites-Lamanites, and (2) this "place of their fathers' first inheritance" actually existed in the west sea locality, west of the "middle" land of Nephi.

Thus, Lehi's landing place on the west sea was west of the land of Nephi and was known to both the Nephites and Lamanites as the land of their fathers' first inheritance. This land of the joint Nephite-Lamanite first inheritance contrasts with the inland "middle" land of Nephi that chief captain Moroni refers to as the land of "our first inheritance" in his epistle to Ammoron (Alma 54:12-13). In this final instance, Moroni is discussing the land of Nephi, or the land of the Nephites' first inheritance, after the separation of the Nephites and the Lamanites at their original west sea settlement.

The association of the "place of their fathers' first inheritance" with the west sea locality is consistent with the information supplied in Mormon 2:27-29 about the Nephite return in A.D. 349. As has been noted above, Mormon states that after mounting a successful offensive to recover their lost territory, the Nephites had "again taken possession of the lands of [their] inheritance." The area was too difficult to control, however, and in the following year, Mormon says, "we made a treaty with the Lamanites and the robbers of Gadianton, in which we did get the lands of our inheritance divided." Mormon then states that he repositioned his forces under the new treaty adjacent to the narrow passage that was strategically situated on the west sea coastal corridor: "And the Lamanites did give unto us the land northward, yea, even to the narrow passage which led into the land southward. And we did give unto the Lamanites all the land southward" (Mormon 2:29).

This variety of references on the "lands of inheritance," coupled with the information developed in chapter 4 on the narrow neck of land defensive complex adjacent to the west sea, reinforces the assumption that Joshua was on the west coast, within or adjacent to the original land of inheritance where Lehi's colony landed, and included within the Nephite territory or "middle" land of Zarahemla as one of the lands of their inheritance until the Nephite withdrawal in A.D. 350.

At the time of the original loss of Joshua (58) in A.D. 345, the Nephites made a rapid retreat into the land northward, and their forces could not be consolidated until they had arrived in the land of Jashon (59) (Mormon 2:16). Jashon's location in the greater land northward is identified by its proximity to the land of Antum (61), where in the hill Shim (62) the religious records of the Nephites had been hidden by Ammaron in ca. A.D. 321 (Mormon 1:2-3; 2:17).[2]

The Nephite defense at Jashon was short-lived. Within the year they were again in full retreat moving northward from Jashon to their next line of defense at the city of Shem (60), as noted in Mormon 2:20-21. No information is given as to whether the hill Shim was also overrun by the Lamanites during this offensive. The record relative to the later period of A.D. 376 relates Mormon's care in removing the records from the hill lest they be destroyed by the Lamanites (Mormon 4:23). Mormon would have been equally concerned with their safety when Jashon was under siege in A.D. 345 had the records' location been threatened. The lack of any similar comment in this earlier portion of his record suggests that the hill Shim may not have been immediately threatened during the Lamanite offensive against Jashon and Shem. For this reason, the land of Antum (61) is shown in figure 14 to be northward beyond the land of Shem (60). The fact that the entire Nephite defense was structured around the city of Shem strongly suggests that Shem, like Jashon and Joshua, was in restricted terrain where the Nephites had a tactical advantage and could not be readily outflanked by their enemy.

Successful in their desperate defense at Shem, Mormon's forces immediately launched a counterattack and by A.D. 349 had regained control not only of Jashon but also of the land of Joshua and the adjacent lands of their inheritance near the west sea in the land southward, as discussed above.

An important point of discussion in the Joshua Network concerns the location of Sherrizah. This locality is mentioned only in Mormon's letter to his son Moroni (Moroni 9:7, 16-17). The information in the letter implies that Sherrizah was a fortified settlement on a high, natural position that he refers to as a tower. The text of the letter does not pinpoint the location of Sherrizah in the Joshua Network, but several factors indicate that Sherrizah was somewhere on the path between Joshua and the land of Shem (60). The first indication is given during the warfare that occurred between the settlements of Joshua (58) and Jashon (59)

(Mormon 2:9). At that time Mormon referred to the presence of his enemy Aaron. This Lamanite leader is also noted in Mormon's letter to Moroni (Moroni 9:17). Secondly, in the letter Mormon notes that he has some records in his possession that he would like to deliver to Moroni if the opportunity should occur. It was at Jashon (Mormon 2:17) that Mormon had access to the records in the hill Shim. This reference to records suggests the letter was prepared before the battle for Shem in A.D. 346.

The final factor that places Sherrizah in the Joshua-Shem (58-60) path relates to Mormon's occupation. During the warfare associated with Sherrizah, Mormon was the chief captain over the Nephite forces. His position as commander is clearly stated in his letter to Moroni, where he discusses his leadership role (see Moroni 9). After the A.D. 362 battle at the city of Desolation (63), however, Mormon resigned his position in disgust with the Nephites because of their wickedness and their intention to mount an offensive war against the Lamanites (Mormon 3:11-16). He did not again participate in a leadership role until the fall of Boaz (65) in about A.D. 376. Only at that later date, seeing that the Lamanites were about to overrun the land, did Mormon resume leadership of the Nephites, a role he retained until his death at Cumorah in A.D. 385. His role as commander-in-chief during the preparation of the letter to Moroni and his mention of his enemy Aaron indicate that the letter was prepared before the treaty of A.D. 350. These various correlations, therefore, place the writing of the letter within the earlier period of warfare associated with the Jashon-Shem complexes. Thus, the location of Sherrizah lies somewhere along the corridor between Joshua (58) and the city of Shem (60).

With the treaty of A.D. 350, the Nephites withdrew into the land of Desolation, where the last phase of their final destruction was initiated (cf. Mormon 2:29; 3:5). Their primary point of control was the fortified city of Desolation (63), which was near the narrow neck of land and blocked Lamanite access into the land northward. Figure 15 demonstrates the newly named places that can be added to the Joshua District model after the A.D. 350 treaty.

The fortified settlement of Desolation (63) was near the boundary line that separated the lands northward and southward. It was also adjacent to the strategic narrow pass (67) that led into the land southward (Mormon 2:29; 3:5). Mormon placed all of his forces in this highly defensive position, for he states: "And there we did place our armies, that we might stop the armies of the Lamanites, that they might not get possession of any of our lands; therefore we did fortify them with all our force" (Mormon 3:6).

The zone that characterized the Nephites' traditional coastal line of defense against Lamanite invasions into the land northward is shown as loci 63 and 67 in figure 15. Within this narrow neck defensive complex were situated two strategic positions. These positions consisted of the narrow pass (67) that blocked the coastal corridor approaches into the land northward and the fortifications at the city of Desolation (63) that served as a backup position behind the narrow pass. The fortified city of Desolation also blocked an inland corridor leading up from the coastal plain into the highlands of the land southward. The control of this corridor up into the highland location shown as locus 68 became crucial to the Nephite defense after A.D. 360. At that time enemy forces became concentrated in the highland positions associated with the eastern periphery that paralleled the coastal corridor on the east (cf. the section on the narrow neck of land in chapter 4) and became a continuous threat to the Nephite defenses at Desolation.

An extended route in figure 15 links the land of David (57) with the highland positions (68) above the city of Desolation. This route symbolizes the Lamanite transportation corridor that provided their armies access into the highlands preparatory to their attacks "down" on the city of Desolation in A.D. 361 and 362.

The accessibility of the narrow pass–Desolation complex to the Lamanites in the coastal region of the land southward is demonstrated by the extended route shown on figure 15 connecting the land of Joshua to that pass. Mormon's successful fortification of this coastal complex preparatory to the Lamanite offensive in A.D. 361 may explain why the Lamanites after the treaty of A.D. 350 chose to initiate their invasions from the unnamed highland position represented as locus 68. By shifting their strategy to invade from the highlands, they had the advantage of elevation and could bypass the primary Nephite defenses at the narrow passage by directly attacking the city of Desolation.

Mormon had ten years of peace to prepare his defenses at Desolation. In A.D. 361 and again the following year, the Nephites successfully defended those lands from their enemies. The second major battle at the city of Desolation resulted in numerous Lamanite casualties. To dispose of the dead Lamanites, the Nephites cast their bodies "into the sea" (Mormon 3:8), establishing the fact that the city of Desolation was adjacent to the west seashore as demonstrated by locus 35d.

Both Lamanite invasions were directed against the city of Desolation from the Lamanites' positions (68) in the higher elevations (Mormon 3:7-8). The consistency of the Lamanite attacks "down" on the Nephite positions and the subsequent Nephite attacks "up" (Mormon 3:10; 4:1) against their enemy indicates that the coastal plain in the land southward adjacent to the narrow pass was not the origin of the Lamanite attacks. Rather, the enemy forces were concentrated in the highland positions associated with the mountainous barrier zone that paralleled on the east the coastal corridor.

The narrow pass (67) near the seashore was probably identical with the location described by Mormon in Alma 50:34 relative to the rebellion of the people of Morianton in 67 B.C. As noted in the previous chapter, the land of Morianton was situated on the border of the east seashore. Its peoples were involved in a land dispute with the Nephites residing in the adjacent land of Lehi (see figure 8). Fearing adverse judgment from chief captain Moroni, Morianton and his colony fled the area, desirous of going into the "land which was northward, which was covered with large bodies of water" (Alma 50:29). This description is similar to other references to the greater land northward given in the text (Mosiah 8:8; Helaman 3:4; Mormon 6:4).

Learning of Morianton's defection and fearing for the safety and liberty of the Nephites in that region, Mormon dispatched an army under the command of Teancum to stop the dissidents. The location where Teancum halted Morianton's movement was on the "borders of the land Desolation . . . by the narrow pass which led by the sea into the land northward, yea, by the sea, on the west and on the east" (Alma 50:34). This narrow pass position was therefore adjacent to the west seashore, possibly in a locality containing bays or estuaries to the east. The location of Morianton's defeat is identical with Mormon's description of the narrow pass used in the Nephite final wars.

The location of Hagoth's shipyard on the west sea (35c) is

also in the vicinity of the narrow passage (67), as shown in figure 15. It was at this site in 55 B.C. that ships were constructed and used for Nephite coastal migrations into the land northward via the west sea. The record states that this location was situated "on the borders of the land Bountiful by the land Desolation . . . by the narrow neck which led into the land northward" (Alma 63:5-7). This position is identical to the references about the location of the defensive line that separated Bountiful and the greater land southward from the land of Desolation, as reviewed in chapter 4 (cf. Alma 22:32; Helaman 4:7). Hence, the Hagoth shipyard (35c) was on the west seashore, directly associated with this defensive line and with both the lands of Desolation and Bountiful.

The narrow pass (67) near the settlement of Desolation (63) noted in Mormon 2:29 and 3:5-6 marks the traditional Nephite line of defense used to protect the greater land northward. It was first referenced by Mormon in Alma 22:32 as "the line Bountiful and the land Desolation," being the distance of a day-and-a-half journey for a Nephite from its eastern end to the west sea. Mormon also describes a period of warfare in 35 B.C. when the Nephites were forced out of the middle land of Zarahemla into the west sea land of Bountiful, probably concentrating their forces near the narrow pass that linked the lands northward and southward. Referring to the Nephites at this location, Mormon states, "And there they did fortify against the Lamanites, from the west sea, even unto the east; it being a day's journey for a Nephite, on the line which they had fortified and stationed their armies to defend their north country" (Helaman 4:7). The fact that this area was adjacent to the land northward in the narrow neck is established by Mormon, who notes in the following verse that the dissenters of the Nephites and an army of Lamanites "had obtained all the possession of the Nephites which was in the land southward."

Northward from the defensive line between the lands of Desolation and Bountiful lay a series of extended and direct routes linking the city of Desolation (63) with the fortified settlement of Teancum (64) and onward to the fortifications of Boaz (65), as shown in figure 15.

The fortified city of Teancum was accessible from both the west sea and the settlement of Desolation, as shown by the direct routes and locus 35e in figure 15. After the fall of the city of Desolation in A.D. 363, the Nephites retreated to Teancum (64), which was "in the borders by the seashore; and it was also near the city Desolation" (Mormon 4:3). The site of Teancum continued to be important to the Nephite defense during the following four years when a series of battles were fought for the control of the Desolation defensive complex.

Nephite control of the city of Desolation was ended by a major Lamanite invasion in A.D. 375. Mormon states:

> And in this year they did come down against the Nephites with all their powers; and they were not numbered because of the greatness of their number.
>
> And from this time forth did the Nephites gain no power over the Lamanites, but began to be swept off by them even as a dew before the sun.
>
> And it came to pass that the Lamanites did come down against the city Desolation; and there was an exceedingly sore battle fought in the land Desolation, in the which they did beat the Nephites (Mormon 4:17-19).

The final loss of the Desolation fortified complex in the narrow neck resulted in the Nephite retreat to the fortifications at Boaz (65), as noted in Mormon 4:20. The Nephite armies halted the Lamanite offensive by holding at Boaz for a short time.

The destruction of the Nephites at Boaz prompted Mormon to return to the hill Shim (62) in the land of Antum (61), where he obtained the remainder of the records (Mormon 4:22-23). As long as Boaz held, the Boaz-Jordan buffer zone existed, ensuring the preservation of the records. With the loss of Boaz, only the fortified settlements associated with the final defensive line at Jordan protected the cached materials.

The land of Antum thus forms a connecting link between the two separate paths into the land northward, enabling the incorporation of figures 14 and 15 into the Joshua District Base Network, as shown in figure 16.

The text states that the hill Shim (62) was near the land of Jashon (59) (Mormon 2:17) and that after the fall of Boaz, Mormon again visited the hill Shim. The various routes on figure 16 symbolize those connections. The Antum–hill Shim (61-62) associations with Boaz (65) and Jordan (66) are not stated. Extended routes have been used in figure 16 to show that other unnamed Nephite settlements existed along these two paths that led to the

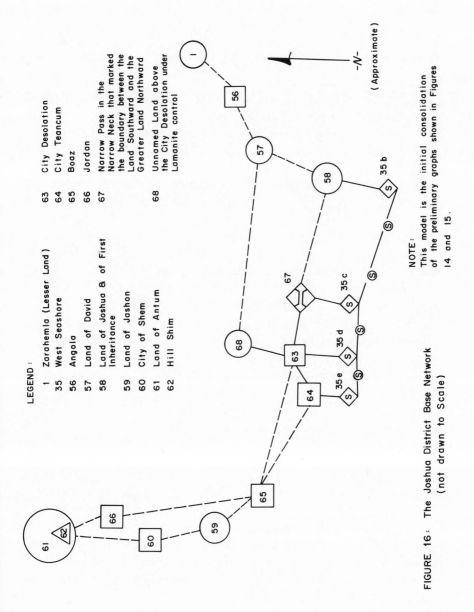

LEGEND:

| | | | |
|---|---|---|---|
| 1 | Zarahemla (Lesser Land) | 63 | City Desolation |
| 35 | West Seashore | 64 | City Teancum |
| 56 | Angola | 65 | Boaz |
| 57 | Land of David | 66 | Jordan |
| 58 | Land of Joshua & of First Inheritance | 67 | Narrow Pass in the Narrow Neck that marked the boundary between the Land Southward and the Greater Land Northward |
| 59 | Land of Jashon | | |
| 60 | City of Shem | | |
| 61 | Land of Antum | 68 | Unnamed Land above the City Desolation under Lamanite control |
| 62 | Hill Shim | | |

-N-

(Approximate)

NOTE:
This model is the initial consolidation of the preliminary graphs shown in Figures 14 and 15.

FIGURE 16: The Joshua District Base Network (not drawn to Scale)

land of Antum. In this network model, the vertices of the land Antum and hill Shim are placed beyond Shem (60) and Jordan (66) based on the assumption that the Lamanite threat to the record repository did not materialize until after the Nephite loss of both Shem and Jordan.

After the defeat of Jordan (66) and its associated strongholds, the Lamanite victors forced a complete rout of the Nephite forces and population. The loss of this final line of defense permitted the Lamanites the freedom of spreading into the interior of the land northward (Mormon 5:4). However, the Nephite forces that survived the battle and exodus still constituted a sufficient threat to Lamanite expansion into the greater land northward. Using this advantage, Mormon concluded an agreement with the Lamanite leader. The Nephite remnants were allowed the time to regroup in the nearby land of Cumorah (Mormon 6:2-4), where the final battle occurred four years later.

Unfortunately, no references exist in the text indicating the spatial associations that existed between Cumorah and the vertices incorporated into the Joshua Network as shown in figure 16. For this reason, Cumorah cannot be integrated into the Book of Mormon spatial system until its relationships to the vertices in the Moron District Network have been established in the following section.

## THE MORON DISTRICT NETWORK

The Moron Network is the last district network to be developed in an analysis of the spatial organization of the Book of Mormon. The Moron system, like the Joshua Network discussed in the preceding section, is set in the land northward and comprises part of the Desolation Regional Network. Named after the Jaredite capital land of Moron, this graph, as shown in its initial development in figures 17 and 18, portrays all the recorded spatial associations provided in the Book of Ether concerning the settlements and lands of the Jaredites.

The temporal span of this network is much more extensive than that of any network previously discussed herein. The Jaredite peoples first colonized the land northward possibly as early as 3,000 B.C. and were culturally destroyed at Ramah (or Cumorah) sometime between the sixth and third centuries B.C., involving a period of perhaps 2,500 years. The record lists a series of 28 rulers that presided during this period.

Although the text contains insufficient evidence to establish a contemporaneous correlation between the Jaredite destruction in the land northward and the Nephite arrival on the west seashore in the land of their first inheritance, the history leaves no doubt of the early sixth century B.C. arrivals of the Nephite and Mulekite peoples. According to the text, no recorded contact existed between the descendants of either culture until about 225 B.C. This contact occurred when Mosiah and his Nephite followers settled at Zarahemla among the descendants of the people of Zarahemla (Omni 1:12-19), a long-established colony that probably included remnants of the preceding Jaredite civilization.

For the length of its history, the book of Ether supplies only limited information on spatial associations. This record consists of Moroni's abridgment of Ether's larger record, a complete text that undoubtedly contained more geographic detail than is available in this abridged format. The majority of the graph shown in figure 18 consists of route complexes traveled during the final Jaredite war. These routes extended from Moron (71) on the northwest, through the land of Corihor (79), to the hill Ramah, or Cumorah (82), as it was known to the Nephites.

The remaining extended routes involving the lands of Nehor (72) and Heth (73) and linking Moron with the plains of Heshlon (75) via the valley of Gilgal (74) have been placed in their positions relative to Moron as a convenience for the model. No information is available in the text about the actual direction or distance from Moron to these locations.

Early in the Jaredite history, the fifth ruler, King Omer, fled Moron (71) upon learning of a plot against his life. The journey took him past the hill Shim (62) and the hill Ramah (82) and then eastward to Ablom (84) near the seashore, (55b) where he found security (Ether 9:3). This Moron-Ablom path provides a general association between the two hills that were first referenced in the preceding section. Since Ablom was near the seashore, and since Omer had traveled there from the vicinity of Ramah to the west, the nearby coastline could have been anywhere in Ablom's northern, eastern, or southern quadrants.

The coastline near Ablom becomes more apparent with an analysis of the main path from Moron (71) to Ramah (82) as

(General associations on this Chart have been developed from Appendix A references.)

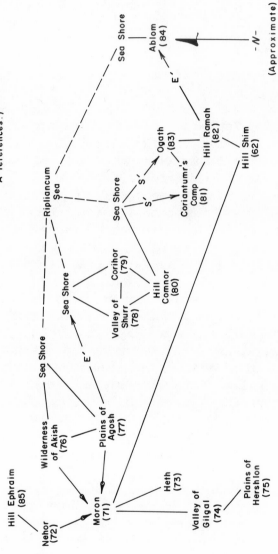

LEGEND:

———— Place to Place Association in the Text

– – – – Place to Open Sea Association in the Text

N-S-E-W Cardinal Direction

➤ Direction Given between Places

➤ Direction of Higher Elevation

Note: Letter N', S' & E' Respectively Indicate Northward, Southward & Eastward directions as established in the Text

FIGURE 17: Chart of the Moron District

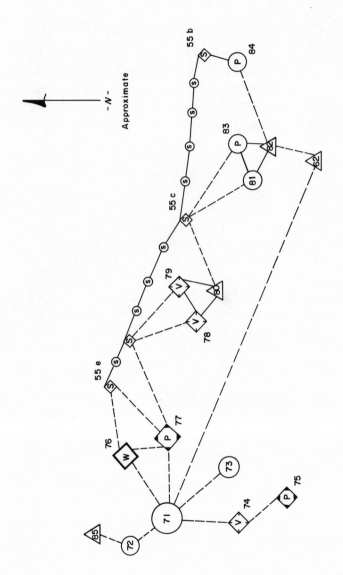

FIGURE 18: The Moron District Base Network
(not drawn to Scale)

shown in figure 18. In order to accomplish this analysis, however, the path can best be followed in reverse of the original movements. The hill Ramah (82) was immediately adjacent to Coriantumr's camp (81) and the place called Ogath (83), where Shiz camped prior to their final battles on Ramah (Ether 15:10-11). Their movement to this locality was southward from the shoreline position described as the "waters of Ripliancum, which, by interpretation, is large, or to exceed all" (55c), as noted by Moroni in Ether 15:8. Earlier a battle had been fought at this seashore position. Thus, a seashore pattern begins to emerge with the sea to the north, northeast, or east of the shore locations 55b and 55c.

This shoreline pattern continues to be consistent farther up the coast, for an earlier engagement at another point on the seashore shown as 55d was eastward from the plains of Agosh (77) (Ether 14:16, 26). And an even earlier battle on the seashore shown as locus 55e (Ether 14:13) was in the vicinity of both the Plains of Agosh and the wilderness of Akish (76). These additional shoreline associations are consistent with the pattern of a seashore extending from the southeast to the northwest. Thus, the coastline can be reconstructed as an extension from points 55b through 55e on the north, northeast, and eastern flank of the connected locations that form the Moron-Ramah-Ablom path.

With this concept of a general coastal layout, the discussion can begin at the land of Moron (71), where the final interrivalry for the rule of the Jaredite people started. The conflict actually began in a series of battles on the Gilgal (74) path between the ruler Coriantumr and a man named Shared, who was slain by Coriantumr at Gilgal.

Shared's brother, Gilead, reinitiated the strife at Moron two years later and was pursued by Coriantumr and his forces into the wilderness of Akish (76), where Coriantumr was subsequently defeated. There Coriantumr remained for two years preparing for an assault on Gilead at Moron (Ether 14:3-7). An extended route in figure 18 shows this association between Moron (71) and the wilderness of Akish (76).

Coriantumr and his forces eventually succeeded in forcing Gilead's successor, Lib, out of the land of Moron. Lib was pursued to the seashore (55e), where in the resulting battle he gained the upper hand. Coriantumr fled back into the wilderness of Akish

(76). Lib, however, went to the Plains of Agosh (77), possibly to block Coriantumr's return. Moroni continues the account, stating that Coriantumr eventually arrived at the plains of Agosh (77), where a battle developed (Ether 14:11-16) and Lib was killed.

Following the death of Lib, his brother Shiz took control. Shiz and his army forced Coriantumr to withdraw from Agosh. Fleeing eastward, Coriantumr again took a stand on the seashore symbolized as locus 55d (Ether 14:16-26).

The general orientation of these troop movements continued in a southeasterly direction. Moron, the land where the Jaredite capital was located throughout most of the Jaredite history, was above the coastal plain where the battles were fought, for movements from that location (71) to the coast (55e) and also to the wilderness of Akish (76) are to lower elevations.

Coriantumr and his forces ultimately triumphed over their opponents during the battle on the seashore shown in figure 18 as locus 55d. They then pursued the retreating Shiz into the interior, apparently to the south or southwest, and the opposing armies made camp to prepare for further conflict on the nearby hill Comnor (80). Ether 14:26-31 further states that Coriantumr's forces stayed in the valley of Shurr (78) while Shiz's army remained nearby in the land of Corihor (79). The associations between these locations are shown by the places and direct routes on figure 18.

Following his defeat on the hill Comnor (80), Coriantumr retreated once again to a position on the seashore (55c) by traveling apparently eastward to the coastline adjacent to the "waters of Ripliancum" (Ether 15:7-8). Coriantumr appears to have been more successful than his opponents in waging seashore battles. Once again he was able to force Shiz's army to retreat from the coast southward (see discussion in chapter 4 on southward as being southeast), where they encamped at Ogath (83) near the hill Ramah (82) (Ether 15:10-11). Just as Coriantumr favored positioning his forces on seashore locations, Shiz had his preference for fighting on large hills. Hence, the associations of Ogath (83) to Coriantumr's camp (81) and the hill Ramah (82) are quite similar to the basic spatial pattern in the Comnor (80) complex, where Shiz had earlier retreated and found temporary success.

This entire series of battles has the appearance of ritualized warfare where the defeated party had preference in selecting the next place of conflict. In addition, although contenders for the kingship may have been slain, the kinship ties were so strong that the conflict was not ended with death, but power to maintain the conflict was shifted to the brother of the deceased.

Both Shiz and Coriantumr remained in the vicinity of Ramah for four years. During that time of preparation for a final battle, both sides gathered together as many people as would participate. This four-year period of waiting and preparation is identical to that observed by the Nephites at the same place nearly a thousand years later. These common factors of time, place, and the marshalling of complete populations for a final battle are not coincidental but suggest a tradition of ritualized warfare.

## THE DESOLATION REGIONAL NETWORK

The Joshua and Moron District Networks described in the preceding sections of this chapter can be incorporated into the preliminary Desolation Regional Network, which is portrayed as an initial graph in figure 19.

The integration of these two districts permits the correlation into this base model of several locations and routes of primary interest. This addition begins on the west seacoast with an unnamed Jaredite city. Referred to by some researchers as the city of Lib, because it was established during the reign of Lib, that settlement was situated in the narrow neck of land near a place where the "sea divides the land" (Ether 10:19-21).

The information provided in Ether 9 concerning a serious drought and famine gives further insight into the position of this Jaredite settlement. Evidently a drought occurred in the land northward, and many inhabitants left the land of Moron to go down into the land southward to find relief. Moron's highland position and the route followed by Omer, as referenced in the preceding section, indicate that a corridor for movement existed going to the southeast past the hill Shim (62) and then on toward the land southward via the narrow neck of land. Much of this path coincides with the route used by the Nephites centuries later as they retreated the distance from the land of Joshua in the land southward to the locality of the hill Shim in the greater land northward.

The description given in Ether 10:19-21 of the terrain asso-

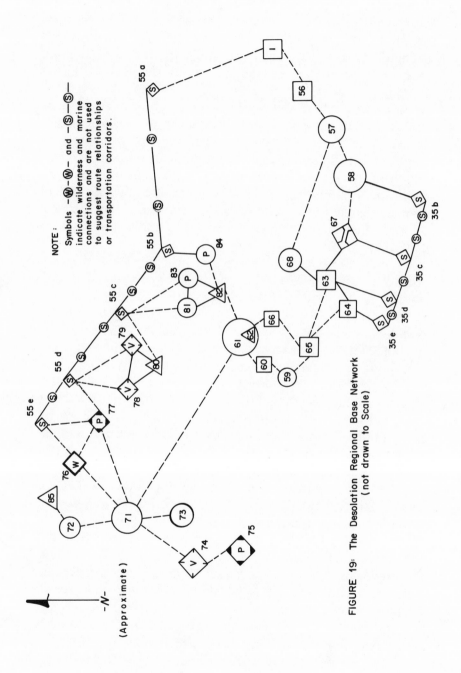

NOTE:

Symbols —Ⓦ—Ⓦ— and —Ⓢ—Ⓢ— indicate wilderness and marine connections and are not used to suggest route relationships or transportation corridors.

FIGURE 19: The Desolation Regional Base Network (not drawn to Scale)

ciated with this Jaredite settlement (86) is identical with that given for the Hagoth shipyard (Alma 63:5) locality shown as locus 35c on figure 19. This similarity places the Jaredite settlement in the west sea coastal corridor within the land of Desolation. There is a strong possibility, therefore, that the city of Desolation fortified by Mormon after A.D. 350 was constructed on or near the ruins of this Jaredite settlement. It may have been the desolate nature of the ruined Jaredite settlement that originally prompted the Nephites to include that area within the land Desolation designation of the greater land northward. This conclusion is reinforced by Near Eastern scholars who have stated that the ancient Semites denoted any scene of defeat with the name *Hormah*, which translates as "Destruction" or "Desolation" (Nibley 1976:195).

The greatest significance apparent in figure 19 is the consistency in the correlation of the Joshua and Moron models based on the pivotal position of the hill Shim (62). Shim is the single locality shared by both district networks. Initially identified in the Nephite Joshua-Shem (58-60) and Joshua-Jordan (58-66) paths, the hill Shim also serves as a fundamental element in the Jaredite Moron-Ablom (71-84) and Moron-Desolation (71-63) paths. Thus, with the addition of the Moron District Network, the Nephite path shown in figure 16 extending to the land Antum (61) can be extended northward to Cumorah-Ramah (82), positively correlating the basic association between Cumorah and the Nephite settlements in the Joshua Network, an association that could not have been established without Ether's record.

The final association that can be developed on this regional model is the extended route linking Zarahemla (1) with the Sea of Ripliancum, or the north sea (55), via the River Sidon. This seacoast-river association is consistent with all the data in the record and is apparent once the relationship of the north sea to the Jaredite battlefields has been established in the Moron District Network. In addition, there is little doubt, because of their contact with Coriantumr, that the Mulekites arrived by ship in the North Sea, and from that coastline their most direct course to Zarahemla would have been to travel up the River Sidon.

The Book of Mormon does not provide a temporal chronology of the Jaredite history, nor is there sufficient information given to establish the demise of that civilization as contemporaneous with the arrival of the Mulekites. Based on the limited information available in the text, two scenarios can be stated, one of which is correct.

1. The Mulekites, or people of Zarahemla, arrived in the Jaredite territory (Alma 22:30) on the north sea coast and traveled from there to establish a colony at Zarahemla (Alma 22:31). This colonization occurred prior to their meeting with Coriantumr as recorded in Omni 1:21.

2. After the death of Shiz at Ramah (82), Coriantumr was residing somewhere on the shore of the north sea when found by the Mulekite colony upon their initial landing on that same coast. After leaving the north seashore in the land northward, this colony immigrated to Zarahemla, probably traveling by boat along the coastline to enter the mouth of the River Sidon (55a) whence they came "up into the south wilderness" (Alma 22:30-31).

## NOTES

1. The settlement of Angola was spelled Angelah in the original 1830 edition of the Book of Mormon, p. 520.

2. Mormon's A.D. 345 arrival in the land of Jashon, which was in the vicinity of the hill Shim, was not his first visit to the record repository. Ammaron's instructions to Mormon as a youth were that when he was about 24 years of age or ca. A.D. 334, he was to retrieve the plates of Nephi from the cache in the hill Shim. Mormon was further instructed to continue recording the history of the Nephites on the plates (Mormon 1:1-3). It can therefore be assumed that Mormon first visited the hill Shim while in command of the Nephite forces at Joshua, some eleven years before their disastrous defeat at that site and subsequent retreat to Jashon.

# 8

# THE INTEGRATION OF THE REGIONAL NETWORKS INTO THE BOOK OF MORMON AREA MODEL

The networks developed for the lands northward and southward are connected in this chapter, providing a general
model of the Book of Mormon area. The topographic features, including seashores, river systems, and mountain
ranges, identified in that comprehensive model are then
extracted to be used in the following chapter to determine
the book's geographic setting on the American continent.

## THE BOOK OF MORMON SPATIAL SYSTEM

In the preceding chapters, the initial series of network models
has been developed on first the district and then the regional
levels of analysis. As a result, the Manti Regional Network of the
land southward can now be integrated with the Desolation Regional model of the greater land northward to identify the Book
of Mormon Area model. This comprehensive area network represents those place and route associations that can be established
at this point in the research. Thus, like the models developed in
the preceding chapters, the graph shown in figure 20 is in its
basic phase of development.

An examination of figure 20 shows three separate seashore
configurations. The east sea on the right, or east side of the model,
is identified by the 22a-i loci. Places shown as 35a-e on the lower
left portion of the model symbolize the west sea. The east and
west seas are separated by the "middle" lands of Zarahemla and
Nephi, centered on their capitals (1 and 43), a relationship that
is completely consistent with the references (cf. Alma 22:32; 50:
7-11).

The third seashore is symbolized by vertices 55a-e located in
the northwestern portion of the model. This coastline represents
the north sea. Information in the text on both the north sea and

the south sea is limited to the following statement concerning Nephite expansion: "They did multiply and spread, and did go forth from the land southward to the land northward, and did spread insomuch that they began to cover the face of the whole earth, from the sea south to the sea north, from the sea west to the sea east" (Helaman 3:8).

The east, west, and north seas are quickly discernible in figure 20, but where is the south sea?

The most apparent explanation for the location of the south sea is given in this same reference. Here Mormon is detailing the expansion of the Nephites in both the lands northward and southward. As figure 20 demonstrates, the land southward, comprising the Manti regional portion of the model, is flanked by seas to the east and to the west. The greater land northward, comprising the Desolation region, is flanked by seacoasts to the north and to the south. If this simple explanation is correct, the seashores were relative designations based on the general direction of each sea from specific points of reference in either the land southward or the greater land northward. Thus, in the land northward, with seashores to the north and south, those bodies of water were referenced as the north and south seas. In the land southward, on the other hand, the seashores were to the east and the west; hence, the east and west seas. The designation of the sea by its direction from the Nephite land of reference is apparent in another context. In Alma 53:8, 22, a careful description is given of the west seashore where, in about 64 B.C., the Lamanites were capturing Nephite fortifications in the vicinity of Antiparah (30). Mormon refers to this area as the "west sea, south." By using this designation is Mormon indirectly indicating that the west sea also had a northern segment? If so, this southern portion of the west sea can be identified in figure 20 as the coastline adjacent to the Antiparah complex (35a), in contrast to the northern segment of the same seashore that is adjacent to the city of Teancum (35e).

This coastline, extending to the southeast of Teancum, permits the following hypothesis: In the land southward, as a Nephite's orientation to the west sea progressed from the northwest to the southwest, a differentiation in nomenclature for the sea also occurred. Thus, in the land southward, the seacoast to the west was identified as the west sea, but the seacoast to the southwest and south of the same location was identified as the "west sea, south."

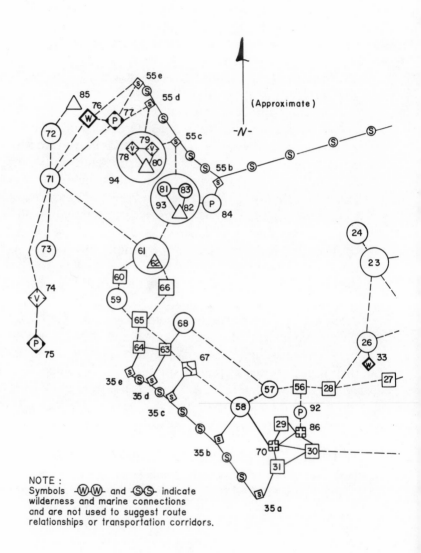

(Approximate)

-N-

NOTE :
Symbols -W-W- and -S-S- indicate
wilderness and marine connections
and are not used to suggest route
relationships or transportation corridors.

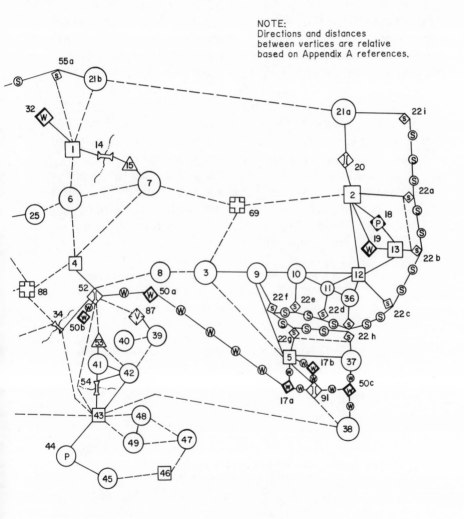

NOTE:
Directions and distances
between vertices are relative
based on Appendix A references.

FIGURE 20: The Book of Mormon
Area Base Network

The correlation shown in figure 20 of the Desolation and Manti Regions contains an additional route and vertex connecting these two systems. These additions consist of the link that existed between the Antiparah complex (30) and the land of Joshua (58), all on the west seashore. Alma 56:31 states that in 66 B.C., the Lamanite armies at the captured settlement of Antiparah (30) were threatening Judea (29) and an unnamed Nephite settlement (31) near both Judea (29) and the west sea (35a). This information is consistent with two previous comments that "the armies of the Lamanites, on the west sea, south, . . . had obtained possession of a number of their cities in that part of the land" (Alma 53:8), which prompted the Nephite leader Helaman to march with his reinforcements "to the support of the people in the borders of the land on the south by the west sea" (Alma 53:22; 56:9).

Upon his arrival at Judea, Helaman relates that the Nephites desired to engage the enemy outside the Lamanites' captured fortifications. The land route past Judea (29) to other unnamed Nephite settlements situated to the northward of Judea is then referenced in Helaman's remark:

> And it came to pass that we kept spies out round about, to watch the movements of the Lamanites, that they might not pass us by night nor by day to make an attack upon our other cities which were on the northward.
>
> For we knew in those cities they were not sufficiently strong to meet them; therefore we were desirous, if they should pass by us, to fall upon them in their rear, and thus bring them up in the rear at the same time they were met in the front. We supposed that we could overpower them; but behold, we were disappointed in this our desire.
>
> They durst not pass by us with their whole army, neither durst they with a part, lest they should not be sufficiently strong and they should fall (Alma 56:22-24).

The trail junction (70) in figure 20 and the extended route northward from the Antiparah complex symbolize the connection that Helaman is discussing. The Lamanites at Antiparah had access northward past Judea and therefore also past the unnamed Nephite seashore settlement (31).

The association of the land of Joshua (58) with the Nephite settlements situated northward along that route is based on an assumption made in the preceding chapter. That discussion identifies Joshua's location in, or adjacent to, the Nephites' "land of first inheritance" on the west seashore. Alma 22:28 establishes the "place of their fathers' first inheritance" as on the west seashore, west of the land of Nephi, as it describes the lands inhabited by the Lamanites before the 72 B.C. war.

The proximity of the Lamanite west sea settlements in the land of Nephi to the Antiparah complex is further signaled by the initiation of the Lamanite west-coast invasion against Antiparah. Therefore, if the land of inheritance incorporated west sea lands extending northward from the Lamanite coastal settlements to Joshua, then the land of inheritance also incorporated the intermediate Antiparah complex.

The validity of this conclusion is reinforced by the use of Judea to name one of the settlements in the land of first inheritance. Since the Nephites originated in Near Eastern Judah and landed on the west sea at the "land of their first inheritance" subsequent to Nephi's relocating his people in the land of Nephi (Mosiah 10:13), it is not coincidental for a location in that land of inheritance to have been named after their original homeland, Judah.

If this conclusion is correct, Joshua is in closer proximity to Judea and Antiparah than is suggested by the relative associations shown in figure 20.

An additional trail junction, vertex 86, and its associated routes have been plotted into figure 20. Like vertices 69, 70, and 88, vertex 86 is not mentioned in the Book of Mormon but becomes apparent only when information being used for the analyses of separate paths indicates a common junction. Located on the path between Antiparah (30) and Judea (29), this junction also contains a direct route to junction 70 and an extended route northward to Angola (56).

The basis for the addition of junction 86 comes from the events related in Alma 56 relative to the recovery of Antiparah by the Nephites in 65 B.C. At that time Antiparah (30) had fallen to the Lamanite army, and the Nephite fortified settlements at Judea (29) and an unnamed city (31) adjacent to the west sea were being threatened from the positions at Antiparah.

To resolve the situation and bring the Lamanites out of their defenses into the open where they could most effectively be fought, the Nephites developed a ploy centered on Helaman and his 2,000 Ammonite warriors. Helaman took his small force near Antiparah (30), giving the impression that they were taking provisions to the unnamed Nephite stronghold (31) on the seashore. The path from Judea (29) to vertex 31 through the trail junction (70) represents the routes taken by this army as detailed in verses 31-33.

The Lamanites, anticipating an easy victory and the bonus of recovering the provisions destined for the Nephite settlement, sent an army to intercept Helaman. Following the plan, Helaman's detachment "did flee before them, northward. And thus we did lead away the most powerful army of the Lamanites" (Alma 56:36). A second Nephite force joined the pursuit, following directly behind the Lamanites. It can be assumed that the northward course taken by Helaman was into a neutral zone, for had the Nephites turned back toward Judea or had they taken the route through the Nephite zone toward Joshua (58), the Lamanites would have sensed a trap and would have been reluctant to continue the pursuit. The northward trail taken by Helaman, therefore, is shown as the path in figure 20 leading from junction 70 through junction 86 and then northward toward Angola (56).

On the third day of the pursuit into the wilderness, the forces locked in battle at the place on the route shown as vertex 92. The Nephites emerged as victors. The large number of captives taken in the conflict posed a problem to the Nephites. In verse 57 Helaman relates: "And as we had no place for our prisoners, that we could guard them to keep them from the armies of the Lamanites, therefore we sent them to the land of Zarahemla, and a part of those men who were not slain of Antipus, with them; and the remainder I took and joined them to my stripling Ammonites, and took our march back to the city of Judea."

This reference demonstrates the route relationship northward to a connection with the main Joshua-Manti path to Zarahemla. While still at the battlefield, the Lamanite captives were taken onward to the land of Zarahemla for detention before Helaman retraced his route "back to the city of Judea."

The extended route from the battlefield (92) to Angola (56) demonstrates a relative connection between the two places. The route connected with the main path somewhere between the land of David (57) and the settlement at Cumeni (28). Cumeni was occupied at the time by Lamanites, which would have discouraged the Nephites from moving their prisoners directly to that location. The land of David was probably more distant from the battlefield than was Angola; hence, the region around Angola has been selected as their probable immediate destination on the journey to Zarahemla.

## THE TOPOGRAPHIC FEATURES ASSOCIATED WITH THE AREA NETWORK

The Base Area Network shown in figure 20 contains a variety of topographic features. Its seashores, rivers, wilderness, and coastal corridor zones are quite distinctive and can be abstracted into the simple topographic map portrayed as figure 21.

The most extensive environments depicted in figures 20 and 21 involve the three separate seas and their associated land masses. These large bodies of water form a triangle with its three points situated to the northwest, west, and east of the main land mass.

Shorelines associated with the northern and western seas extend northwest to southeast. References considered in the reconstruction of the Joshua District Network concerning travel along the west seashore (35) into the greater land northward consistently cite a northward or northwestern orientation. North is never used.

The north sea shoreline (55) as reconstructed in the Moron District also extends from the southeast to the northwest, based on the movement of the Jaredite combatants. Continually traveling in an easterly and southerly direction, the opposing forces made periodic stops along the seacoast. They moved eastward to the seashore both from the Plains of Ogash (77) and from Ramah (82). Travel from the seashore at locus 55c was southward to Ramah.

The general location of the east sea to the lands of Nephi and Zarahemla is apparent, based on the references used in reconstructing the Moroni and Nephi District Networks in chapter 6. The relative north-south associations of the lands of Bountiful, Jershon, and Antionum that were near the east sea, as shown in the Nephi Network (see figure 12), further demonstrate the eastern position of the east sea.

The east seashore's northward orientation between Mulek

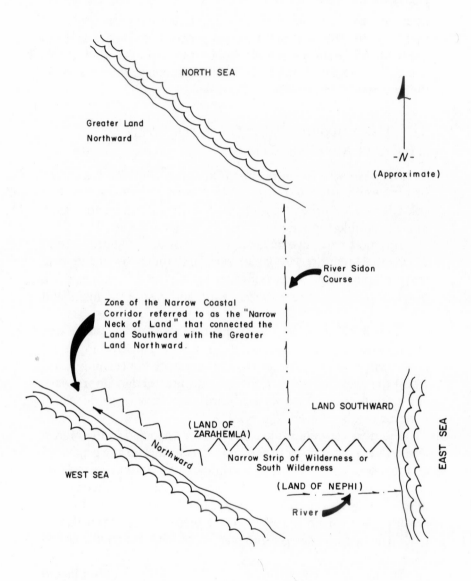

NORTH SEA

Greater Land
Northward

-N-
(Approximate)

River Sidon
Course

Zone of the Narrow Coastal
Corridor referred to as the "Narrow
Neck of Land" that connected the
Land Southward with the Greater
Land Northward.

LAND SOUTHWARD

(LAND OF
ZARAHEMLA)

Northward

Narrow Strip of Wilderness or
South Wilderness

WEST SEA

EAST SEA

(LAND OF NEPHI)

River

FIGURE 21: Topographic Features in the
Area Base Network

(13) and Bountiful (2) is stated in Alma 52:23. This is the only reference to the cardinal orientation of the seashore and is therefore insufficient for postulating a north-south or northwest-southeast extension of the entire seacoast. The reconstructions of the Moroni and Nephi Networks demonstrate a complex association of routes and settlements in the east sea locality. This complexity is the result of a diverse shoreline topography, as partially demonstrated in the Manti Regional Network.

Three separate River Sidon crossings are demonstrated in figures 12 and 20 using vertices 14, 16, and 34. This river originated in the highlands beyond the land of Manti (4) in the narrow strip of wilderness (50), a mountainous zone that extended from the east sea to the west sea. Other wilderness locations in figure 20, including vertices 17 and 33, were probably segments of this barrier. The narrow strip of wilderness mountain chain spanned the Nephites' continent, creating a definite barrier between the "middle" lands of Zarahemla and Nephi (cf. the discussion on this barrier in chapter 3).

Thus, the River Sidon, with its northward flow down past the city of Zarahemla coupled with the extensive wilderness barrier zone, creates a definite river-mountain complex in the center of the land southward with associations to the north, east, and west seas as shown in figure 21.

The hypothesized east-west drainage system (54) associated with the land of Nephi is also provided in figure 21. This system was discussed in the section on the Nephi District Network in chapter 6. Its existence is based on the identification of the Shemlon-Ishmael-Middoni settlements as being east of the city of Nephi (43) and at consecutively lower elevations.

The final topographic feature to be discussed in this section involves the west sea coastal corridor that served as the land route between the land southward and the greater land northward. Its northwest-southeast orientation is discussed in chapter 4 and in the preceding section. Associated in the Book of Mormon with the narrow neck of land and the narrow pass or passage (67), this highly strategic coastal shelf afforded the Nephites excellent control over Lamanite access into the greater land northward. The development of the network models in chapters 4, 5, and 6 discuss the associations and references relative to this topographic locality. Of special significance to the topographic map shown as figure 21 is the highland zone that flanked the coastal corridor on the east. This mountain barrier evidently contained an access route that linked the coastal city of Desolation (63) with an important area under Lamanite control in the highlands (68) (see figure 20).

# 9

## DEFINING THE AMERICAN TOPOGRAPHIC SETTING OF THE AREA MODEL

This chapter presents a correlation of the basic topography of southern Mesoamerica with the terrain and coastal configurations identified in the Book of Mormon model.

The identification of the ancient American locale of the Book of Mormon's area network proceeds in three successive stages. Initially, the area model's topography is compared with the geography of the American continent to determine the setting of the ancient history. With the field narrowed to the southeastern portion of Mesoamerica, the correspondences between model and setting are examined in the second section. Finally, the Mesoamerican locations of the area network are integrated into the area model, resulting in a map of the Book of Mormon localities.

### TOPOGRAPHIC COMPARISONS: MODEL TO AMERICAN GEOGRAPHY

In the preceding chapter the preliminary model of the area network of the Book of Mormon is identified as figure 20. The topographic features associated with that model were then abstracted into figure 21, a basic topographic map of the area. This map is a simplified compilation of rivers, coastlines, and mountain-wilderness barrier systems. It is useful in identifying the topographic setting of the Book of Mormon lands in the Americas.

An examination of the land mass and coastal configurations of the American continent begins with the southern tip of South America and proceeds northward to the Arctic. The major land masses in both North and South America can be discarded from the search because they lack the mountainous east-west barrier system that spanned the distance from the east sea to a west seashore. In addition, the north, east, and west coastline configurations as defined in figures 20 and 21 have marginal similarity with the coastlines on these large land masses.

With the elimination of North and South America, the area of investigation shifts to the linking territories of Mexico and Central America as shown in figure 22. Like a long spinal column, this topographic system extends from modern Mexico on the north to the present boundary between Colombia and Panama on the south. This 2,500-mile-long land bridge consists of complex mountain and valley systems containing diverse environments. It is flanked by extensive coastlines that are swept by the Caribbean and Pacific currents as demonstrated in figure 22.

The comparison of the Book of Mormon topography abstracted into figure 21 can begin with Panama and proceed northward. The Caribbean Sea on the north and east and the Gulf of Panama on the south present the same basic configuration as is shown in figure 21. This area can be discarded, however, for it lacks an east-west mountain barrier connecting the potential east and west seas.

The next possible area to consider consists of western Panama. This region has the Caribbean on the north, the Gulf of Panama on the east, and the Gulf of Chiriqui on the west. The peaks of the Serrania de Tabasara mountains, ranging from 6,000 to 11,000 feet above sea level, create an east-west barrier across the region. This range, however, is the eastern extension of the Cordillera de Talamanca, running the length of the country from its origin in Costa Rica to the northwest. Thus, the main barrier system does not extend between the east and west seashores as required by the topographic model of the Book of Mormon.

A review of the topography of the modern state of Costa Rica furnishes a similar condition to Panama. When either the Gulfo Dulce or the Gulfo de Nicoya on the Pacific is considered as possible east seas, no barrier system exists from those gulfs westward to the corresponding shorelines on the Bahia de Coronado and Golfo del Papagayo.

Farther northward, the diverse coastlines, estuaries, and lakes of Nicaragua, Honduras, and El Salvador furnish a variety of possible associations with the area model. The most apparent correlation features the Gulf of Honduras and the Caribbean as the

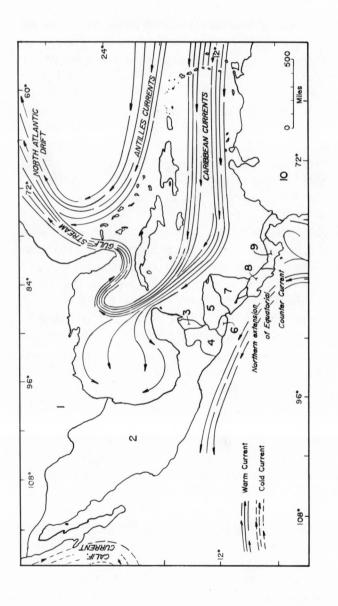

FIGURE 22: The present-day Countries
of Middle America and the Currents of
the Pacific and Atlantic Oceans.

(after West and
Augelli 1966:38)

Legend:

1. The United States
   of America
2. Mexico
3. Belice
4. Guatemala
5. Honduras
6. El Salvador

7. Nicaragua
8. Costa Rica
9. Panama
10. South America

north sea, the Caribbean shoreline on the east of Nicaragua as the east sea, and the Pacific Ocean as the west sea.

The terrain situated within this 500-by-300-mile region is very complex. Extensive faulting has resulted in a series of mountain chains paralleled by long river valleys. These mountain-valley systems are generally oriented northeast to southwest and drain into the Caribbean. The mountain complexes begin on the east in Nicaragua and continue across the region to the Gulf of Honduras, where they extend into Guatemala. No mountains are adjacent to the east shoreline of the Caribbean; the higher elevations merge into the coastal shelf some 60 miles west of that sea. Hence, a specific east-west mountain-wilderness barrier system extending from the east shoreline to the west shoreline does not exist in this region.

One final region in the Central American land bridge remains to be examined for possible correlation with the Book of Mormon model. This region involves the territory of southern Mexico and Guatemala consisting of an area measuring roughly 200 miles (northeast to southwest) by 600 miles (northwest to southeast). Figure 23 has been prepared to aid the correlation of this geographic region with the topographic map abstracted from the Book of Mormon area model (i.e., figure 21) reintroduced to aid comparison as inset B in figure 23. The Gulf of Mexico, Caribbean Sea, and the Pacific Ocean correspond respectively with the north, east, and west seas as shown by comparing figures 23A and 23B.

An examination of the terrain between the Caribbean Sea on the east and the Pacific coastline on the west results in the identification of several parallel mountain-river valley complexes. This mountain barrier begins on the east with the Sierra de las Minas, adjacent to the Gulf of Honduras, and the inland sea Lago de Izabel. It continues to the west, linking with the Sierra de los Cuchumatanes range in central Guatemala. This impressive inland mountain range consists of a formidable barrier, with its highest peaks ranging between 10,000 and 12,500 feet in elevation. The rugged Cuchumatanes connect in western Guatemala with the high Pacific coastal Sierra Madre range known in southern Mexico as the Sierra de Soconusco.[1] Thus, a definite barrier system created by the junction of two of the earth's geological plates spans the continent from the narrow shorelines of the east sea, or Caribbean, extending westward to the Pacific Ocean, or west sea.

The Soconusco range barrier parallels the narrow Pacific coastal shelf. It extends to the southeast from the Isthmus of Tehuantepec through Mexico, connecting with the Sierra Madres which continue to the southeast through Guatemala and into El Salvador.

Two additional correlations to the model shown in figure 23 exist. These consist of river systems. To the south of the mountainous barrier system is the long, narrow Motagua River valley. This drainage system is situated in a fault that parallels the mountain chain. Its flow to the east into the Gulf of Honduras is similar to the river system hypothesized in figure 23B. In that figure, a drainage system having an eastward flow is proposed for the mountain barrier's slopes that face to the south. The initial identification of the existence and orientation of this drainage is based on the following assumptions: First, the Shemlon-Middoni complex was in the "middle" land of Nephi's eastern quadrant; second, the gradual loss of elevation recorded by travelers going from Nephi to Shemlon, Ishmael, and Middoni indicates that progressively lower elevations were encountered to the east of the capital of Nephi and that those lower elevations were drained by a river system that flowed in that direction. The Motagua River system, which drains eastward, correlates with this basic model.

The River Sidon system was a completely separate system in the Book of Mormon. It flowed northward, having its headwaters in the interior of the highland barrier system as shown in figure 22B. This river model has a direct correspondence with the Usumacinta River system of southern Mexico and its Chixoy and Pasion channels in Guatemala.[2] The Usumacinta River system flows generally north to northwest. The direct line distance that it drains measures some 250 miles from its headwaters in the Cuchumatanes northwest to its mouth in the Gulf of Mexico.

In summary, the topography of southern Mexico and Guatemala as shown in figure 23A contains a pattern of coastal, river, and mountain features that are complementary to the topography identified for the Book of Mormon as abstracted from the area network into figures 21 and 23B. This similarity in topographies means that the "best fit" for the Book of Mormon Area Network in the Americas is located in the geography of the modern countries of southern Mexico and Guatemala, comprising the ancient cultural region known to archeologists as southeastern Mesoamerica.

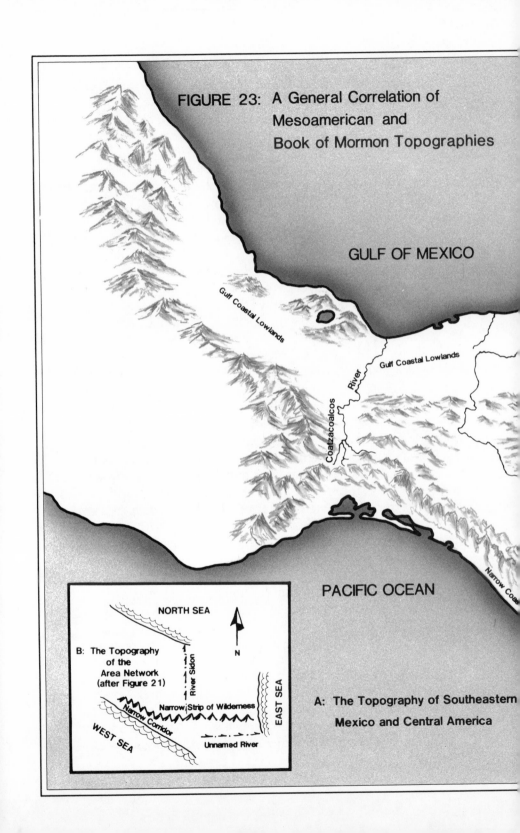

FIGURE 23: A General Correlation of
Mesoamerican and
Book of Mormon Topographies

GULF OF MEXICO

Gulf Coastal Lowlands

Gulf Coastal Lowlands

River

Coatzacoalcos

PACIFIC OCEAN

Narrow Coas

NORTH SEA

B: The Topography
of the
Area Network
(after Figure 21)

River Sidon

N

EAST SEA

Narrow Strip of Wilderness

Narrow Corridor

WEST SEA

Unnamed River

A: The Topography of Southeastern
Mexico and Central America

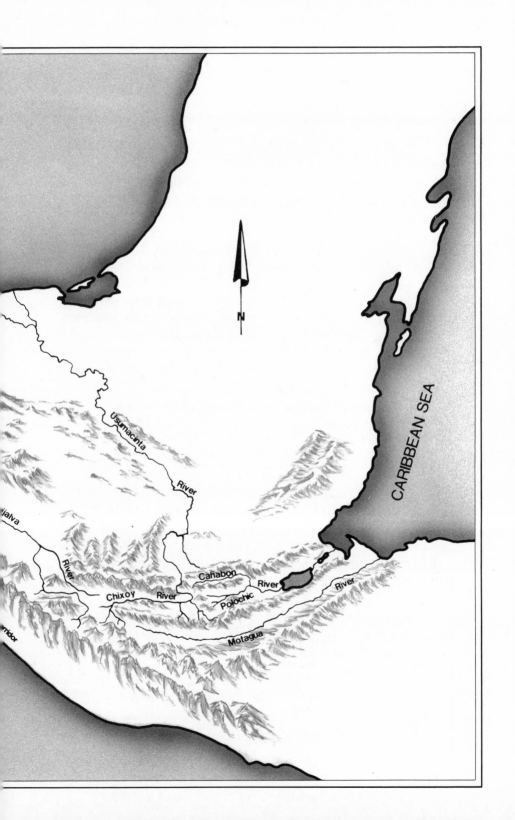

## SOUTHERN MESOAMERICA AND THE SPATIAL NETWORK OF THE BOOK OF MORMON

The term *Mesoamerica* is used to designate an ancient cultural area of high development that existed prior to the Spanish conquest. This area extended from the Rio Panuco–Sinaloa regions of central Mexico southward to the mouth of the Motagua and the Gulf of Nicoya in Honduras and Nicaragua. The designation of this cultural area as Mesoamerica was first used by Paul Kirchhoff in his 1943 article entitled "Mesoamerica: Its Geographic Limits, Ethnic Composition, and Cultural Character" (Kirchhoff 1981:1-10).

Mesoamerica was an area of high cultural achievement in religion, technology, architecture, art, literacy, agriculture, calendrics, and astronomy. Southern Mesoamerica was the region where the Olmec, Zapotec, and Mayan civilizations flourished in the first millennia before and/or after Christ. This region therefore contains a rich cultural heritage.

The balance of this section is devoted to examining the Book of Mormon area network within its Mesoamerican setting.[3] The final product of this endeavor is a combined area model–Mesoamerican map that facilitates further research and explanation. The network models developed in the previous chapters have been designated as the initial series of models. The revised models in this chapter are referred to as secondary models, or as the secondary series, for they are in the second phase of system development. In addition, the general placements of the Book of Mormon locations in the following maps are the results of combining the textual analyses of the preceding chapters with field testing and a knowledge of the existing landscape. The abstract graphs of the initial series of models have required careful adjustment with the existing landforms to simplify this presentation and to identify the "best fit" correlations that can then be used for further field testing.

### EAST SEA CORRELATIONS

The land of Jershon was apparently recolonized by the Nephites in about 73 B.C. after the migration of the people of Ammon

124

to Melek (cf. Alma 35:13-14 with Alma 50:7-15). Because of Jershon's proximity to the Zoramites and the Lamanite territory, a series of fortified settlements as engineered by the early chief captain Moroni were established for the new colonists' protection. From the similarities of the descriptions given of these locations, the original land of Jershon was apparently incorporated into the lands of Mulek (13) and Gid (12) (see Alma 27:22; 28:1; 31:3).

In the preceding section, the area model's east sea topography was correlated with the Gulf of Honduras on the Caribbean and the Lago de Izabel–Sierra de las Minas localities. The diversity of topography in this Mesoamerican locality enables the compatible integration of all the text's lands and settlements situated near the east sea. This can be accomplished by tentatively identifying the east sea land of Bountiful as the Caribbean coastal shelf bounded on the northwest and north by the Maya Mountains and on the south by the Rio Sarstun drainage. Figure 24 demonstrates this association. The narrow strip of wilderness (50c) that separated the Zoramite land of Antionum (37) from the Lamanite land of Siron (38)(cf. Alma 31:3; 39:3) fits into the topography of the locality.

The land of Jershon (36) can be situated in the lowlands to the north of the Rio Dulce and the El Golfete bodies of water. Jershon is the locality where the people of Ammon were initially settled and where the Nephite armies assembled when threatened by the combined Zoramite-Lamanite forces. Its position across the Rio Dulce as shown in figure 24 is reinforced by the numerous references in Alma 35 of travel going "over" between Jershon and Antionum. The variety of contexts where "over" is used to describe travel between two locations indicates this term was used relative to movement across physical barriers. In certain cases those barriers can be identified as wilderness or mountainous terrain — for example, in Alma 30:21, 39:3. Alma chapter 35 contains a variety of references to travelers going "over" between Jershon and Antionum. The description of these two lands in Alma 31:3 states:

"Now the Zoramites had gathered themselves together in a land which they called Antionum, which was east of the land of Zarahemla, which lay nearly bordering upon the seashore, which was south of the land of Jershon, which also bordered upon the wilderness south, which wilderness was full of Lamanites."

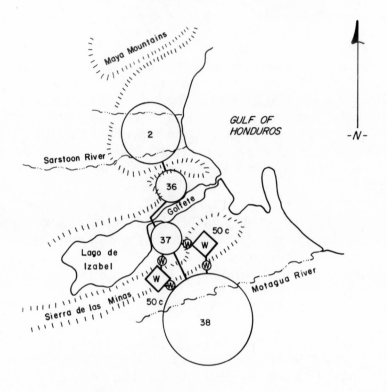

-N-

Legend:

2   Land of Bountiful
36  Land Jershon
37  Land of Antionum
38  Land of Siron
50  Narrow Strip of Wilderness

FIGURE 24:  The Bountiful – Siron Path
            As Located in the Lago de Izabel
            or East Sea Locality

This description gives no indication of a wilderness barrier between the two lands, although it stipulates that Antionum and possibly Jershon bordered the wilderness south (the narrow strip of wilderness barrier zone) that can be identified in this locality with the Sierra de las Minas mountain chain.

The barrier between Jershon and Antionum suggested by the repetition of "over" in describing travel between these two places, therefore, was probably not mountainous nor wilderness terrain but rather a narrow channel in the Rio Dulce–El Golfete waterway associated with the outlet of the Lago de Izabel as shown in figure 24.

The correlation of the east sea settlements that were first developed in the Moroni District Network (see figure 8) with the Gulf of Honduras locality is shown in figure 25. This figure gives the basic distribution of the lands of Lehi and Morianton and the settlements of Omner, Gid, and Mulek (9, 10, 11, 12, and 13) along the north shore of the Lago de Izabel, Rio Dulce, and El Golfete waterways. Omner, Gid, and Mulek would have been placed in strategic positions to control Lamanite access across the Rio Dulce narrows. Lehi and Morianton would have been used to block east-west movement along the narrow north shore of the sea. Moroni (5) was north and west of wilderness zones 17a and 17b. This wilderness barrier, east and south of Moroni, correlates with the narrow strip of wilderness barrier that separated the Nephites from the Lamanites. Moroni was very close to the east sea, for in A.D. 34 it "did sink into the depths of the sea, and the inhabitants thereof were drowned" (3 Nephi 8:9; 9:4). Moroni's strategic position in figure 25 further demonstrates why it was the first Nephite settlement to fall to the Lamanites in the 72-60 B.C. war and the last settlement to be retaken by Moroni at the close of the war.

Figure 26 is a composite map of the Bountiful-Siron-Moroni settlement complex on the east sea. It combines the settlement positions shown in figures 24 and 25. This basic correlation of model to the Gulf of Honduras locale is useful for research purposes. Field research in these ancient site locations will result in the further refinement of this model.

The Lago de Izabel locations shown on figures 24-26 are the present-day lake shoreline. The ancient waterway known to the Nephites as the east sea, an extension of the larger Caribbean

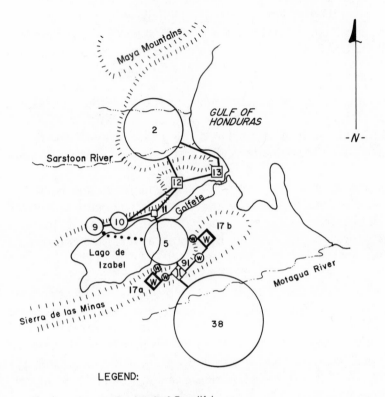

LEGEND:

2    Land of Bountiful
5    Land of Moroni
9    Land of Lehi
10   Land of Morianton
11   Omner
12   Gid
13   Mulek
17   Narrow Strip of Wilderness or South
       Wilderness
38   Land of Siron
91   Passage through the Wilderness

NOTE: Symbol • • • • denotes submerged route in the Lago de Izabel
when the surface dropped during the past tectonic disturbances

FIGURE 25:   The Bountiful – Moroni Path
As Located in the Lago de Izabel
or East Sea Locality

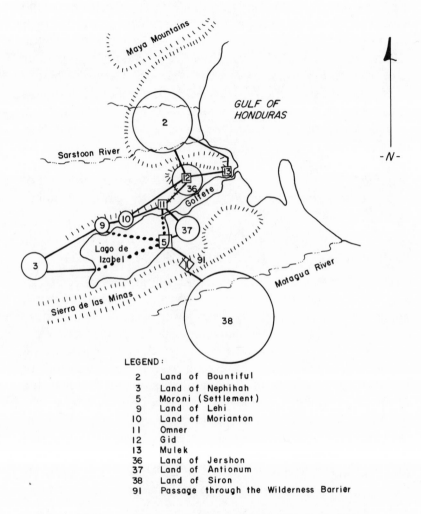

Maya Mountains

GULF OF
HONDURAS

Sarstoon River

-N-

②

⑫

◇36

⑬

Golfete

□11

⑨ ⑩

◇37

Lago de
Izabel

⑤

◇91

③

Motagua River

Sierra de las Minas

38

LEGEND:

| | |
|---|---|
| 2 | Land of Bountiful |
| 3 | Land of Nephihah |
| 5 | Moroni (Settlement) |
| 9 | Land of Lehi |
| 10 | Land of Morianton |
| 11 | Omner |
| 12 | Gid |
| 13 | Mulek |
| 36 | Land of Jershon |
| 37 | Land of Antionum |
| 38 | Land of Siron |
| 91 | Passage through the Wilderness Barrier |

NOTE: symbol ••• denotes submerged route in the Lago
de Izabel when the Surface dropped during the past
tectonic disturbances

FIGURE 26: The Bountiful - Siron - Moroni
Settlement Complex As Located in the
Lago de Izabel or East Sea Locality

Sea, was not as extensive as its modern shoreline; hence, the western routes from Moroni (5) to Nephihah (3) and Lehi (9) are presently covered by the sea as shown in figure 26. Lago de Izabel and the Polochic River Valley are situated in a graben, or deep depression, caused by tectonic faulting along the earth's plates that meet in this locality. Some time after Moroni was constructed, a movement in the plates occurred, resulting in the collapse of a large segment of the Polochic Valley. The waters of the Caribbean rushed in to fill the depression, resulting in the large lake complex that is presently visible. This seismic disturbance may have been the event of A.D. 34 wherein the Book of Mormon, in 3 Nephi 8:9 and 9:4, describes the city of Moroni as having been sunk into the depths of the sea.

## CORRELATIONS OF THE JERSHON TO MANTI PATH

Moving westward from the east sea–Lago de Izabel/Gulf of Honduras locality, the narrow strip of wilderness barrier that is paralleled by a series of connected faultline depressions can be used to demonstrate the scale of the Manti Regional Network.

The earlier discussion of this network in chapter 6 noted the apparent ease of travelers in moving from the east sea lands of Jershon and Morianton up into the land of Manti. The Polochic River Valley, which is the eastern portion of a major east-west faultline, affords such a convenient transportation corridor from the Caribbean and Lago de Izabel area into the highlands. This river valley drains the north slope of the narrow strip of wilderness that equates with the Sierra de las Minas range. From its mouth at the west end of the Lago de Izabel, the Polochic River extends west past the village of Tucuru into the Alta Verapaz highlands, which comprise the narrow strip of wilderness in this region. These highlands are associated with the headwaters of the Cahabon River and drain also into the adjacent Chixoy River. Ancient Manti correlates in this model with these 5,000-foot elevation valleys and their steep conifer-wooded slopes of the Alta Verapaz. The villages of Tactic and San Cristobal Verapaz and the town of Coban are the current population centers in this locality.

Figure 27 is a map demonstrating the topographic and model correlations in the eastern segment of the fault corridor.

The extended route from Manti to the east sea is first referenced concerning the journey around 77 B.C. of the people of Ammon from the land of Nephi to Jershon via the wilderness near Manti (cf. Alma 27:14, 22, 26; 17:1). About three to four years later, these converted Lamanite people left Jershon for the safer territory at Melek (Alma 35:13). The topography of the region explains how Melek could be directly accessible to people coming from Jershon. They traveled westward from the north shore of the Lago de Izabel locality (land of Jershon) up the Polochic Valley into highland Manti, the vicinity of the present-day towns of Tactic and Coban. Crossing the Chixoy River (River Sidon) they continued westward in the natural corridor until they reached ancient Melek (26).

This Polochic Valley corridor into the highlands was subsequently used by Moroni and his army when they left Jershon to halt an imminent Lamanite invasion of Manti. Mormon relates this action in the following statement:

"Now Moroni, leaving a part of his army in the land of Jershon, lest by any means a part of the Lamanites should come into that land and take possession of the city, took the remaining part of his army and marched over into the land of Manti" (Alma 43:25).

In Alma chapters 43 and 44, Mormon then describes Moroni's development of the Nephite ambush at the river crossing near Manti and the subsequent battle at that location (not shown in figure 27). The Nephites had the advantage over their enemy from the beginning. They used good intelligence sources to determine the area in jeopardy, and then they had access to a route that facilitated their advance into the locality and deployment at the river site before the arrival of the Lamanite advance force.

## CORRELATIONS OF THE MANTI TO JUDEA PATH

The next portion of this analysis concerns the western corridor extending from Manti to Judea. So critical to the Nephite defense during the 72-60 B.C. war, this path can be identified in the topography of central Guatemala and southeastern Mexico.

Figure 28 is a map of the topography of the region beginning on the east with the continuation of the valley from the highlands of the Alta Verapaz locality, where ancient Manti was positioned, westward to the coastal range above the Pacific Ocean, or west sea of the text. This ancient system of linked river valley corridors

## BOOK OF MORMON LOCALITIES

| | |
|---|---|
| 3 | Land of Nephihah |
| 4 | Land of Manti |
| 5 | Moroni |
| 8 | Land of Aaron |
| 9 | Land of Lehi |
| 10 | Land of Morianton |
| 11 | Omner |
| 12 | Gid |
| 13 | Mulek |
| 17 | Wilderness |
| 36 | Land of Jershon |
| 37 | Land of Antionum |

## PRESENT - DAY TOWNS & CITIES

| | | | |
|---|---|---|---|
| a. | Coban | i. | Cunen |
| b. | San Cristobal Verapaz | j. | Sacapulas |
| c. | Gualan | k. | Rabinal |
| d. | Panzos | l. | Salama |
| e. | Tucuru | m. | Granados |
| f. | Tactic | n. | El Progreso |
| g. | Livingston | o. | Guatemala City |
| h. | Puerto Barrias | | |

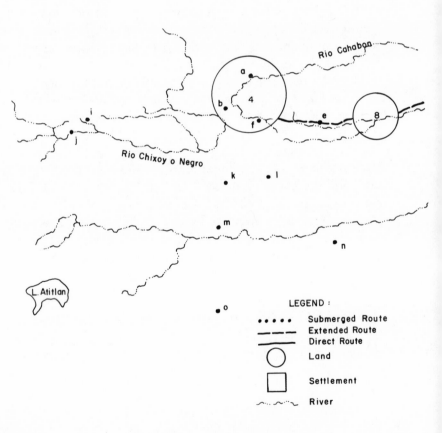

LEGEND :

•••• Submerged Route

– – – Extended Route

——— Direct Route

◯ Land

▢ Settlement

～～ River

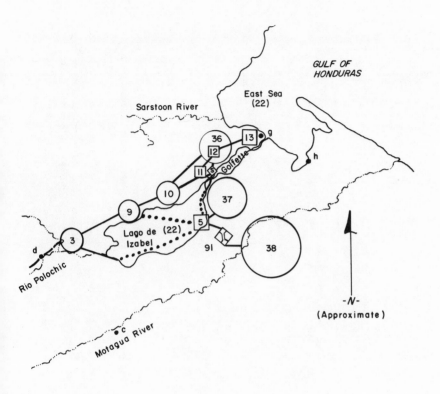

GULF OF
HONDURAS

East Sea
(22)

Sarstoon River

36 · 13 · g

12

· h

11 S Golfette

10

37

9

5

Lago de (22)
Izabel

3

91

38

d ·

Rio Polochic

-N-
(Approximate)

· c

Motagua River

Map Scale 1 : 1,000,000

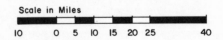

Scale in Miles

10    0   5   10  15  20  25              40

FIGURE 27 :  The Manti - Jershon - Antionum
Paths as Located in the
Polochic River Drainage

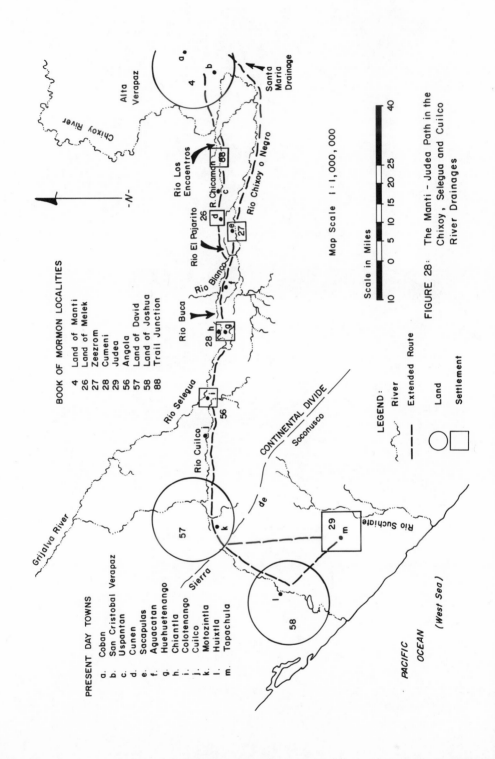

BOOK OF MORMON LOCALITIES

4   Land of Manti
26  Land of Melek
27  Zeezrom
28  Cumeni
29  Judea
56  Angola
57  Land of David
58  Land of Joshua
88  Trail Junction

PRESENT DAY TOWNS

a. Coban
b. San Cristobal Verapaz
c. Uspantan
d. Cunen
e. Sacapulas
f. Aguacatan
g. Huehuetenango
h. Chiantla
i. Colotenango
j. Cuilco
k. Motozintla
l. Huixtla
m. Tapachula

LEGEND:

River
Extended Route
Land
Settlement

Map Scale 1:1,000,000

Scale in Miles

10   0   5   10  15  20  25      40

FIGURE 28:  The Manti - Judea Path in the
            Chixoy, Selegua and Cuilco
            River Drainages

-N-

Grijalva River

Chixoy River

Alta Verapaz

Santa Maria Drainage

Rio Los Encaentros

Rio Chicaman

Rio El Pajarito

Rio Chixoy o Negro

Rio Blanco

Rio Buca

Rio Selegua

Rio Cuilco

CONTINENTAL DIVIDE

Soconusco

Sierra de

Rio Suchiate

PACIFIC OCEAN
(West Sea)

contains two east-to-west-trending parallel faults both beginning in the San Cristobal Verapaz and Tactic valleys on the east of the Chixoy River. These faults then extend west across the Chixoy gorge to meet at the junction of the Blanco and El Pajarito rivers east of Aguacatan. In figure 28, the northern fault line is associated with Rios Los Encuentros and El Pajarito, while the southern fault is followed by the Rio Chixoy or Negro.

The first route simply continues in the faultline from the town of Tactic west to the head of the Santa Maria drainage. The Santa Maria gorge then descends some 2,400 feet to the river, ending where the Chixoy Dam has recently been constructed. The narrow Chixoy River canyon is a continuation of this fault, extending upriver past the town of Sacapulas, which may be in the vicinity of ancient Zeezrom (27), to the Rio Blanco junction.

A second route on the north and parallel to this first corridor begins in the ancient Manti locality of the San Cristobal Verapaz valley on the east of the river and descends down to the vicinity of the existing bridge across the Chixoy. The route then proceeds westward up the Rio Chicaman valley past the towns of Uspantan and Cunen, which may correlate with the localities of the ancient trail junction (88) and Melek (26). West of Cunen, the route descends down the Rio El Pajarito valley to the junction of the Rio Blanco on the headwaters of the Chixoy, or Negro, River.

The Rio Blanco valley is an intermediate segment of the long system of fault corridors that extend from the Alta Verapaz to the Continental Divide on the Pacific coastal range. The route westward follows this valley past the town of Aguacatan to the head of the narrow Rio Buca canyon. At this point a saddle is crossed on the narrow ridge that descends southward from the high escarpment of the Cuchumatanes range. This high mountain chain comprises the western segment of the narrow strip of wilderness barrier zone that separated the lands of Zarahemla and Nephi.

The ridge at the head of the Rio Buca separates the headwaters of the two major river systems in southern Mesoamerica: the Chixoy-Usumacinta on the east and the Selegua-Grijalva on the west.

After crossing the ridge into the Grijalva drainage, the valley corridor system proceeds westerly past the town of Chiantla in the Huehuetenango basin, where ancient Cumeni (28) may have been located, to descend the Rio Selegua past the town of San

Sabastian Huehuetenango. At the low ridge where the village of Colotenango is situated, the route leaves the Selegua River canyon, ascends the saddle possibly at the locale of ancient Angola (56), and immediately drops down into the Cuilco River canyon. This river valley, also a tributary of the Grijalva River, is a continuation of the westward faultline that begins in the Gulf of Honduras.

The Cuilco River canyon extends past the town of Cuilco to the Mexico-Guatemala border. On the Mexican side of the border, the Cuilco River junctions with other Grijalva tributaries flowing into the Grijalva Depression to the north. These river canyons may mark the location of the ancient land of David (57). Here the route to the Pacific continues south, up the river valley past the town of Motozintla, and over the narrow pass that at its 6,000-foot elevation marks the Continental Divide. This pass separates the Gulf of Mexico drainage of the Grijalva system from the Pacific drainages on the south slopes of the coastal Sierra de Soconusco range. After ascending this pass, the route to the Pacific seashore divides into two branches, each branch of the trail descending to the separate lowland Mexican towns of Huixtla and Tapachula, which may be the sites of ancient Joshua (58) and Judea (29) respectively.

It is interesting that only as the result of a long series of connecting faultlines can such a direct, linear route exist in such a topographically complex area. Southern Guatemala and southeastern Mexico are dominated by abrupt and very difficult mountain, canyon, and valley associations that restrict overland travel. Other than the Pacific coastal shelf, there are only two other areas where direct lines of surface travel can be accomplished in Guatemala. These consist of the Motagua River valley and the nearly 270-mile-long fault system that, as described above, links the Caribbean Sea with the Pacific coast.

Movement from the east sea to the west sea along this series of fault valleys in the Polochic, Chixoy, and Grijilva drainages is first noted in the text concerning the flight of the people of Morianton (10) from their settlement on the east sea to the narrow pass on the west sea (Alma 50:25-36). Teancum and his army were sent by Moroni from the east sea area to halt the exodus. So rapid was their flight that Teancum could not intercept Morianton until they had arrived on the west seashore. In the ensuing battle Morianton was killed and his people defeated before Teancum could bring those Nephites back into their homeland. The defeated rebels were undoubtedly returned to Moroni's camp by this same corridor that had been used for their attempted migration into the greater land northward.

The later use of this corridor by the Nephites during the 72-60 B.C. war is referenced by Helaman in his letter to Moroni concerning the Nephite recovery of the captured settlements of Antiparah (30), Cumeni (28), and Manti (4) as recorded in Alma 56-58.

Helaman and the Nephite armies began the recovery of their lands by first reinforcing the west sea defenses at Judea (29) and then recapturing Antiparah (30). Helaman's arrival at Judea with the 2,000 Ammonite warriors from Melek (26) indicates that the Nephites had retained a safe route for travel between Zarahemla and their west sea fortified settlements. This route is alluded to in Alma 56:57, which states that Lamanite prisoners taken in this locality were sent to the land of Zarahemla for safekeeping. The Nephite fortifications at Antiparah, Judea, and the unnamed coastal settlement (31) had been established to curtail Lamanite advances northward beyond this complex against other Nephite settlements (see Alma 56:22). It is logical, therefore, that this Antiparah defensive complex also protected the route that led back to the land of Zarahemla.

If the Manti-Judea path in figure 6 is identical with the Alta Verapaz–Tapachula route described above and shown in figure 28, the Antiparah defensive complex was situated on the Pacific coastal shelf to the southeast of modern Huixtla. To afford maximum protection, the Nephites would have placed one fortified settlement in the Tapachula vicinity to block that branch of the route leading up into the mountains. The important Preclassic ceremonial site of Izapa is located just to the east of Tapachula and was probably situated within the Antiparah defensive complex. Izapa may have been a unit in the Judea settlement system since the Nephite need for defense in depth would have required Antiparah, as a forward position, to be situated farther to the southeast away from the trail system that led into the land of Zarahemla.

With the recovery of Antiparah, Helaman and his Ammonite warriors traveled back on the Manti-Judea path to the vicinity of Cumeni (28). The Nephites gained control of Cumeni by intercepting the Lamanite supply column and starving the hostile forces into surrender. The Lamanites' vulnerability to having their supply lines disrupted demonstrates that Cumeni was not readily accessible from their homeland. The Lamanite army isolation at the besieged site of Cumeni is further substantiated by the fact that their needed reinforcements were dispatched from Manti (Alma 57:22), along the fault corridor to the east of Cumeni.

Cumeni's position on or near the main east-west route in the fault system is indicated in Alma 57:11. This reference states that after its recovery by the Nephites, the prisoners were sent to the land of Zarahemla and the captured provisions taken to Judea. The Huehuetenango basin is situated at such a strategic location. At the base of the Cuchumatanes range, this basin is accessible to the east-west faultline corridor, which correlates with the Manti-Judea path. The Huehuetenango basin also blocks any access to the north or the west coming from the Lamanite homeland in the Motagua River corridor to the southeast.

Zeezrom (27) evidently sat along the Manti-Judea path, based on its inclusion in the list of captured settlements provided in Alma 56:13-15. Its omission from Helaman's account of the recovered settlements given in the subsequent chapter is probably not an oversight. Zeezrom was most likely situated between Cumeni and Manti in a position that it could be bypassed by Helaman in his march toward Manti. If Zeezrom were situated on the main Chixoy channel in the Sacapulas area, for instance, it could have been easily bypassed by Helaman traveling the upper Cunen-Uspantan corridor to the Chixoy crossing west of San Cristobal Verapaz. In addition, a continued Lamanite presence in the Sacapulas depression would not have presented a threat to Helaman's forces at Manti as long as the Nephites could watch and defend the entrance to that route in the Tactic locality. From the head of the Santa Maria drainage, the Nephites could easily observe the Chixoy River route and have ample warning of any force advancing from Sacapulas. It would take time for a hostile force to ascend the steep slope, some 2,400 feet from the river up to Manti in the highland valleys of the Alta Verapaz.

The control of the southern and western approaches into Manti appears to have been Helaman's intent, for, upon arriving in the land of Manti, he positioned his forces south of the fortified settlement adjacent to the "wilderness side which was near to the city" (Alma 58:13). This wilderness was a segment of the narrow strip of wilderness barrier zone. Helaman's army was therefore situated in the San Cristobal–Tactic locality, an excellent tactical position. It afforded Helaman the necessary protection from being flanked by a hostile force coming from Sacapulas along the Chixoy depression, and it also blocked any Lamanite supply and reinforcement columns coming from the south up from Nephi on the main trail. Helaman's threat of interdicting the Lamanite supply lines into Manti from the "middle" land of Nephi eventually pressured the Lamanites into coming out of the fortified positions; this military action cost the Lamanite forces the control of the city of Manti.

## MANTI TO ZARAHEMLA PATH CORRELATIONS

The correlation of the narrow strip of wilderness barrier with southern Mesoamerica's connected mountain ranges and their associated faulted valleys provides the basis for coordinating the Zarahemla-Manti-Nephi paths. Figure 29 is the map of these paths situated in the Motagua, Cahabon, and Chixoy River systems of central Guatemala. Spatial associations on these paths and their linked settlements and environmental features have been discussed in chapter 6 relative to both the Moroni and Nephi District networks.

The Zarahemla-Manti-Nephi paths are centered on the land of Manti (4), which has been established as existing in the Alta Verapaz locality where the towns of Coban, San Cristobal Verapaz, and Tactic are presently situated. This highland area is drained by the headwaters of the Polochic and Cahabon rivers, which flow into the Caribbean, and the Chixoy–Usumacinta River, which empties into the Gulf of Mexico.

From Manti, two extended routes led northward into the lowlands of the Nephite homeland. One route led to the valley of Gideon (7), as stated in Alma 17:1: "Alma was journeying from the land of Gideon southward, away to the land of Manti." The land of Gideon has been placed in the general vicinity of the present-day village of Chisec. This village is in a large valley system that has excellent overland connections to the north, south, and east. Travel to the west and northwest is restricted by the complex limestone karst topography of the region.

This natural restriction to travel westward from Chisec is another reason for placing the valley of Gideon in the Chisec locality. Alma chapter 2 relates the 87 B.C. Amlicite defeat near the lower River Sidon crossing east of Zarahemla. To escape Alma and his Nephite army, the Amlicites retreated southward through the valley of Gideon and then evidently to the southwest to the land of Minon (6), where they joined a Lamanite army. These combined forces then were free to move northward into the land of Zarahemla, which they proceeded to sack. Alma and the Nephites in the valley of Gideon could not travel directly into Zarahemla to block the threat, but were forced to return to the lower River Sidon crossing to gain entry into their capital. This brief account of the Amlicite struggle, therefore, indicates the existence of a topographic barrier of some type that curtailed direct travel between Gideon and Zarahemla. That barrier very possibly was the karst terrain that forms the western and northwestern peripheries of the Chisec valley.

The other route north from Manti went to the land of Minon (6), which was "above the land of Zarahemla, in the course of the land of Nephi." (Alma 2:24). As noted in this reference and in the discussion above on Gideon, Minon was evidently closer to the River Sidon than was the valley of Gideon and had access northward into the lesser land of Zarahemla (1) and southward via Manti (4) to Nephi (43).

The lesser land of Zarahemla (1) has been located in the Laguna Lachua–Montana Nueve Cerros locality of the northern Alta Verapaz lowlands. This large, centrally located lowland area has excellent overland and riverine access throughout the southern Peten tropics. The Usumacinta River is navigable from the rapids in the Laguna Lachua vicinity all the way downstream to its mouth in the Gulf of Mexico. The eastern periphery of the Laguna Lachua basin is drained by the Icbolay River, an extensive tributary in the Usumacinta system. The eastern crossing of the River Sidon (14) was either on the main channel of the Chixoy to the west of the Laguna Lachua or was on the Rio Icbolay as shown in figure 29.

In addition to its environmental position and centrality, this locale offered the Nephites exceptional agricultural and trade potential. A subterranean salt resource exists in this location.[4] These salt deposits are the only known salt resource in the in-

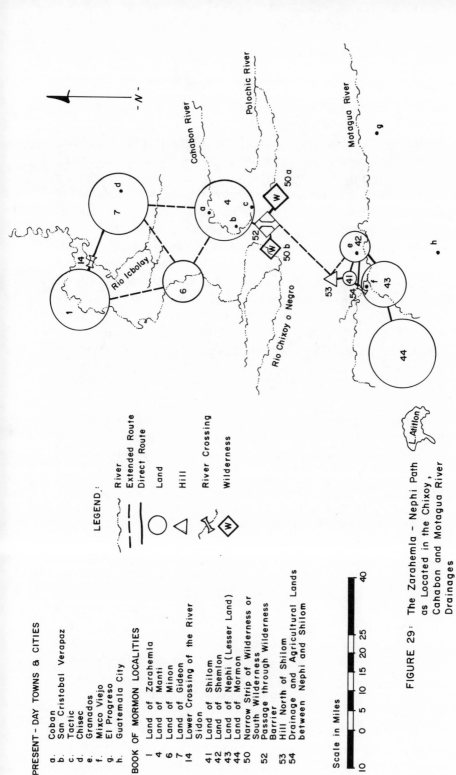

PRESENT - DAY TOWNS & CITIES

a. Coban
b. San Cristobal Verapaz
c. Tactic
d. Chisec
e. Granados
f. Mixco Viejo
g. El Progreso
h. Guatemala City

BOOK OF MORMON LOCALITIES

1    Land of Zarahemla
4    Land of Manti
6    Land of Minon
7    Land of Gideon
14   Lower Crossing of the River
     Sidon
41   Land of Shilom
42   Land of Shemlon
43   Land of Nephi (Lesser Land)
44   Land of Mormon
50   Narrow Strip of Wilderness or
     South Wilderness
52   Passage through Wilderness
     Barrier
53   Hill North of Shilom
54   Drainage and Agricultural Lands
     between Nephi and Shilom

LEGEND:

~~~  River
———  Extended Route
- - - Direct Route
◯    Land
△    Hill
⋈    River Crossing
◈W   Wilderness

FIGURE 29: The Zarahemla – Nephi Path
           as Located in the Chixoy,
           Cahabon and Motagua River
           Drainages

Map Scale: 1" = 1,000,000

Scale in Miles

10   0   5   10   15   20   25        40

terior. Anciently the closest known competing salt sources were on the distant Caribbean coast of Northern Yucatan. A spring on the west slope of the Mesa de Tortugas brings diluted salt to the surface. This spring flows into the Arroyo Salinas at the base of this mesa and then northward to empty its mineral content into the Rio Salinas segment of the Usumacinta. The Maya Indians for centuries have used artificial evaporation ponds in the Arroyo Salinas for gathering this valuable resource from the stream.

The primary known archeological site in this locality is situated along the Arroyo Salinas to the east of the Montana Nueva Cerros or Nine Hills from which it has derived its name. Limited archeological survey and testing have been conducted on this site by Brian Dillon during a number of visits between 1975 and 1978 (Dillon 1977 and 1979). Dillon's work demonstrates a Preclassic and Classic Maya period of occupation in the vicinity of the Arroyo Salinas drainage dating roughly from 300 B.C. until A.D. 900 (1979:243-47). After the abandonment of the interior lowland Mayan sites about A.D. 900, Salinas de Los Nueve Cerros was also abandoned, but not forgotten. The Maya Indians continued to visit this site to obtain salt until recent times, for Dillon notes that "seasonal extraction of salt by boiling brine from the salt stream ... continued until 1936 under concession from Coban" (1979:7).

This entire locality is still awaiting intensive exploration and mapping. During a visit to the site in 1981, this author observed extensive ruins covered by centuries of accumulated soil, debris, and the lofty, ever-present rain forest.

## MANTI TO NEPHI PATH CORRELATIONS

Figure 29 also shows the path connecting Manti (4) on the north to the "lesser" land of Nephi (43) on the south. The south wilderness or narrow strip of wilderness (50) existed to the south of Manti (cf. Alma 16:6-7; 22:27; 43:22; 50:11; 58:13-24) and served as a barrier between the Nephites on the north and the Lamanites to the south in the land of Nephi. A passage through this wilderness barrier into Manti has been postulated and is shown as symbol 52 in figure 29.

An extended route links the wilderness barrier zone (50) and its passage (52) with the hill on the north of the lands of Shilom

(41) and Nephi (43), as stated in Mosiah 7:4-6, 16 and Mosiah 11:13. This hill was not only accessible to Shilom and Nephi, as stated in these references, but also to the Lamanite settlement at Shemlon (42), as referenced in Mosiah 10:8. The north hill can be correlated with the Sierra de Chuacus range that forms the northern periphery of the Motagua River drainage. To the north of this 6,000-to-7,000 foot elevation range are the Cubilco, Rabinal, and Salama valleys that drain northwest into the Negro, or Chixoy, River. Trail routes extending north of these valleys climb over the next range, which correlates with the narrow strip of wilderness (50) before descending into the valleys of the Alta Verapaz, where ancient Manti (4) existed.

The hostile Lamanites at Shemlon initiated an attack against the Nephites in the drainage (54) that lay between Nephi and Shilom (Mosiah 9:14-15). They also launched attacks against Nephi (cf. Mosiah 19:4-10; 20:7-9). The close proximity of these three settlements is further indicated in Mosiah 11:12, which states that King Noah could stand on the tower in the city of Nephi-Lehi (43) and overlook both lands of Shilom (41) and Shemlon (42). These associations are shown in the network given in figure 29.

The Nephi-Shilom-Shemlon localities correlate with the Granados locality of the narrow Motagua River valley. This area is about 20 miles directly north of Guatemala City. However, the intervening terrain contains a 3,000-foot drop in elevation from Guatemala City down into the Motagua River valley. This complex topography consists of numerous ridge and canyon systems that preclude both direct observation and ready access from the conifer-forested region of Guatemala City down into the arid river bottom of the Motagua.

The lesser land of Nephi can be correlated with the locality of Mixco Viejo, or Ancient Mixco, situated on the south side of the Motagua River. This archeological site is situated near the river flood plain on a plateau containing fertile volcanic ash deposits. The ash plateau contains evidences of seismic faulting. Extensive erosion along the faults and the faces of the plateau have resulted in numerous vertical faces that provide Mixco Viejo with excellent natural fortifications. This was the site of a major battle in 1525 between the Spanish Conquistadores led by Captain Pedro de Alvarado and the Pokomam Maya Indians. The Spanish captured the late Maya capital only after an informant had told them of a secret passage into the fortified settlement. The Spanish sent a small force into the fortification through that passageway, established a defensive perimeter, and defeated the Maya. The passage used by the Spanish was probably not identical with the secret passage used by the Nephites; however, research in the locality may establish a correlation between the two corridors.

Intermittent archeological excavations at Mixco Viejo in the period from 1954 through 1966 were oriented toward the evaluation and reconstruction of many Late Postclassic Maya structures. Some evidences of earlier occupations on the site were identified by the team during the course of their investigations. There is a very good probability that extensive evidence of this site's earlier occupations exists, but it may be buried under the ash deposits upon which the Late Postclassic site was constructed before the Spanish arrival.

The Pixcaya River joins the Motagua just to the east of the site of Mixco Viejo. The highlands up the Pixcaya River to the west and southwest of Mixco Viejo are considered to be the ancient land of Mormon (44) with its forests and flowing waters (Mosiah 18:4-5, 30-31).

## WEST SEA CORRELATIONS

The Joshua complex identified in chapter 7 can now be related with the Manti-Judea path shown in figure 28. The proximity of the land of Joshua (58) to Judea (29), as discussed above, is predicated on both settlements having been situated in the "land of first inheritance." Mormon's withdrawal from the land of Zarahemla (1) to Joshua (58) during the final Nephite-Lamanite war was probably accomplished by their traveling to Joshua on the faultline corridor route. The Nephite defense in that war was centered on the control of the west sea positions needed to protect their final area of withdrawal, the greater land northward. It would have been logical, therefore, for them to take the most direct and secure route available to move from the center of the land at Zarahemla to the west sea. The faultline corridor from Manti to Judea would have afforded Mormon those important criteria—security and mobility.

If the route into the Huixtla locality could afford Mormon rapid transit into the west sea coastal plain, he knew that it also could provide his Lamanite adversaries with the same advantage. For this reason, Mormon could not place his major population down the coast to the southeast of Huixtla in the Tapachula locality. Had he done so, and had a major Lamanite advance been mounted down the route from Manti to break through into his rear at Huixtla, the Nephite population farther south around Tapachula would have been cut off, unable to retreat into the land northward. For this reason, Mormon had to maintain the majority of his population to the northwest along the coastal corridor from the exit of the overland route at Huixtla. The land of Joshua would therefore have been centered on Huixtla in order to maintain a strong defense at the northern coastal exit of the Manti route. The land of Joshua probably extended from Huixtla northward for some distance up the coastal shelf and to the southeast of Huixtla, encompassing the earlier "lesser" lands of Judea and possibly Antiparah.

Mormon's military sphere of influence on the west sea was probably not limited to the Huixtla locality. He would have been susceptible to attack not only from the route into the interior, but from southward down the coast. For this reason, he probably established a coastal defense system with depth to ensure adequate protection from a major coastal attack launched from the southeast. To do so, he would need a secondary defensive system down the coast, possibly in the vicinity of Judea. To enhance that protection, Mormon would have occupied forward positions at strategic points, possibly as far southward as the Antiparah locality.

Such an extensive defense system would have required a large force, especially in the Tapachula-Huixtla area. As the war continued, the attrition to Mormon's forces would have increased the difficulty of holding these positions at Joshua. The Nephites' psychological need for controlling the "lands of [their] inheritance" (Mormon 2:27-29) could not justify further occupation after the recovery of the area in A.D. 349. Mormon, knowing that his forces could no longer adequately defend the Joshua locality, secured the treaty of A.D. 350 and moved his people farther to the northwest into the land of Desolation, where they could establish a better defensive system.

The land of Desolation provided the Nephites with an ideal defensive situation that did not exist at Joshua. Marking the entrance into the greater land northward, the land of Desolation featured a restricted coastal shelf and the strategic position of the narrow passage that led into the land southward. These were important factors in Mormon's defense and the Nephites' survival. The negative factor was the existence of an inland trail. This route led up from the coast into a highland area in the land southward that Mormon, under the provisions of the treaty, could not occupy. Lamanite invasions "down" against the city of Desolation resulted in Nephite reprisal attacks "up" against the enemy and the eventual loss of Nephite control on the west sea.

In chapter 7 a variety of topographic features associated with the land of Desolation was identified. These topographic factors include the following: a restrictive coastal corridor paralleled by the west sea on one side and a range of mountains on the other; a strategic narrow pass blocking northward coastal movement coming from the south; estuaries and lagoons near the narrow passage where Hagoth constructed his ships; and a trail that provided access from the coastal plain up into the highlands above Desolation.

One place on the Pacific coastal shelf northwest of Huixtla meets all of these conditions. This is the Tonala-Arriaga locality on Mexico's Gulf of Tehuantepec. Figure 23A contains the basic topographic features of the Pacific coastal shelf. An ancient trail extends from Arriaga north into the interior highlands, which drain northward into the Grijalva Depression. In the Tonala–Tres Picos vicinity, the Pacific coastal shelf is at its narrowest width. Here a strategic ridge complex extends down from the mountains across the shelf to form an escarpment above the ocean. This ridge forms a natural barrier restricting movement northward up the coast. The defensive system was anchored on the steep mountain slopes to the east and extended west along this ridge to the escarpment above the ocean. Also in this locality are large lagoons where fishing villages now stand near ancient archeological sites.

Assuming that the Tres Picos–Tonala–Arriaga localities were that portion of the land of Desolation in the narrow neck region, this locality marks the ancient Nephite transition zone between the greater land northward and the land southward. This is the position of the narrow neck of land that separated the west sea land of Bountiful on the south from the major land of Desolation on the northwest.

The pronounced aridity of the coastal shelf north of this

location contrasts dramatically with the increase in vegetation along the coast to the south of Tonala. West from Arriaga to Tehuantepec is a dry coastal plain continually exposed to the desiccant wind that blows south across the Isthmus of Tehuantepec from the Gulf of Mexico. Agriculture in this area is presently supported through extensive irrigation. The native vegetation of the area consists of dense thorn forests that lose their leaves in the dry winter. This arid zone is a natural "land of desolation."

From Tonala southward along the coast, the effects of moisture from the Pacific begin to be more pronounced. The western slopes of the Sierra de Soconusco begin to support a greater variety of vegetation, not just the thorn thickets that dominate to the north. Sugar-cane cultivation is practiced on the hillsides, and natural grasslands there remain green throughout the year. This abundance in flora and fauna naturally increases the farther down the coast one proceeds. At Tapachula all of the species of the tropical rain forest can be encountered. This area, with its abundance, is truly a "land of Bountiful."

## GREATER LAND NORTHWARD CORRELATIONS

The Nephites' final loss of the land of Desolation occurred in A.D. 375 when they were driven deeper into the greater land northward. Their subsequent efforts to hold at Boaz and again in the Jordan locality suggest a restricted corridor where they could, with difficulty, halt any Lamanite flanking attempts and still retain a secure rear area for their large noncombatant population (cf. Mormon 5:3-4). This advantage was lost with the decimation of the defensive complex centered on Jordan.

The important topography of the west and the north seas indicates that these actions occurred in the Isthmus of Tehuantepec of southeastern Mexico. The narrow corridor that was defended in the instance of Boaz and Jordan, and also in Mormon's earlier experience at Jashon and Shem, was in the interior. This corridor linked two important segments of the greater land northward — the west sea coastal segment containing the cities of Desolation and Teancum on the south, and the north sea segment on the north. The north sea segment contained the large territory that was scene of the Jaredite struggles. With the Gulf of Mexico fitting the requirements of the north sea and the Pacific Ocean meeting the requirements of the west sea (or south sea as described in relation to the greater land northward in Helaman 3:3-12), the Isthmus of Tehuantepec becomes the corridor between these two shores. This isthmus becomes the logical place where Mormon would have established his defensive system to halt the Lamanite invasion into the Gulf coastal lowlands.

With the loss of his defensive system at Jordan, Mormon had no other recourse than to select a final defensive position in the land northward where he could gather the remnants of his people. The land of Cumorah furnished him with that position. Cumorah was in a land of "many waters, rivers, and fountains" (Mormon 6:4). Here Mormon hoped to gain a strategical advantage by concentrating his forces on the hill named Cumorah by the Nephites (Mormon 6:2). The hill Cumorah was also known as the hill Ramah to the earlier descendants of Jared's party, who were destroyed at this same location. Indeed, as Moroni states, the hill Ramah "was that same hill where my father Mormon did hide up the records unto the Lord, which were sacred" (Ether 15:11).[5]

The Desolation Regional Network described in chapter 7 and its model shown in figure 19 establish the land of Cumorah in the vicinity of the north seashore northward of the Shem-Jordan defensive complex. A review of the topography along the Gulf of Mexico shoreline in the Isthmus of Tehuantepec demonstrates two very important topographic complexes that correlate directly with the descriptions given in the text. First, this locality is a land of waterways; it contains extensive estuary and riverine water systems. Second, the Gulf shoreline on the north side of the isthmus is dominated by the Tuxtla Mountains. This volcanic peak and ridge complex rise as high as 6,600 feet above the gulf shoreline.

The correlation of the Tuxtla Mountains with the land of Cumorah-Ramah is not a recent development. Previous researchers (cf. Sorenson 1985:47, 347; Palmer 1981:89-123) have placed Cumorah in the Tuxtla Mountains. Their correlations have been based on the proximity of that mountain complex to the Isthmus of Tehuantepec and also on the fact that the Tuxtla locality contains extensive estuaries, lakes, and rivers as noted in Mormon 6:4.

The Tuxtla Mountains would have furnished Mormon and the remaining Nephites with a valuable strategic position. With their backs to the sea, the Nephites had no other option but to stand their ground and fight against forces attacking upslope from the lowlands. In addition, the Nephites had extensive water resources and fertile volcanic soils for growing the food needed to feed their refugee population. The adjacent coastline and river-lagoon systems were a valuable source of fish, but they were also important waterways needed to maintain communication and trade with the more remote Nephite settlements in the land northward. Centuries of Nephite occupation in this region had provided them with an extensive knowledge of the complex waterways adjacent to Cumorah. After the fall of Jordan, the Lamanites had unrestricted access by land into the land northward. Thus, the Nephites would not have been able to rely exclusively on land routes for their communication and transportation. The waterway networks would have been critical assets to the Nephites during that final period of gathering.

A review of the Moron District model given in figure 18 demonstrates that from Cumorah/Ramah a major complex of Jaredite routes and battlefields stretched along the coast to the northwest. This complex apparently extended along the gulf coast from the Tuxtla Mountains past the present city of Veracruz. Moron's location has been hypothesized as being in the highlands of Oaxaca, 150 miles by direct line to the south of Veracruz (cf. Sorenson 1985:47; Palmer 1981:126, 129). This distance and the difficulty in travel from Oaxaca down to the gulf coast north of Veracruz appear to be excessive when viewed in the perspective of the areas covered by both the Jaredites and the Nephites between major battles. In addition, the wilderness of Akish was situated near the coast and also in the general vicinity of Moron. If the mountainous terrain that forms the western and northwestern border of the gulf lowlands northwest of Veracruz can be correlated with the wilderness of Akish, the site of Moron may have been somewhere along the highland arc between the existing population centers of Jalapa and Huatuxco as shown in figure 23.

## THE MESOAMERICAN SETTING OF THE AREA MODEL

The correlations of the east and west sea localities, the narrow strip of wilderness, and the greater land northward developed in the preceding section permit the general coordination of southern Mesoamerica with the area network as shown in figure 30.

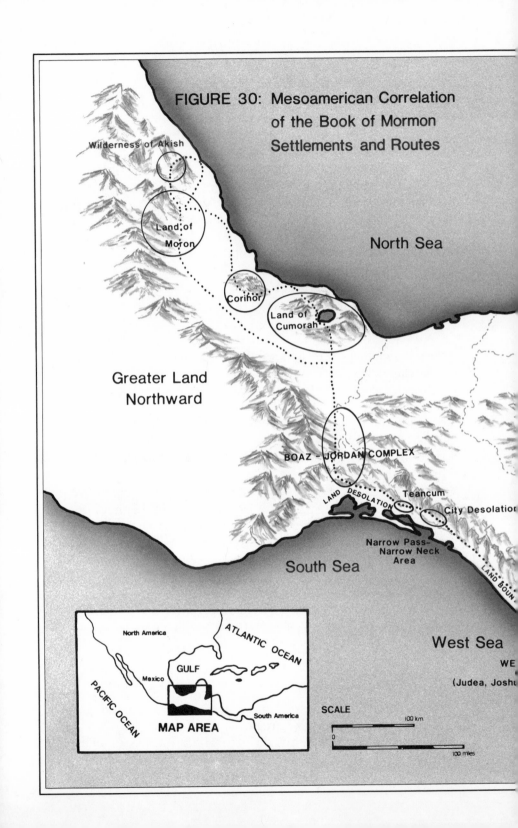

FIGURE 30: Mesoamerican Correlation
of the Book of Mormon
Settlements and Routes

Wilderness of Akish

Land of Moron

Corihor

Land of Cumorah

North Sea

Greater Land Northward

BOAZ – JORDAN COMPLEX

LAND DESOLATION

Teancum

City Desolation

Narrow Pass–
Narrow Neck
Area

South Sea

LAND BOUN

West Sea

WE

(Judea, Joshu

North America

ATLANTIC OCEAN

GULF

Mexico

PACIFIC OCEAN

South America

MAP AREA

SCALE

100 km

0

100 miles

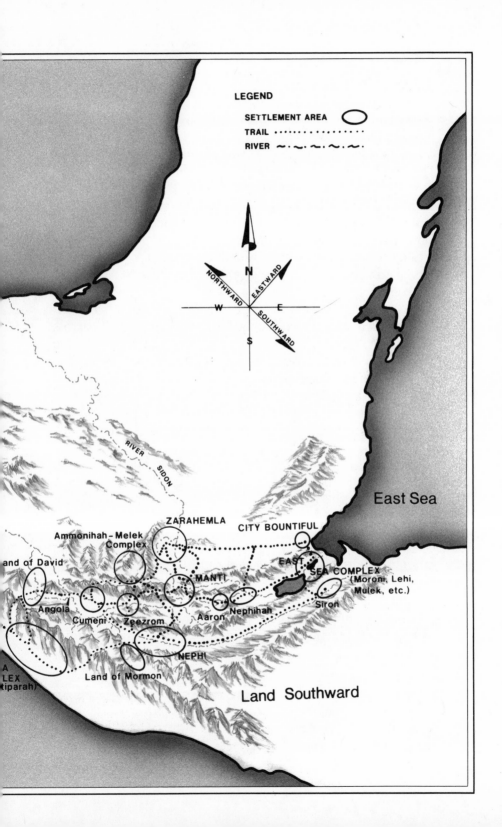

LEGEND

SETTLEMENT AREA ⬭
TRAIL ⋯⋯⋯⋯⋯⋯
RIVER ∿∿∿∿∿

NORTHWARD
EASTWARD
N
W • E
SOUTHWARD
S

RIVER SIDON

East Sea

ZARAHEMLA

CITY BOUNTIFUL

Ammonihah–Melek
Complex

and of David

EAST

SEA COMPLEX
(Moroni, Lehi,
Mulek, etc.)

MANTI

Angola

Cumeni   Zeezrom

Aaron   Nephihah

Siron

NEPHI

A
LEX
(iparah)

Land of Mormon

Land  Southward

Figure 30 is a revised Book of Mormon Area Model incorporating the correlations of the east sea to west sea settlements shown in figures 13 and 27 with the faultline corridors that connect the Alta Verapaz highlands with both the Gulf of Honduras on the east and the Huixtla-Tapachula locality on the Pacific coast. This composite map contains the path from the land of Jershon (36) via Lehi (9) along the north shore of the east sea (22) and then up the Polochic River Valley past the ancient sites of Nephihah (3) and Aaron (8) into the Manti (4) locality in the highlands presently known as the Alta Verapaz. Here in the Manti locality, the north-south path extending from the population centers of Zarahemla (1) to Nephi (43) crosses the east sea to west sea path.

The western portion of the path that linked the east and west seas can then be observed to continue west from Manti (4), across the Chixoy River and west through the trail junction (88) and the Melek locality (26), which was possibly near Cunen-Nebaj. The route continues along the southern base of the Cuchumatanes escarpment that forms the western portion of the narrow strip of wilderness barrier system. On entering the Grijalva drainage system, the route passes through the Huehuetenango basin, which is the prime candidate for the land where Cumeni (28) was situated. The route eventually crosses the Continental Divide in the Sierra de Soconusco Mountain range and then descends the Pacific slope into the vicinities of Huixtla and Tapachula. These localities correlate with Joshua (58) and Judea (29) in the west sea land of Bountiful.

With the addition of the Joshua-Cumorah and Cumorah-Moron paths, figure 30 is provided with a scale of distance from the eastern periphery of the model, or the east sea, to the western periphery in the Moron locality of the greater land northward. This scale permits an understanding of the general distances and proportions of the area model within its Mesoamerican setting.

### Notes

1. This correlation of the narrow strip of wilderness with the Sierra de las Minas and the Cuchumatanes range was first suggested to the author by archeologist V. Garth Norman in 1978. Initial evaluations of this possible correlation led to the research program that is described in this volume.

2. The Grijalva River, with its headwaters in the Cuchumatanes Mountains, has been proposed as an alternative model for the River Sidon (cf. Sorenson 1985 and Palmer 1981). The Grijalva theory is based on the correlation of the east sea with the Gulf of Mexico, which is situated to the north of the land mass. In order to justify the east sea being to the north, proponents of this theory interpret all references to north in the Book of Mormon as being "Nephite North," meaning that to the Nephites north was situated in a west-northwest direction (Sorenson 1985:38-42, Palmer 1981:35-36).

3. The Book of Mormon records extensive surface disturbance in the lands northward and southward in A.D. 34 at the time of Christ's crucifixion at Jerusalem (cf. 3 Nephi 8 and 9). These references provide a list of destroyed settlements, some of which probably cannot be archeologically identified. This does not mean that the land changed so completely that all of the earlier topographic and settlement associations were obliterated. Two factors demonstrate that the ancient, pre-34 A.D. land form and settlements of the text can still be identified. First of all, Mormon and Moroni, living in the fourth century A.D., were able to correlate the positions of earlier locations with their contemporary topography and settlements (cf. Sorenson 1985:45-46). In addition, archeologists have identified and studied numerous cultural sites in southern Mesoamerica that existed before A.D. 34. The intact existence of those early sites and the continuity of their association with adjacent major land forms indicate the viability of seeking correlations between the text's spatial structure and the existing topograpy of the Americas.

4. The name *Zarahemla* may have had a variety of meanings to the Nephites. Its use certainly included a designation of the leader and descendants of the Mulekite colony who settled in the locality in the sixth century B.C. (Omni 1:14-16). The Hebrew peoples are known for their use of puns in proper names. There is a possibility that *Zarahemla* may have been both a title and a description of some special feature in the local environment. For instance, the name may have been developed by combining the two Hebrew words *zarah* and *mla* as identified in Genesius' *Lexicon* (see Tregelles 1949). *Zarah* is a derivative of the ancient Hebrew root צרח (zeriah) meaning "to cleave" or "to make a cleft." The term *mla*, or in ancient Hebrew מלח (melach), means "salt." Perhaps Zarahemla was a descriptive name of the salt stream at the ancient site of Salinas de Los Nueve Cerros. This saline stream surfaces in a natural cleft in the west slope of the high, salt dome presently named Mesa de Los Tortugas. Should this correlation be correct, the locality's name of Zarahemla was derived from a composite word describing the cleft and its unusual salty fountain.

5. It has been noted by David Palmer that the term *cumorah* can be interpreted as "arise-o-light" or "arise-revelation" (1981:21). Another

interpretation may be even more appropriate. The word *cumorah,* like so many other nonsettlement place names used in the Book of Mormon, is a descriptive term that, through the process of the original English translation, has become a proper noun. *Cumorah* is a composite of ancient Hebrew words as identified in Gesenius' *Lexicon* (see Tregelles 1949). The *cum* is very possibly a derivative of the root קָמַה (*kamah*) meaning "to gather together" or "to collect," and also possibly is tied to the root כָמַן (*caman*) meaning "to hide away" or "to lay up." The *orah* is derived from the word אוֹר (*aor-aoor*) which means "light," but in this case the type of light associated with "knowledge, doctrine, teachings" or "revelations." Thus, if these analyses are correct, the term *cumorah,* to the Nephites described a place where special knowledge had been gathered together and hidden away. In a more specific context, a cumorah is a secret repository of sacred records. The term cumorah may therefore have been used to designate each sacred record cache situated in any one of a variety of geographical locations, whether in New York State or in Mesoamerica.

# 10

## INTERWEAVING TIME AND SPACE

This chapter sequentially relates the historic events recorded in the Book of Mormon, using maps of Mesoamerica, to portray the ancient American settings of those experiences.

The spatial organization of settlements, routes, and places of the Book of Mormon as reconstructed in the preceding chapters was not as static or two dimensional as is suggested by the graphs. In reality, that model is quite dynamic and can be studied through its various phases of development. The graphs used to portray the system are similar to a photograph of the night sky. One comprehends the placement and association of the stars in the photograph but has little indication of the complex operation and depth within the system. The way mankind has used their space upon the earth's surface is as dynamic, incorporating many processes through time. This dynamic aspect of the Book of Mormon's general system is addressed in this chapter as a means of furthering an understanding and appreciation of the text and its spatial organization.

The text of the Book of Mormon provides an exotic tapestry richly portraying man's struggle with his nature in a unique environment. The settlement model that has been extracted from this tapestry is actually an incomplete abstraction of 3,000 years of human experiences in a relatively small and isolated area. The incompleteness of the spatial model stems from three factors. First, the book is not a complete history of its peoples. Second, the writers of those ancient records had only marginal interest in describing their locality. Their main purposes were to express their faith and to convey theological information to future readers. Finally, the data provided in the text are processed through our modern understanding and insights, which although greatly serviceable, are by no means infallible. As J. William Fulbright once remarked, "There is an inevitable divergence, attributable to the imperfections of the human mind, between the world as it is and the world as men perceive it."

The approximate 3,000 years of human experience contained in the Book of Mormon can be interwoven into the topography of southern Mesoamerica through the use of six overlapping stages of cultural development. These stages begin with the Jaredite Period and include the Nephite Expansion in the Land Southward, the Nephite Wars, the Nephite Expansion into the Greater Land Northward, the Intermediate Phase, and the Final War.

The simple Jaredite spatial model developed in chapter 7 rapidly expands through the Nephite development phase extending roughly from 590 to 87 B.C. The period of Nephite-Lamanite wars extending from 87 to 60 B.C. was a phase of Nephite consolidation as detailed in the book of Alma. This phase provides the most detailed information available in the text on settlement planning, fortifications, and place associations. Nephite expansion through the west sea corridor and into the ancient Jaredite homeland extended between ca. 125-28 B.C. based on the fragmentary information provided in the text. The general model expands at a much slower rate in the following 385 years contained in the Intermediate Phase of Nephite history (60 B.C. to A.D. 325). The final war of the Nephites extended through the period A.D. 325 to 385 and was ended with the destruction of the Nephite civilization in the lands of the earlier Jaredite people. This correlation between the two civilizations provides an important link between the Jaredite portions of the model and the Nephite settlements in the land southward.

## THE JAREDITE PERIOD (CA. 3000–? B.C.)

No information is available in the text concerning spatial organization of the Jaredite peoples before their arrival at Moron, the capital land. Hugh Nibley has indicated that this migration possibly crossed the north Pacific (Nibley 1952:176). The model developed in the preceding chapters places the Jaredite capital of Moron in closer proximity to the Gulf of Mexico than to the Pacific shore. This proximity indicates that the people of Jared may have disembarked from their eight boats on the shore of the Gulf of Mexico in the Moron vicinity rather than on the distant Pacific coast.

Moron thus becomes the point from which all movement originates within the initial spatial system. Since it is referenced only in terms of a land, Moron was an upland zone occupied by a number of small dispersed settlements. Although these villages gradually expanded in population and size, their designation as a land continued throughout Moroni's abridgment of Ether's record; Moron is never accorded city status in the book of Ether.

The earliest travel occurred when Corihor journeyed from Moron to the land of Nehor to establish a rival kingdom. The location of Nehor and the adjacent hill called Ephraim cannot be determined by direction or distance from Moron; hence, for convenience, that extended route on the network was placed northwest from Moron in figure 18. Moroni, in his abridgment of the book of Ether, relates in verse 5 of chapter 7 how Corihor left the land of Nehor and "came up" to Moron to depose his father Kib. In the next verse Moroni states that Moron was near the land of Desolation, where both the Jaredites and the Nephites perished. The association of these two verses is an indication that the land of Nehor was in the land of Desolation and was situated at a lower elevation than Moron in the coastal lowlands, later known to the Nephites as the greater land northward.

With the imprisonment of the king, Kib, the political power of the Nehor locality became established under Corihor's leadership. At this point two competing capitals were established, with Nehor being the residence of the leaders until Noah seized control of the Moron locality referenced as the "land of their first inheritance" (Ether 7:16). In the following verse Noah captures the ruler, his cousin Shule, and brings him into exile at Moron. The reality of the two kingdoms is emphasized in Ether 7:20, which states, "And the country was divided; and there were two kingdoms, the kingdom of Shule, and the kingdom of Cohor, the son of Noah." The text indicates that the kingdom of Shule was centered at Nehor, while the kingdom of Cohor was located at Moron. Sorenson has noted (1985:27) that this lowland locality was evidently a longtime political rival with the upland capital of Moron. This major and bitter rivalry began as early as Corihor's occupation at Nehor.

It is curious that Nehor, being such an important political

rival, is last refered to during Corihor's reign. The land and city of Nehor are never again mentioned in the record. Perhaps the land of Nehor was renamed in honor of the ruler Corihor and became the land and valley of Corihor in remembrance of the first political rival.

Several factors in the text suggest the plausibility of the Nehor-Corihor association. First, the area around the land of Corihor contained a large population and numerous settlements (Ether 14:16-30; 15:1-14). This is why the area became the scene of the final Jaredite wars. The contending leaders brought the conflict along the coastal plain into the populated area in order to recruit to their causes all the available manpower.

The second factor that indicates the viability of the Nehor-Corihor association has to do with political and religious ideology. The important land of Nehor is never again mentioned in the Jaredite history after the reign of Corihor. The influence of the Nehors, however, continues throughout the history of the Book of Mormon. Could it be that the land of Nehor was the origin and political seat of the philosophy of the Nehors, a rival political and religious dogma that not only endured for centuries to fan the flames of contention among the Jaredites, but persisted into the Nephite period, causing extensive disruption to that society? It is not certain that the land of Nehor was the place of origin and capital of the Nehor philosophy. One thing appears certain, however — individual Jaredites survived that war (cf. Sorenson 1985:119). Those survivors and their posterity may have retained and perpetuated the philosophy of the Nehors into the time of the Nephite dominance. Thus, in Alma's day, the persistent expansion of the philosophy of the Nehors had become a serious threat to the dominant cultures (Alma 14:16-18; 15:15; 16:11; 21:4; 24:28-29).

Later in the record of Ether, Jared, the son of the ruler at that time, withdrew from Moron and traveled into the land of Heth (Ether 8:2), where he plotted the overthrow of his father, Omer. This event occurred two generations after Corihor's rebellion. Heth can be shown linked by an extended path to Moron, but distance and direction are presently unknown (see figure 18).

Jared's unsuccessful attempt to depose Omer ultimately led to his daughter's plot with Akish to take her grandfather's life. Learning of this plot, Omer fled Moron, apparently traveling to the southeast, for he ultimately passed the hill Shim and then the hill Ramah. At this point Omer altered his course to travel eastward, or to the northeast, toward Ablom on the gulf coast. Ablom became his home for many years until a civil war eliminating his enemies at Moron provided him a safe return to the seat of power (Ether 9:3-13).

Omer's journeys are shown in figure 31. Also shown is the continuation of the route past the hill Shim down into the land southward, which was used by the Jaredites a few years later to flee from the ravages of famine at Moron (Ether 9:30-35). The position of the unnamed city (86) built on the land southward side of the isthmus, or narrow neck of land, during the reign of Lib is also included. No dates are given for when this unnamed city was first occupied, but it was apparently past the midway point of the Jaredite period, for Lib ruled at Moron some twelve generations of rulers after Omer, or sixteen generations after Jared. After Lib, about thirteen generations of rulers reigned before the last king, Coriantumr.

The majority of geographic information available in the book of Ether is established during the final civil war as observed and recorded by the prophet Ether. The initial clashes between the ruler Coriantumr and his rival Shared in the valley Gilgal and on the plains of Heshlon are shown for convenience as extended routes in figure 18. Like Heth, these places were linked to Moron by extended routes, but their distance and direction are unknown. For this reason, these locations are not identified on figure 30.

As the civil war progressed, the various localities extending from the wilderness of Akish to Coriantumr's camp near the hill Ramah are added to the expanding graph (see figure 32). Thus, the association of the Jaredite sites in the land Desolation is established within the zone flanked by seashores to the north and south and by the Isthmus of Tehuantepec on the east.

## NEPHITE EXPANSION IN THE LAND SOUTHWARD (CA. 590-87 B.C.)

Even before the demise of the Jaredite civilization at Ramah, the expansion of new ethnic populations into the region was underway. The separate arrivals of the Nephite and Mulekite immigrants on the west and north seashores respectively precipitated major cultural changes in those regions.

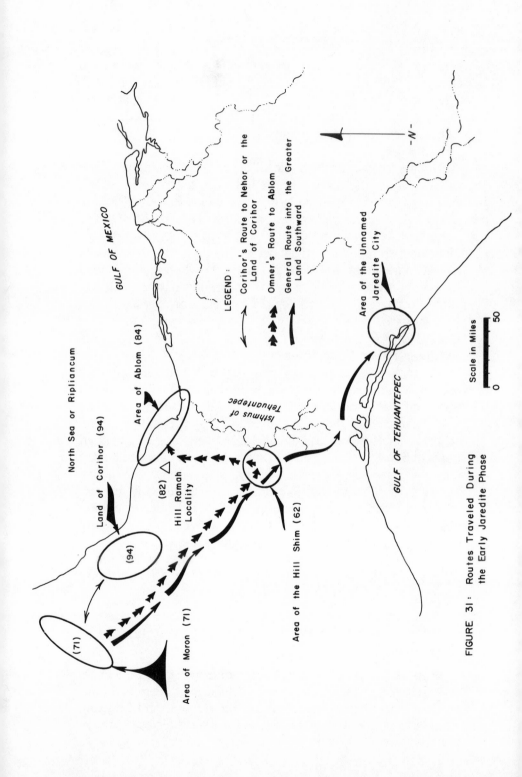

FIGURE 31: Routes Traveled During the Early Jaredite Phase

LEGEND:

Corihor's Route to Nehor or the Land of Corihor

Omner's Route to Ablom

General Route into the Greater Land Southward

-N-

GULF OF MEXICO

North Sea or Ripliancum

Land of Corihor (94)

(94)

(71)

Area of Moron (71)

Area of Ablom (84)

Hill Ramah Locality

(82)

Isthmus of Tehuantepec

Area of the Hill Shim (62)

GULF OF TEHUANTEPEC

Area of the Unnamed Jaredite City

Scale in Miles

0          50

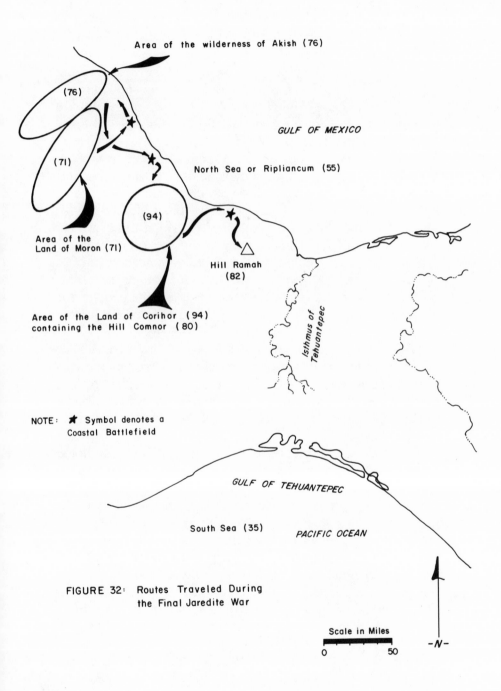

Area of the wilderness of Akish (76)

(76)

GULF OF MEXICO

(71)

North Sea or Ripliancum (55)

Area of the
Land of Moron (71)

(94)

Hill Ramah
(82)

Area of the Land of Corihor (94)
containing the Hill Comnor (80)

Isthmus of
Tehuantepec

NOTE: ✸ Symbol denotes a
Coastal Battlefield

GULF OF TEHUANTEPEC

South Sea (35)          PACIFIC OCEAN

FIGURE 32: Routes Traveled During
the Final Jaredite War

Scale in Miles

0          50          -N-

Figure 33 shows this initial phase of expansion. Judea has been tentatively identified in the preceding chapters as the location of the initial Nephite settlement near the west seashore. This association is based not only on the name similarity with the Nephites' original homeland in Asia, but also on the description of the "place of their fathers' first inheritance" given by Mormon in Alma 22:28.

The Mulekites, or people of Zarahemla, landed on the Gulf of Mexico or north seashore in the land of Desolation; then they traveled via the Sidon or Usumacinta River into the Zarahemla locality of the southern Peten zone in Guatemala, where they settled. Although the record gives no information about how and why these people chose Zarahemla as the site to colonize, it is probable that the Jaredites, with their access to centuries of accumulated information on the land southward, had some influence on that decision. We can also surmise that Jaredite peoples participated in that settlement based on the perpetuation of Jaredite names throughout the text (Nibley 1952:243-48).

The Nephite expansion within the land southward took a new direction a short time after their arrival near Judea on the Pacific coast. Dissension within the group, kindled by the elder brothers' hostility, forced Nephi and other members of the extended family to withdraw from the coast and travel through the wilderness into the interior (2 Nephi 5:5-8). Their new settlement became known as the land of Nephi, or Lehi-Nephi, an important homeland for both the Nephites and the Lamanites in the centuries to follow (see figure 33). The primary Nephite occupation of the land of Nephi covered a period of perhaps 360 years. The various leaders and descendants of Nephi kept records about the periods of peace and hostilities with the descendants of Nephi's brothers Laman and Lemuel and the other indigenous peoples of the area, who were all collectively referred to as Lamanites. The abridged records available on that initial period of Nephite expansion provide no information on the geography and settlements in the land of Nephi.

About 225 B.C. the early Nephite prophet Mosiah and a number of his people left the land of Nephi and traveled to a new and safer land. Evidently they abandoned their homeland under some duress, for they assembled on the hill north of the cities of Nephi and Shilom (Mosiah 11:13) whence they began their northward

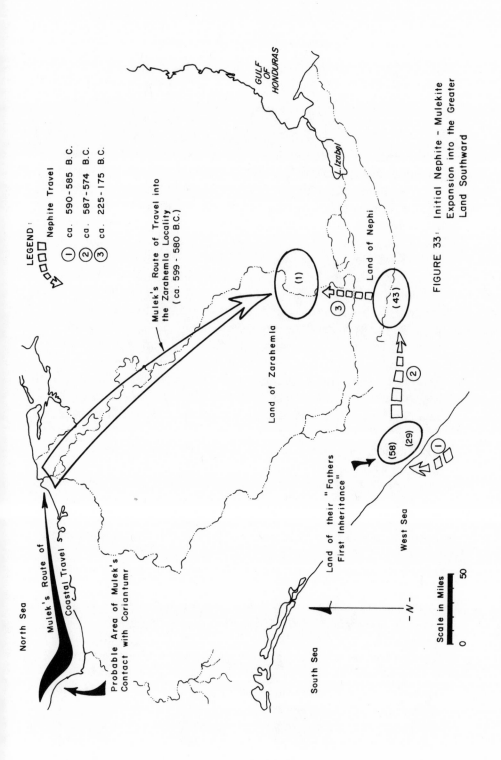

trek. The route they followed is not detailed in the text, but it was undoubtedly the main Nephi-Zarahemla trail system that was used frequently by later travelers. This connection of Nephi via the hill north of Shilom to Zarahemla is first shown in figure 3. Arriving in the land of Zarahemla, the people of Mosiah united with the people of Zarahemla, an established colony that evidently included descendents of the Jaredite peoples.

A Nephite colony led by Zeniff left Zarahemla about the year 200 B.C., hoping to recover their earlier homeland at Nephi. Zeniff was able to establish a treaty with the Lamanites who resided in the vicinity, and the Nephites reoccupied the cities and lands of Shilom and Nephi, which were apparently in the vicinity of Granados and Pachalum near the archeological site of Mixco Viejo.

Further contact between the sites of Nephi and Zarahemla was not recorded until about 121 B.C., when a Nephite search party set out from Zarahemla to seek the descendants of the Zeniff colony (Mosiah 7:2). This party was led by the early Ammon and traveled on this main route from Zarahemla to Nephi. The difficulty of the journey and their problems in locating Nephi indicate that no further contact had been maintained between these two Nephite settlements during the intervening 70-plus years. Ammon and his small party, upon arriving at Nephi, found the descendants of Zeniff's original colony in bondage to the Lamanites who occupied nearby Shemlon and Shilom. Limhi, the grandson of Zeniff and current leader of the Nephite settlements, initiated a plan for escaping at night through a secret pass in the back wall. Thus, the people of Limhi were able to evade their Lamanite guards by traveling around Shilom, which had evidently been occupied by the Lamanite invaders, eventually to arrive at Zarahemla.

The pursuit of the Limhi party resulted in the Lamanites' discovery and capture of two small, separate Nephite colonies, Amulon and Helam. Figures 12 and 30 show the general associations of the settlements of Helam and Amulon in the Rabinal-Cubilco locality of Guatemala along with Alma's subsequent route to Zarahemla via the valley of Alma. The pursuing Lamanites' route for return to Shemlon in the Motagua River valley via Helam is also indicated (Mosiah 21-23).

Figures 12 and 30 are also representations of the spatial distribution of identifiable lands in the "middle" land of Nephi, where Nephite missionaries taught among the Lamanites between 91 and 72 B.C. Lamanite harrassment and hostility toward the Lamanite converts, known as the people of Ammon, resulted in abandonment of their homes at Ishmael, Nephi, Shilom, and Middoni (Alma 23:8-13) and their departure on the route north to Zarahemla under the guidance of the Nephite missionaries. Halting the large body of refugees in the wilderness zone near Manti (see figure 30), the Nephite sons of Mosiah traveled on alone north through Manti to meet Alma the younger on the route between Gideon and Manti (Alma 17:1; 27:14). The reunited friends then continued northward to Zarahemla, where by popular mandate the land of Jershon was awarded to the refugees. With their acceptance by the Nephites, the people of Ammon were allowed unrestricted passage from Manti in the Alta Verapaz down the Polochic River valley to Jershon on the north shore of the Lago de Izabel–Golfete waterway as shown in figure 30.

## THE NEPHITE WARS (CA. 87-60 B.C.)

Nephite expansion in the land southward was accelerated by a series of conflicts that began about 87 B.C.

During the fourteen years that the sons of Mosiah were proselyting among the Lamanites, a major rebellion led by Amlici occurred in the vicinity of Zarahemla. Figures 29 and 30 show the place near the Icbolay River segment of the Sidon where this warfare was initiated around 87 B.C. The first major engagement began at the hill named Amnihu (15), which was near Zarahemla on the east side of the lower River Sidon crossing (Alma 2:15-38). The Amlicites withdrew from that bloody exchange and were pursued by the Nephites through the valley of Gideon, which has been correlated with the valley complex presently found near the village of Chisec. Their southward retreat to the land of Minon resulted in the Amlicites joining with a large Lamanite force. The combined armies then moved north to attack the city of Zarahemla.

The Nephite army, in the meantime, had been recovering in the valley of Gideon. Upon hearing of the turn of events, and to counter the hostile attack, they returned northward through the valley, passed the original battleground near the hill Amnihu, and arrived at the river crossing, where they successfully launched a counterattack against the Amlicites and Lamanites. The resulting battle in Zarahemla led to the defeat of Amlici. Lamanite-Amlicite survivors were driven northwestward into the wilderness of Hermounts, where they perished.

This decisive action not only demonstrates the association of Gideon, Hermounts, and Minon with Zarahemla, but it also shows that no other alternative routes linked Gideon to Zarahemla. Access between Gideon and Zarahemla was either southward via Minon or to the east via the hill Amnihu and the lower River Sidon crossing. In addition, the distance from Minon to Zarahemla appears to have been shorter and perhaps more direct than the distance from Gideon to the capital, since the hostile forces were able to arrive in Zarahemla before Alma and the Nephite army.

Following the Amlicite defeat and while the sons of Mosiah were still proselyting among the Lamanites in the middle land of Nephi, Alma the younger in about 83 B.C. embarked upon an extensive missionary program among the Nephites (Alma 5–15). His initial travels in the lesser land of Zarahemla and in Gideon would eventually lead him to Melek, Ammonihah, and Sidom as shown in figures 10 and 30.

Shortly after Alma's agonizing departure from Ammonihah with Amulek, a Lamanite force destroyed that settlement and raided the adjacent land of Noah. During their return to the middle land of Nephi, the raiders were ambushed at the upper crossing of the River Sidon by the Nephite chief captain Zoram, who had traveled there via Manti along the west side of the River Sidon (see figure 30).

A third crossing of the River Sidon is the scene of a later Nephite ambush. In 74 B.C., after the war in Jershon near the east sea, the Lamanite converts who had settled in that land were resettled in the land of Melek, where they could be secure from Lamanite aggression. At that time the Nephites prepared for further conflict by concentrating their forces in the land of Jershon opposing the Zoramite-Lamanite armies in adjacent Antionum. Realizing that they could not be successful on the east seacoast, the Lamanites withdrew a majority of their troops and "marched round about in the wilderness, that they might come over into the land of Manti, that they might commence an attack upon the weaker part of the people" (Alma 43:24). The Lamanite force evidently pulled back from a confrontation with the Nephites in the Golfete locality east of the Lago de Izabel. They traveled back over the Sierra de las Minas chain (the narrow strip of wilderness) to the Motagua River valley and then westward up the valley to a point where they could ascend the mountain and drop down into the Chixoy drainage in the Rabinal valley region. By following a minor tributary of the Chixoy, the Lamanite force could travel to the ford near Alta Verapaz, or Manti. The settlement and route configurations in figure 30 incorporate all these troop movements.

Moroni, the Nephite chief captain, upon learning of the Lamanite plan to attack in the vicinity of Manti, moved a large portion of his army from Jershon to Manti via the Polochic River corridor. He set up the ambush on both the east and west sides of the river, placing men from the crossing "down into the borders of the land Manti," which was evidently nearby (Alma 43:32). Expecting the Lamanites to arrive from the east, Moroni hid part of his force on the south of the hill Riplah, which was on the east bank of the river. Upon the enemy's arrival at the ford from the east, the trap was sprung; the Nephites on the south of the hill moved behind the Lamanites to curtail any retreat eastward and subsequently defeated the enemy.

After the victory at this third crossing of the Sidon, Moroni, aware that an extensive period of hostilities lay ahead, began securing Nephite colonies in fortified settlements at the vulnerable frontier points between the "middle" lands of Nephi and Zarahemla. Figures 26 and 27 show deployment of the east sea fortified sites between the Lamanite land of Siron on the south and the land of Bountiful on the north. Of these eastern fortified settlements, only Nephihah was inland. The land of Nephihah was between the border of the land of Moroni on the east and the border of the land of Aaron to the northwest or north.

The record indicates that similar fortifications were developed on the west seashore and in the interior lands of Manti, Ammonihah, and Noah as shown in figure 34. These associations help demonstrate the vulnerability of Nephite border positions to Lamanite attack as noted in the text.

This period of colonization and construction of defensive settlements along the border lands was a time of great internal stress for the Nephites as shown by the Morianton incident. In 68 B.C. a border dispute in the Lago de Izabel area of the east

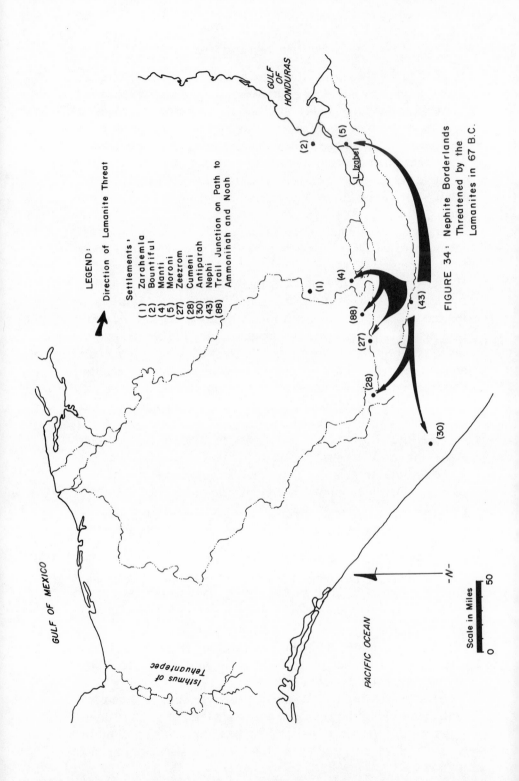

LEGEND:

→ Direction of Lamanite Threat

Settlements:

(1) Zarahemla
(2) Bountiful
(4) Manti
(5) Moroni
(27) Zeezrom
(28) Cumeni
(30) Antiparah
(43) Nephi
(88) Trail Junction on Path to Ammonihah and Noah

GULF OF MEXICO

Isthmus of Tehuantepec

GULF OF HONDURAS

L. Izabel

PACIFIC OCEAN

-N-

Scale in Miles

0          50

FIGURE 34: Nephite Borderlands Threatened by the Lamanites in 67 B.C.

seashore occurred between the adjacent colonies of Lehi and Morianton. The conflict resulted in the temporary abandonment of the Lehi settlement. Morianton took his people westward through the Polochic, Chixoy, and Cuilco river corridors in an attempt to flee through the narrow neck of land on the west seashore and resettle in the greater land northward. According to Mormon, this group was able to travel as far as the narrow neck of land before they were stopped and defeated by a Nephite army led by Teancum. The description of the topography where Morianton was stopped (Alma 50:34) is identical to that used for both the unnamed Jaredite city (Ether 10:20) and for the place where Hagoth would later construct ships to emigrate to the land northward (Alma 63:5). This narrow pass leading into the land northward and associated on the west sea coastline with a complex of bays or estuaries is probably near present-day Tonala and Arriaga. These Mexican towns mark the entrance into the arid Pacific coastal corridor that connects the west seashore via the low ridges of the Isthmus of Tehuantepec with the lowlands of the Gulf of Mexico of the greater land northward.

In 67 B.C. the Lamanites launched their major attacks against the Nephites, beginning on the east sea area near the sea now known as Lago de Izabel. Their rapid capture of the fortified sites along the seashore is named in an order that is consistent with later references to the associations between those cities. Only Nephihah, in the interior, and the east sea entrance into the land Bountiful were retained by the Nephites, the latter as a result of a successful battle on the seashore at the border of the land of Bountiful.

Moroni, under attack on the west sea, wrote to Teancum that he was to "fortify the land Bountiful, and secure the narrow pass which led into the land northward" (Alma 52:9). Since Teancum and his army were positioned to begin the recovery of Mulek and the other captured east sea cities, the fortified city in the land Bountiful and its adjacent narrow pass leading northward are in the immediate vicinity of the east sea. Therefore, this narrow pass and its adjacent "land northward" are not identical with the narrow pass leading into the greater land northward that was situated on the west sea. This is further apparent in verse 11 where Moroni gives his present position as being on the "borders of the west sea." If the narrow pass he refers to in his letter was on the west seashore, Moroni would have been in a better position to protect the zone than was Teancum, who was locked into a defensive position on the east seashore to the east of Zarahemla and north of Moroni. Figure 34 shows the areas threatened during this critical period in Nephite history.

After the Lamanites obtained control of the east sea settlements, they mounted a successful drive on the west sea coastline. Nephite operations to regain the Antiparah fortifications near the west seashore were enhanced by the arrival at Judea of Helaman and his force of two thousand warriors, sons of the people of Ammon who had earlier been resettled at Melek. Their journey to Judea in 65 B.C. was a result of the Lamanite capture of Manti and the other interior sites of Zeezrom and Cumeni. Thus, by 65 B.C., as shown in figure 35, the Lamanites had captured Nephite frontier positions on the east sea, on the west sea, and at Manti on the main north-south route. They had also captured two previously unidentified sites that also were evidently on the Nephite border controlling transportation routes along the base of the narrow strip of wilderness—that is, in the Chixoy and the Selegua river corridors. Figure 30 shows the general route from Zarahemla to Judea along the fault corridor system that was followed by Helaman and his force during their journey to provide support for the outnumbered Nephites at Judea.

With the recapture of Antiparah, Helaman and the Nephite armies sent their Lamanite captives to Zarahemla and finished preparing the security of the west sea corridor leading into the greater land northward. By 63 B.C. Helaman was able to advance inland, as shown in figure 36, to recover the next strategically significant settlement, Cumeni. This captured Nephite settlement was apparently in the vicinity of the modern city of Huehuetenango. Helaman's plan to recover Cumeni was simple. He surrounded the site and maintained control of the Lamanite supply lines in order to starve the defenders into submission. Recovering the main supply column and obtaining the surrender of the local garrison, Helaman sent the captured provisions to Judea and his prisoners on to Zarahemla. His success was nearly lost, however, when a large Lamanite force from Manti initiated a counterattack. A last-minute arrival of Nephite support led to a defeat of the counterattacking army, which was driven back to Manti (Alma 57:22).

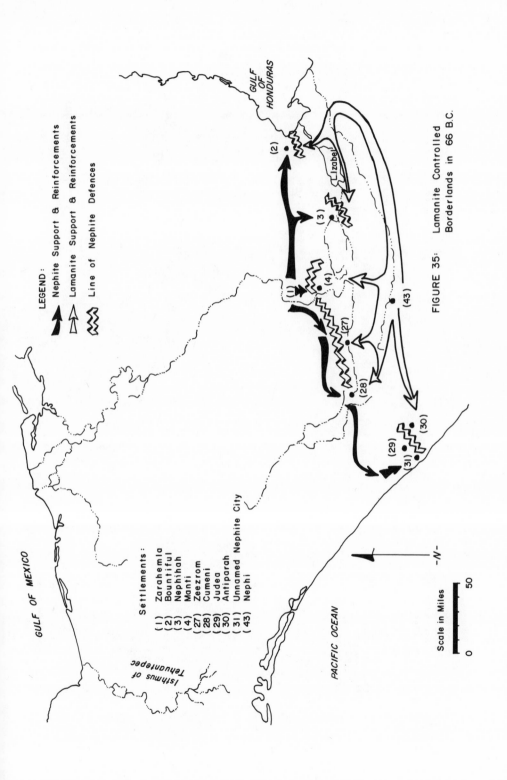

LEGEND:

Nephite Support & Reinforcements

Lamanite Support & Reinforcements

Line of Nephite Defences

Settlements:

(1) Zarahemla
(2) Bountiful
(3) Nephihah
(4) Manti
(27) Zeezrom
(28) Cumeni
(29) Judea
(30) Antiparah
(31) Unnamed Nephite City
(43) Nephi

GULF OF MEXICO

Isthmus of Tehuantepec

GULF OF HONDURAS

Izabel

PACIFIC OCEAN

-N-

Scale in Miles

0        50

FIGURE 35:  Lamanite Controlled Borderlands in 66 B.C.

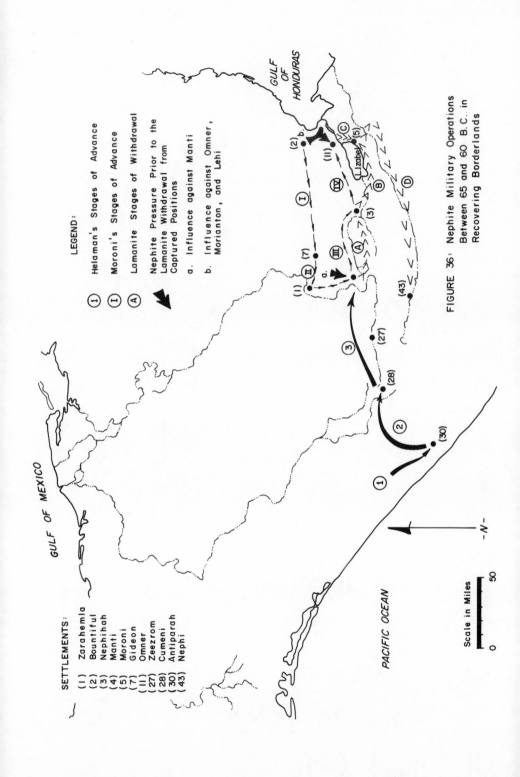

LEGEND:

①　Helaman's Stages of Advance

Ⅰ　Moroni's Stages of Advance

Ⓐ　Lamanite Stages of Withdrawal

➤　Nephite Pressure Prior to the
Lamanite Withdrawal from
Captured Positions

a. Influence against Manti

b. Influence against Omner,
Morianton, and Lehi

SETTLEMENTS:

(1)　Zarahemla
(2)　Bountiful
(3)　Nephihah
(4)　Manti
(5)　Moroni
(7)　Gideon
(11)　Omner
(27)　Zeezrom
(28)　Cumeni
(30)　Antiparah
(43)　Nephi

GULF OF MEXICO

GULF
OF
HONDURAS

PACIFIC OCEAN

- N -

Scale in Miles

0      50

FIGURE 36: Nephite Military Operations
Between 65 and 60 B.C. in
Recovering Borderlands

No information is given on the recapture of Zeezrom, which was probably in the Sacapulas region on the Chixoy corridor, a strategic position on the route between Manti and Cumeni based on its placement in Alma 56:14. With the recovery of Antiparah, Cumeni, and the northern route to Manti bypassing Zeezrom, the Nephites were in position for attacking the Lamanite forces at Manti through their exposed western and northern flanks. The Lamanite positions at Manti are described by Helaman and Mormon as strongholds that were so well fortified that only through extensive losses could they be captured by direct assault. The Nephites could not sustain heavy losses. Thus, they prepared to fight a holding war at Manti by controlling the surrounding terrain and threatening the Lamanite supply columns coming from the south up into the Alta Verapaz. This is the same successful strategy that was used to recover Antiparah and capture Cumeni. Helaman's plan for the recovery of Manti without heavy losses was to use this strategy once the route to Cumeni and the upper crossing of the Sidon had been secured.

The large Lamanite army in the city of Manti, or modern Coban, was lured away in a strategy similar to that used at Mulek and Antiparah, for they left their defensive position to chase a weaker Nephite army into a neutral zone on the wilderness (south) side of Manti. The Nephites then secured Manti by returning to the undermanned strongholds to gain control of the fortifications before the enemy force could return.

This strategy conserved Nephite strength at Manti in the Alta Verapaz but had a disastrous effect on their people defending Nephihah in the Polochic River valley. While still in control of Manti, the Lamanites were not sufficiently strong to hold that site and launch an attack either northward against Zarahemla or to the east across the river and "down" to Nephihah (Alma 56:25). With the release of the large force that had previously maintained Manti, the Lamanites, by uniting with their local forces around Nephihah, gained sufficient strength to take that major fortification.

Figure 36 gives the routes followed by the Nephite army as a result of the fall of Nephihah in 62 B.C. Survivors of Nephihah fled the area to join Moroni's army, which at that time was at Gid, Mulek, and Bountiful. Moroni, incensed at the loss of Nephihah and the news of a Nephite revolt at Zarahemla, departed probably from the city of Bountiful, where the main body of his army was secured, and traveled to Gideon, gaining reinforcements along the way. At Gideon he combined forces with the ousted chief judge Pahoran and led a successful assault against the rebel government at Zarahemla.

Having recovered control of the Nephite government, Moroni then moved to recapture Nephihah, traveling possibly via Manti and Aaron.[1]

After surrounding the fortifications at Nephihah, Moroni recaptured that settlement through a plan similar to the one used to recover Gid. While the Lamanite defenders were concentrated at the east entrance, a fortified pass that opened on a plain where the Nephite forces were assembled, Moroni had his men scale the west wall under the cover of darkness, carrying extra weapons for the captive Nephites. At daybreak the Lamanites discovered the large force within the stronghold and fled en masse through the pass.

Outside the fortification, they were attacked by Nephite forces waiting on the plain. Those Lamanites who were not captured or slain fled to the safety of the occupying force in the land of Moroni. Since no mention is made of these survivors also fleeing to Lehi, it can be assumed that the Nephite forces at Nephihah controlled access on that route. They did this to ensure that the Lamanite garrison at Lehi would not receive any additional strength, for the next phase of Moroni's attack would be in that direction (Alma 62:30).

By 60 B.C. Moroni was ready to launch counterattacks to recover the east sea settlements of Omner, Morianton, Lehi, and Moroni. His plan was quite simple. While he attacked from Nephihah against the cities of Lehi and Morianton, his junior officers would attack from Gid on the north shore of Lago de Izabel, forcing the retreating Lamanites to withdraw to the seashore, where their only escape was southward to the fortifications at Moroni. This site, which was still in Lamanite control, became a safety valve providing refuge for their retreating armies. Had the Nephites boxed them in and forced them to stand their ground, the recovery of the intermediate settlements would have been delayed and possibly jeopardized, resulting in costly casualties for the Nephites.

Figures 26 and 27 provide the addition of these new routes

and the identification of the wilderness zone to the east and south of Moroni in the Sierra de las Minas mountain range. It was from this wilderness area overlooking the fortifications of Moroni that the Nephites successfully launched their final attack against the forces at Moroni, bringing an end to the long and bloody struggle.

## NEPHITE EXPANSION INTO THE
## GREATER LAND NORTHWARD (CA. 125-28 B.C.)

Nephite immigration into the greater land northward is not well documented in the Book of Mormon. Mass migrations out of the land southward are noted as having occurred in 55 B.C. (Alma 63:4-10) and again in 46 B.C. (Helaman 3:3-12). Little information exists, however, on the exploratory phases that preceded those migrations.

Although the Nephites settled in the land southward as early as around 589 B.C. and were established in the land of Nephi by 569 B.C. (2 Nephi 5:28), their knowledge of the area outside their immediate homelands appears to have been very limited for the next 450 years. By about 121 B.C. the Nephites at both Zarahemla and Nephi had trouble finding the route between these two key settlements. This is evident in the problems encountered by Ammon's party from Zarahemla in their search for the remnants of the Zeniff colony at Nephi (Mosiah 7:2-4) and in King Limhi's search party from Nephi that traveled into the greater land northward while trying to find the route to Zarahemla (Mosiah 8:7-11).

It is interesting that in the 56 intervening years between these tentative exploratory probes and the mass migrations into the greater land northward as noted above, the Nephites acquired an extensive knowledge of the surrounding geography. This period must have been a time of extensive exploration and reconnaissance, especially relative to the routes leading into the land northward.

Two catalysts may have brought about the Nephite exploration and expansion into the north countries—the discovery and interpretation of Ether's record concerning the existence and collapse of the Jaredite civilization, and the Nephite-Lamanite war of 72-60 B.C. These were important events that altered the Nephites' territory and traditional economic base. The history and description of geography in the greater land northward furnished by Ether's record and substantiated by King Limhi's explorers provided the Nephites with an interest in expanding northward into new resource areas. The major war, on the other hand, forced Nephite resettlement into both the east sea and west sea localities, supplying the motivation for further expansion beyond the zones of conflict once peace had been established.

Consider the impact that Ether's record must have had on the relatively isolated Nephite leaders at Zarahemla. The geographic and economic potential of the greater land northward was undoubtedly more thoroughly documented in Ether's original records than is available in Moroni's abridged version found in the book of Ether. Ether's original record also provided further veracity and substance to the earlier account of the liaison between the people of Zarahemla and Coriantumr, the last ruler of the Jaredites. That record, evidently the first written information that the Nephites had about the Jaredite civilization, had existed among the Nephite rulers since its translation around 200 B.C. by Mosiah (Omni 1:20-22) after his arrival at Zarahemla.

One of the most intriguing puzzles of the Book of Mormon concerns King Limhi's expedition sent from the land of Nephi to find the land of Zarahemla. How could this expedition have set out for Zarahemla but instead arrived in the greater land northward? How could they have confused the ruins of the Jaredite civilization with their forefathers' homeland at Zarahemla? The answer to these questions can partially be found in reviewing the graph of the area network as shown in figure 30. Knowing from tradition that Zarahemla lay to the north of Nephi, this party evidently traveled northward over the Sierra de Chuacus mountains that form the northern watershed of the Motagua River drainage. Descending one of the drainages of the Chixoy system, the group arrived in the arid Chixoy canyon. The steep canyon walls downstream from the bend in the Chixoy precluded travel to the north down the canyon.

The explorers were faced with a difficult decision. Should they ascend the steep east slope of the canyon wall (the route that, unbeknownst to them, would lead them into Manti and ultimately to Zarahemla)? Or should they turn westward and travel up the Chixoy River to find the unknown passage through the mountains that led to Zarahemla? The expedition evidently decided to stay with the river, and they turned westward.

The route up the Chixoy channeled the explorers within that series of long, open river valleys that are part of the linear fault corridor that parallels the narrow strip of wilderness from the Caribbean on the east to the east slope of the Sierra Madre range above the Pacific on the west. By continuing in this system of valleys, they traveled through the locality Nephite settlers would later name Zeezrom. Ascending the narrow Rio Buca canyon, they left the headwaters of the Chixoy and dropped down into the basin where the modern town of Huehuetenango is situated. A few years later, Nephite settlers, retracing the route taken by this expedition, would establish the settlement of Cumeni in this same basin.

From the Huehuetenango basin the problem of tracing the route followed by these explorers becomes more complex. Two schools of thought presently exist as to the route this expedition took after departing from the Huehuetenango basin: (1) the ancient explorers traveled into the nearby Grijalva River valley, or (2) they selected a separate route that would have led via the west sea corridor and the Isthmus of Tehuantepec into the Jaredite homeland in the greater land northward.

The text provides explicit references that the Limhi expedition found Ether's record in the greater land northward. The Book of Mormon states that they "traveled in a land among many waters, having discovered a land which was covered with bones of men, and of beasts, and was also covered with ruins of buildings of every kind, having discovered a land which had been peopled with a people who were as numerous as the hosts of Israel" (Mosiah 8:8, cf. Mosiah 21:26). A third reference notes that Ether, after viewing the destruction of the Jaredite civilization, "finished his record; . . . and he hid them in a manner that the people of Limhi did find them" (Ether 15:33). These three references leave no doubt that the Limhi expedition made their way into the Jaredite homeland and especially into the locality of Cumorah, the only stated place in the Book of Mormon consistently noted for containing "many waters."

The question then arises, Which route did the expedition follow? Did they remain in the Rio Selegua drainage gradually working their way down through that difficult canyon gorge until they emerged into the open valley that leads downstream into the arid Grijalva Depression? Perhaps then they floated down am-

177

icable stretches of the Grijalva River, canoed through the vast rivers of the lowlands, eventually emerging in the Gulf of Mexico to the east of the Jaredite homeland. At that point, they could have traveled westward along the coastal waterways until, arriving under the shadow of the Tuxtla Mountains, they could march overland to the locality of Ramah/Cumorah, where they would witness the destruction described above.

The Grijalva Depression has not been the major land route connecting the highlands of Guatemala with the gulf lowlands to the west of the Tuxtlas. The historic trail systems leading from the highlands of Guatemala through the Grijalva zone into the gulf lowlands have traditionally been of secondary value to the inhabitants, because of the difficulty of the terrain and the proximity of the more accessible route along the Pacific coast via the Isthmus of Tehuantepec. In addition, the area network developed from the references of the Book of Mormon contains no topographic features, routes, or settlements that correlate with the Grijalva Depression and its major waterway.

Traditional trail systems, difficult topography, and the lack of network associations therefore suggest that the Limhi expedition followed the more direct route westward from the Huehuetenango basin. Instead of descending into the Rio Selegua gorge, they crossed over the low summit in the vicinity of the modern village of Colotenango, descended into the Rio Cuilco valley, and traveled to the vicinity of the modern Mexican village of Motozintla.

A short climb from Motozintla would bring the expedition to the summit of the Sierra Madre range, where they could look west down on the Pacific coast and the west sea land of Bountiful, the setting for the future Nephite settlements of Joshua and Judea.

At that point the explorers must have known that they had missed the route to Zarahemla. It is fortunate that they continued on, for had they turned back they would have postponed to a later date the discoveries of the greater land northward and the records of Ether.

Descending to the coastal corridor, the party turned northwest, their course gradually bringing them into the confines of the narrow neck of land that marked the distinction between the lush, verdant environment of Bountiful to the south and the harsh, parched environment of the land northward on the Pacific side of the Isthmus of Tehuantepec.

Their course past the desolate ruins of the Jaredite city in the narrow neck of the coastal corridor and their subsequent experience in the desiccated environment leading to the Isthmus of Tehuantepec may have led them to consider that region as a land of desolation.

Arriving at the low, hilly range that marks the watersheds in the isthmus between the Pacific and the Gulf of Mexico, the explorers continued northward across the Continental Divide. Soon they found themselves in a more familiar environment. The gradual abundance of water was evidenced by the change in vegetation. Flora adapted to the harsh, arid regime of the Pacific slope were being replaced by species that could remain green throughout the dry season.

In the Isthmus of Tehuantepec, the party found the ancient trail system, which they followed north down into the lush tropical forests of the gulf coastal lowlands. The trail to the north led directly toward the Tuxtla Mountains and the adjacent lowlands containing numerous waterways and lagoons—the land of Cumorah. It was here on this final portion of the trek, unable to continue farther north because of the sea, that they discovered the hill Ramah. The extensive evidences of the earlier Jaredite occupation and destruction convinced the group that their excursion had indeed led them to Zarahemla and that their efforts had been in vain. They concluded that Zarahemla had been destroyed before their arrival (Mosiah 21:26).[2]

The search party gathered artifacts from the battleground to serve as additional evidence for their report to King Limhi. Undoubtedly believing their mission to be a failure, they turned back toward Nephi.

The text is silent about where and how the explorers discovered Ether's 24 gold plates, the record of the Jaredites. It is certain, however, that the recovery of that ancient report was the most important occurrence of their travels, a round-trip journey that covered a minimum of 1,000 miles. This long and difficult expedition ultimately proved to be very important to the Nephites, for it pioneered their future land migrations into the greater land northward.

Nephite expansion beyond the immediate land of Zarahemla can be partially traced in the text beginning with the return of Ammon and King Limhi's people to Zarahemla in about 121 B.C.

and the subsequent entry into Zarahemla of Alma and his followers within the year. By 82 B.C., Alma the younger was traveling between the Nephite settlements of Zarahemla and Melek and later onward toward Aaron. As figure 30 demonstrates, both settlements were accessible through Manti. Melek was accessible via the fault valley to the west of Manti, and Aaron via the fault valley to the east of the highlands of the Alta Verapaz. In 81 B.C. the Nephite chief captain Zoram was moving troops through Manti well into the south wilderness on the east of the river at the upper crossing of the Chixoy to intercept and destroy the Lamanite raiders of Ammonihah.

Nephite expansion into the fault valleys both east and west of Manti continued in the following years. The people of Ammon and subsequent Zoramite colonizations of Jershon around 78 B.C. (Alma 17:1; 27:14, 20-26) and Antionum around 74 B.C. (Alma 31:3) demonstrate the expansion of Nephite domination down the Polochic River fault valley into the east sea regions associated with the Lago de Izabel. When the need came to send missionaries among the Zoramites, Alma and two sons left Zarahemla and were aided by Amulek and Zeezrom (Alma 31:6). These last individuals were at Melek among the people of Ammon, who had recently been resettled from Jershon via the Polochic River Valley route. This reference suggests that Alma traveled from Zarahemla to Manti and then westward to Melek to get Amulek and Zeezrom. Their route eastward to Antionum would then have been back through Manti and down the Polochic River valley into the Caribbean lowlands.

No information is provided about the settlement of the Nephite colonies along the fault valley to the west of Manti. These colonies would have included Zeezrom through Cumeni to the Antiparah-Judea complex near the west sea. There is good reason to believe that occupation along this corridor was underway before 90 B.C., based on the description of that date concerning Nephite areas of occupation on the west sea (see Alma 22:27-34). Certainly their control of the east-to-west sea fault corridors was well established by the 72-65 B.C. period when the war with the Lamanites forced the Nephites to prepare extensive fortifications along their border settlements and move defensive colonies into the east sea locality (see Alma 50).

Nephite expansion into the greater land northward increased

markedly after the conclusion of the 72-60 B.C. war. Alma chapter 63 records the departure of numerous Nephite colonists. By 55 B.C. shiploads of emigrants were embarking under Hagoth's direction in the narrow neck of land on the west sea to travel northward along the Pacific coast to settle in the land northward. The account further records that in 46 B.C., due to contentions and dissension among the Nephites, numerous colonists, including both Nephites and the people of Ammon, left Zarahemla for the land northward (Helaman 3:3-12). By the year 28 B.C., Lamanites were also leaving their homelands to emigrate into the greater land northward (Helaman 6:6).

## THE INTERMEDIATE PHASE
## (CA. 60 B.C. to A.D. 325)

During this phase of Nephite history, three major incidents occurred that can be associated with the spatial organization of that civilization; all these occurrences were related to battles.

Figure 30 shows the route between Zarahemla and the city of Bountiful via Gideon. In 51 B.C. a large Lamanite army penetrated the Nephite defenses on the frontier and assaulted the city of Zarahemla. Destroying the government at that capital and finding little opposition, the leader, Coriantumr, directed his army eastward with the intent of capturing the city of Bountiful "that he might obtain the north parts of the lands" (Helaman 1:23). Mormon notes in verse 27 that Coriantumr pursued his course through "the center of the land" and "the most capital parts of the land" before he was stopped by Moronihah short of the east sea land of Bountiful. These references are important in two ways—first, that Zarahemla was in the center of the land southward; second, that an important and heavily populated route led from that capital east to the city of Bountiful. Other cities involved in this warfare are not named in the record, further demonstrating the incompleteness of the general system that has been developed from the text.

The second incident involves a major rebellion among the Nephites as recorded in Helaman 4:5-16. The dissenters gathered enough Lamanite support that by 35 B.C. they had taken possession of the middle land of Zarahemla, driving the loyal Nephites into an unnamed land noted in verse 5. As shown in figure 37, the

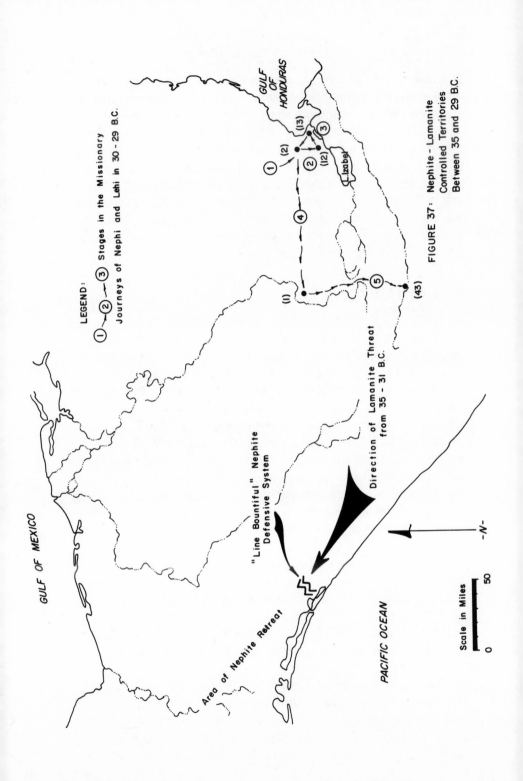

GULF OF MEXICO

GULF OF HONDURAS

LEGEND:

①—②—③ Stages in the Missionary Journeys of Nephi and Lehi in 30 - 29 B.C.

(13)

③

(2)

①

②

(12)

L. Izabel

④

⑤

(1)

(43)

"Line Bountiful" Nephite Defensive System

Direction of Lamanite Threat from 35 - 31 B.C.

Area of Nephite Retreat

PACIFIC OCEAN

-N-

Scale in Miles

0          50

FIGURE 37: Nephite - Lamanite Controlled Territories Between 35 and 29 B.C.

Nephites were primarily concentrated in the west sea land of Bountiful, which extended northward to the narrow neck separating the lands northward and southward (Helaman 4:5-6). In this narrow coastal corridor, the Nephites fortified a line extending from the west seashore to a point one day's journey to the east, where evidently the mountainous terrain served as sufficient protection from being flanked from the east (Helaman 4:7). Mormon states that this Nephite defensive line was established to defend their north country, meaning the greater land northward. A second and similar description of this important defensive line is given in Alma 22:32-34.

Figure 37 portrays this defensive line, anchored on the east by the impassable terrain of the Sierra Madre, or Soconusco mountains. The west end of the defensive line was on the west seashore, or Pacific. Within the line and near the escarpment overlooking the west sea was the narrow pass that led into the land southward.

The Nephite armies under Moronihah's leadership were able to recover only "one-half of their property and the one-half of all their lands" by 31 B.C. (Helaman 4:16). Realizing that the conflict could not be resolved by warfare, two religious leaders, Nephi and Lehi, embarked upon a mission "among all the people of Nephi" (Helaman 5:14). Beginning at the city of Bountiful near the east sea, they progressed south to the city of Gid and then to Mulek as shown on figure 37.

Helaman 5:16 states that when they had completed their work "among all the people of Nephi who were in the land southward," they then went into the land of Zarahemla among the Lamanites. Evidently the populations at the cities of Bountiful, Gid, and Mulek were the only loyal Nephites left in the land, and their support and assistance were required before the two brothers could begin work among the Lamanite populations and the Nephite dissenters at Zarahemla. Finding success among the populations in the land of Zarahemla, the brothers went from there south into Lamanite territory (Helaman 5:20). Their ultimate success in the land of Nephi resulted in many Lamanite converts who also traveled north into Zarahemla to conduct missionary work among the Nephite rebels (Helaman 6:4). The peace that gradually developed through these efforts ultimately allowed the Nephites to return to their lands. Open frontiers were eventually established for the two cultures, leading to economic prosperity and extensive immigration into the greater land northward (Helaman 6:6-9).

The third incident that occurred, beginning in the year A.D. 17, involved a large temporary displacement of the Nephite population. A significant number of Nephites had joined forces with a large secret society known as the Gadianton robbers (3 Nephi 3 and 4). Giddianhi, the leader of this warlike sect, desired complete control of the Nephite lands, resources, and culture, and through terror and destruction he initiated his purposes. The loyal Nephites, realizing that they were too sparsely spread for an adequate defense of all their lands and settlements, abandoned much of the land southward. Their plan was simply to unite within a single consolidated region (see figure 38) where they could ensure mutual protection through the erection of a large fortification system. In addition, they used a scorched-earth policy to deny the robbers access to the surplus food that they could not take with them to cover the projected seven-year siege.

The place they chose for their defense was in the land southward in an unnamed land "between the land of Zarahemla and the land Bountiful, yea, to the line which was between the land Bountiful and the land Desolation" (3 Nephi 3:22-25). The reference to the fortified line in this quotation indicates that this fortified area was in the same Pacific coastal locality of Tonala previously used as a retreat by the Nephites during the 35-29 B.C. conflict as noted above and referenced in Helaman 4:5.[3]

The robber's siege of the Nephites' fortified position in this coastal zone could not be maintained, for the robbers had to rely on the local resources for food and provisions. As the siege continued, the robbers gradually exhausted their food resources. The increasing shortage of wild game in the adjacent wilderness areas ultimately forced the terrorists to end their occupation and begin a withdrawal toward lands far to the north where they could escape Nephite reprisals. The Nephites curtailed this plan in A.D. 22 by positioning an army in ambush on the route northward up the coast ahead of the robbers and then attacking their rear on the south. This operation, which marked the temporary destruction of this secret society, occurred in the area between Arriaga and the Isthmus of Tehuantepec to the northwest of the Tonala-Arriaga locality.

With the conclusion of the Gadianton conflict, the Nephites

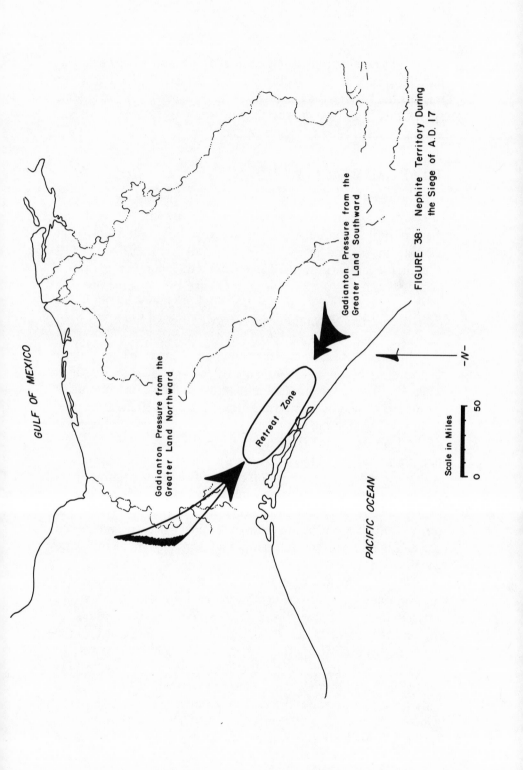

GULF OF MEXICO

Gadianton Pressure from the
Greater Land Northward

Retreat Zone

Gadianton Pressure from the
Greater Land Southward

PACIFIC OCEAN

-N-

Scale in Miles

0          50

FIGURE 38: Nephite Territory During
the Siege of A.D. 17

returned to their original settlements in the land southward, and little reference to geographic location is made in the text from this period through the ensuing 300 years, which marked a golden age of peace and prosperity for the Nephites as a result of the advent of Jesus Christ in their midst.

## THE FINAL WAR (A.D. 325-385)

The era of peace and prosperity for the peoples of the Book of Mormon began to close about A.D. 200. By A.D. 321, realizing that a period of conflict was about to erupt, the prophet Ammaron took all the sacred religious records and hid them in the hill Shim in the land northward. He informed the young boy Mormon of the location of the repository and gave him instructions that when he was of age he should go to the hill Shim, take the plates from the cache, and continue the record of the Nephites (Mormon 1:2-4).

The final war between the Nephites and the Lamanites began by the River Sidon about A.D. 325. By the year 327 the Nephites were in full retreat from Zarahemla toward their north countries in the greater land northward. As figures 14 and 39 indicate, they withdrew through the settlement of Angola to be later driven out of the land of David. Their attempt to establish a defensive settlement in the land of Joshua near the west sea ultimately failed, and by A.D. 345 they were in full retreat through the narrow pass that led into the land northward. While fortifying the city of Jashon, somewhere in the Isthmus of Tehuantepec, Mormon visited the nearby hill of Shim in the land of Antum, where he recovered some of the records that Ammaron had deposited in the hill some 24 years earlier.

With the eventual collapse of the Nephite defense at Jashon, the Nephites were driven northward into the land of Shem. In A.D. 346 they were able to hold at the city of Shem, causing the Lamanites to retreat back along the Pacific coastal shelf into the land southward. Mormon notes that the Nephite drive was so successful that they recovered the lands of their inheritance. This probably does not mean all the land of Zarahemla, however, but rather the Joshua zone in the land southward that was infested with the robber sect (Mormon 2:8, 28). The newly recovered territory in the land southward could not be adequately defended

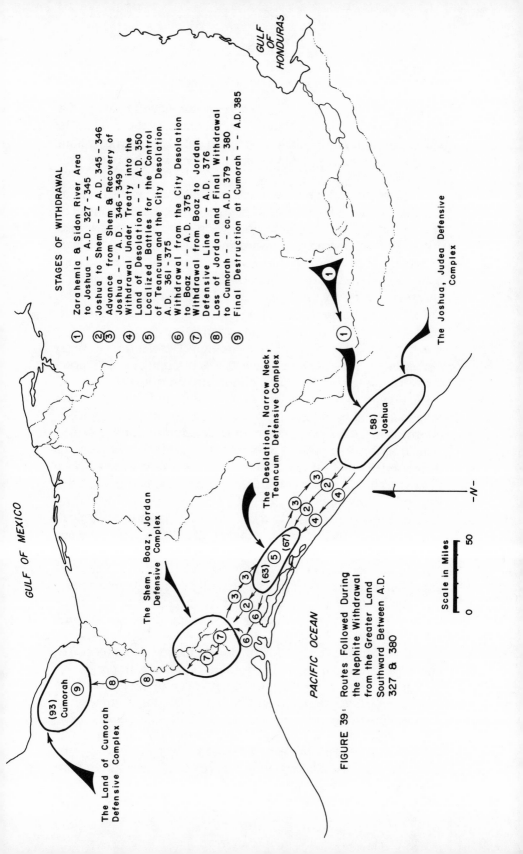

STAGES OF WITHDRAWAL

1. Zarahemla & Sidon River Area to Joshua – A.D. 327–345
2. Joshua to Shem – A.D. 345–346
3. Advance from Shem & Recovery of Joshua – A.D. 346–349
4. Withdrawal Under Treaty into the Land of Desolation – A.D. 350
5. Localized Battles for the Control of Teancum and the City Desolation A.D. 361–375
6. Withdrawal from the City Desolation to Boaz – A.D. 375
7. Withdrawal from Boaz to Jordan Defensive Line – A.D. 376
8. Loss of Jordan and Final Withdrawal to Cumorah – ca. A.D. 379 – 380
9. Final Destruction at Cumorah – A.D. 385

The Joshua, Judea Defensive Complex

The Desolation, Narrow Neck, Teancum Defensive Complex

The Shem, Boaz, Jordan Defensive Complex

The Land of Cumorah Defensive Complex

GULF OF MEXICO

GULF OF HONDURAS

PACIFIC OCEAN

-N-

Scale in Miles

0        50

FIGURE 39: Routes Followed During the Nephite Withdrawal from the Greater Land Southward Between A.D. 327 & 380

by the Nephites; thus by A.D. 350 a treaty was signed between the opposing forces, and the Nephites took control of the land northward at the defensive line that extended one day's journey within the coastal corridor separating the land northward from the land southward.

Figures 30 and 39 show the locations used by Mormon to establish in-depth fortifications relative to the Nephite control of the land access into the land northward. Near the narrow pass that led into the land southward, he constructed the fortified settlement of Desolation. To the west or northwest of that stronghold near the seashore was the fortified settlement of Teancum. The west sea or Pacific Ocean must have been adjacent to the city of Desolation, for during a major battle in A.D. 362 the Lamanite dead were "cast into the sea" (Mormon 3:8).

By A.D. 367 the cities of Teancum and Desolation had been lost and recaptured several times. It was not until A.D. 375, however, that the Lamanites gained dominance. In that year "they did come down against the Nephites with all their power; and they were not numbered because of the greatness of their number" (Mormon 4:17). Losing the cities of Desolation and probably also Teancum, the Nephites withdrew to a secondary stronghold at Boaz (see figures 30 and 39), where they attempted without success to hold a defensive line. Mormon, who had not led the Nephite armies since A.D. 362, when he resigned in protest of their corruption, decided to take action. Knowing that the Boaz defense would not last, he went to the hill of Shim in the adjacent land of Antum and took the remainder of the records out of that repository lest they should fall into Lamanite control. Then, relinquishing his role as an idle witness of the Nephite destruction, he assumed command at Jordan, where he used a series of fortified cities to establish a final defensive line (Mormon 4:19-23; 5:3-4).

Those fortifications at Jordan in the narrow Isthmus of Tehuantepec were the Nephites' last line of defense in protecting their populations and resources concentrated in the greater land northward. Thus, when Jordan fell in A.D. 379, the Nephites had no additional defensive positions that could halt Lamanite expansion northward, and a rout ensued. Those Nephites who could outdistance the Lamanite forces reached safety; those who were too slow were annihilated on the spot or sacrificed at a later time to the Lamanite idols (Mormon 5:5-7).

Pockets of Nephite resistance must have continued to exist after the loss of the Jordan line. These must have presented some threat to the Lamanites, giving Mormon the political leverage to establish a temporary treaty with the Lamanite forces. Under the terms of the treaty, Mormon was granted four years to gather all the remainder of his people together northward in the land of Cumorah for the final battle of A.D. 385.

Figures 30 and 39 depict the route from Jordan to Cumorah that was marched by the vanquished Nephite survivors. This is probably the same general route used several thousand years earlier by the deposed Jaredite ruler Omer as he traveled from Moron past the hill Shim and on beyond the hill Ramah to his exile at Ablom on the gulf. It appears to be more traditional than circumstantial that the Cumorah of the Nephite destruction was identical to the hill Ramah where the Jaredite civilization met its demise.

Moroni, the son of Mormon and one of the few survivors of the Cumorah tragedy, retained several of the Nephite records and concluded the documentation of the account. His final entry was made about 36 years after the battle on Cumorah, some 421 years after the original sign had been given of Christ's birth in Palestine (Moroni 10:1). During the preceding 35 years, Moroni had lived apparently alone, wandering wherever he was directed through inspiration. Thus it is that by A.D. 421 he was able to prepare a cache for the records on the west slope of an obscure hill in a land far from his own home, a hill situated in a rural upper New York state locality where 1,400 years later a young boy named Joseph Smith would reside.

## NOTES

1. The record does not detail the route used by Moroni to march on Nephihah after leaving Zarahemla. In Alma 62:14-18 an incident that occurs during their march suggests that they may have been taking the Polochic Valley corridor from Manti eastward through Aaron. While traveling, Moroni's force defeats a "large body of men of the Lamanites." After accepting their captives' covenant of peace, Moroni sends the 4,000 Lamanites "to dwell with the people of Ammon" who were at Melek. The Polochic River route westward through Manti to Melek would have been the most direct corridor for the Lamanites to travel; Moroni would have been reluctant to have them make the journey through the Nephite

heartland. Therefore, the Lamanite force was probably encountered at a strategic position along the Polochic route where they were protecting the Manti corridor into Nephihah.

2. Although traditional teachings correlate the Jaredite demise with the Mulekite arrival, some scholars are of the opinion that the destruction of the Jaredites did not coincide with the arrival of the Mulekites in the early decades of the sixth century B.C. They believe rather that Coriantumr's visit with the people of Zarahemla occurred sometime after the Mulekite settlement was established at Zarahemla. This theory would mean that the Jaredite demise could have occurred as late as 200 or 300 B.C. This conclusion has been based on the supposition that the state of preservation of the human remains, artifacts, and buildings described by the Limhi expedition suggests that the demise of the Jaredite civilization occurred within a relatively short time before the ca. 125 B.C. arrival of Limhi's explorers.

Omni 1:15-22 sheds some light on this question. Verses 15 and 16 state that the people of Zarahemla departed from Palestine and traveled to the land of Zarahemla at ca. 600 B.C. Verses 17 and 18 state that sufficient time had passed after their arrival at Zarahemla for the population to expand and numerous wars to transpire. Furthermore, due to the absence of written records, the language had become corrupted to the degree that the collective memory of these past events was maintained only by oral histories and geneologies. The final verses note that after the Nephite's arrival in Zarahemla and the subsequent merging of the two populations, which occurred at ca. 225 B.C., a large stone containing unknown inscriptions was brought to King Mosiah by the people of Zarahemla. The summary of his interpretation states that this record "gave an account of one Coriantumr, and the slain of his people. And Coriantumr was discovered by the people of Zarahemla; and he dwelt with them for the space of nine moons." Thus, by ca. 225 B.C., perhaps a century before the arrival of the Limhi expedition in the greater land northward, the people of Zarahemla needed Mosiah's translation to help restore the memory of their meeting with Coriantumr.

This reference does not warrant the assumption that the demise of the Jaredites and the arrival of the Mulekites were contemporaneous incidents. This reference simply provides the insight that the meeting between Coriantumr and the people of Zarahemla was before Mosiah's arrival at Zarahemla and probably occurred sometime between 500 and 300 B.C.

3. This coastal territory was used at least three times by the Nephites as a safe corridor for withdrawal toward the greater land northward through the narrow neck of land. The first use of this zone was during the 35 B.C. conflict noted above when the Nephites withdrew from the "middle" land of Zarahemla westward into the west sea land of Bountiful.

Their second involvement was during this conflict of A.D. 17-22 when they consolidated their forces under siege in this same coastal zone. The third instance occurred in A.D. 350 when chief captain Mormon fortified this region as the land of Desolation after abandoning the land of Joshua to the Lamanites.

# CONCLUSION

The preceding chapters have reconstructed and analyzed the relationships among the places of the Book of Mormon. The development of the basic model of the text's geographic layout led to the correlation of that model's topography with the topographic features of the Americas. The setting of the Book of Mormon lands was thus identified in the geographic area of southern Mexico and Guatemala. Through the subsequent comparisons of the model with the natural conditions of the setting, the area network has been further refined into its secondary stage of development, a model useful for conducting field evaluations. Field research using this model as a guide will permit further refinement and modification leading toward the primary and final models of the area network in southern Mesoamerica.

The study of the Book of Mormon secondary area model within its Mesoamerican setting could well be the largest archeological project ever initiated. Its objective will be to examine and explain 3,000 years of cultural development in some 144,000 square miles of complex tropical topography. Present knowledge of the ancient peoples and places of this area during its Classic and Postclassic phases (A.D. 250-1500) is limited, based on fragmented native folklore, Spanish histories, modern archeological field investigations, and the recent discoveries in the decipherment of Maya hieroglyphic texts. The Preclassic and Early Classic phases of cultural development in this area of southeastern Mesoamerica are even less understood. The secondary model, with its general geographic coverage ranging from about 2500 B.C. to A.D. 400, furnishes the temporal and spatial structure needed to expand our understanding of this unique culture area.

Presently it is not possible to predict when, if ever, reseachers will achieve a more thorough understanding of the lands and peoples of the Book of Mormon in its southern Mesoamerican setting. It is certain, however, that the research will continue through the years as a result of the labor and commitment of numerous contributors.

The studies of the Book of Mormon settlements and routes in this volume are a further verification of the authenticity of the Book of Mormon, for they show that complete consistency exists in its fragmented spatial relationships. This consistency and internal integrity are the result of ancient authorship, for such order could neither occur by chance nor be invented in the early nineteenth century A.D.

The research information presently capable of confirming or refuting the spatial validity of the Book of Mormon is of recent date, having been developed within the past thirty years. Even now, it would be very difficult for a modern researcher applying this new theoretical capability to fabricate the book's setting and attain this level of integrity among all the scattered fragments of geographical information.

In the 1827-29 period when the Book of Mormon was being translated by Joseph Smith, it would have been impossible to create this consistency, either from an active imagination or from available information. In the first quarter of the 19th century, the world knew nothing about systems theory and was equally ignorant about the ancient cultures of Mesoamerica. In addition, the geographic information available at that time on Mexico and Guatemela was too inadequate to permit the planned development of a spatial model that some 150 years later could be reconstructed and both culturally and geographically verified using the systemic approach.

The impossibility of a 19th-century fabrication, the consistency of the data, and the clarity of explanation provided in matching the model with the geography of southern Mesoamerica all demonstrate that the geographic information provided in the Book of Mormon is the remnant of a complex and extensive settlement system of ancient origin. The Book of Mormon, its peoples, its message, and its geographic relationships all warrant our respect and attention.

Joseph Smith's comment provided in the introduction to the Book of Mormon, "I told the brethren that the Book of Mormon was the most correct of any book on earth," was not solely confined to doctrine. Joseph Smith knew that the fragmentary geographic references contained in the book were all completely consistent. He understood this consistency because of his unique experience in the translation. It has taken an additional 150 years before scientists and scholars, using an expanding science, could begin to appreciate and understand the geographic precision of the Book of Mormon.

# Addendum to Chapter 4

# The Theoretical Background for This Study

A settlement pattern in any cultural system has form or organization. This organization can be effectively studied through systems theory applications, resulting in the development of models demonstrating the interaction among settlements and their environments. By abstracting the Book of Mormon into a system of elements, including environmental features, settlements, transportation routes, and miscellaneous activity locations, the researcher can understand the system's structure, examine its quantitative and qualitative values, and study associations within sets of elements.

## Systems Theory in the Study of Geography and Culture

This volume has been prepared from a systems perspective in that the spatial associations of settlements, topographic features, and routes are considered as units that interact to form a comprehensive and unique settlement structure. These spatial structures are referred to as *models*. Although these models are simple abstractions of the original system that existed in antiquity, they can be studied in a variety of ways to understand and quantify the nature of the system described in the book.

A number of variables exist that are useful for describing network models. These involve different systems concepts (for example, network centrality, content, magnitude, size, temporal duration, directionality, and complexity). Geographers have developed statistical techniques for conducting quantitative studies of networks in order to assess some of these variables. The settlement system developed from the spatial analysis of the Book of Mormon can be evaluated using such techniques. The information ultimately derived from this approach thus expands our understanding of the text and its peoples.

The use of systems in studying geographical associations is a by-product of a general systems theory[1] that, as its author states, is "a general science of 'wholeness' " ascertainable within a variety of sciences. Biologist Ludwig von Bertalanffy further notes: "There appear to exist general system laws which apply to any system of a certain type, irrespective of the particular properties of the system and the elements involved. These considerations lead to the postulate of a new scientific discipline which we call general system theory. Its subject matter is formulation of principles that are valid for 'systems' in general, whatever the nature of their component elements and the relations or 'forces' between them" (1968:37).

Systems to von Bertalanffy, are defined as "complexes of elements standing in interaction" (1963:33). This abstract concept can be better understood when applied to a specific system such as the human body. Our physical system consists of various organ complexes that interact to maintain the life of the complete organism. The organs of the human system are all interdependent and interrelated.

In a different perspective, human cultures can also be considered as a variety of systems. Culture, as a general term, has been defined by archeologist Lewis R. Binford as "an extrasomatic adoptive system that is employed in the integration of a society with its environment and with other sociocultural systems. Culture in this sense is not necessarily shared; it is participated in by men. In cultural systems, people, things, and places are components in a field that consists of environmental and sociocultural subsystems, and the focus of cultural process is in the dynamic articulations of these subsystems" (Binford 1972:198; see also Kroeber and Kluckholm n.d.:369).

Human culture thus involves the interaction of people in association with time, space, environment, and social conditions. This cultural, systemic approach is most pertinent to the analysis of the settlement associations noted in the Book of Mormon. This is because, as its ancient authors state, the paucity of writing space, the difficulty of engraving the characters on the plates, and the writers' emphasis on theological concepts rather than on cultural circumstances resulted in the inclusion of very little information about time, space, and environment. Because information about the Book of Mormon's cultural subsystems is limited, the data that are available in the Book of Mormon must be used with maximum efficiency. This can be done by using the holistic approach that systems theory affords. Thus this volume is a reconstruction of the spatial subsystem contained in the Book of Mormon using the interaction of numerous settlements and their transportation-communication routes. This emphasis on space requires the application of temporal, environmental, and cultural factors to establish the most correct approximation of the ancient spatial system.

## ORDER, REALITY, AND SCIENCE

Although volumes have been written about the meaning of science and how its various disciplines are structured and oriented, science is essentially concerned with the act and result of understanding or knowing. Science incorporates philosophies and methods, attempting to explain and manipulate aspects of our shared reality. Understanding science and its applications for conducting studies of this nature is important, for it is the springboard for the inquiry that lies in the chapters of this volume.

A discussion of the methods and development of certain sciences must begin with the concept of reality, or the physical world that we as humans share. That this reality is common to all people stems from the fact that we all share an existence that can be subjected to scientific inquiry. All can relate to our shared experiences regardless of the variations associated with cultural or temporal factors. If this were not so, people would not exist. Reality is shared; scientists jointly perceive problems, communicate their findings, and ultimately arrive at a common understanding of reality and thereby alter and hopefully better our world. As has been so well stated, "All scientific inquiry is pattern- and relation-seeking activity, and the perception of pattern and order in a seeming chaos of events is a creative act founded upon a touchstone of faith that orderly relationships are there in the first place" (Abler et al. 1971:112). We do not live separate realities, but we do perceive aspects of that reality in our own separate, individualistic ways.

Reality contains order, the critical factor that permits explanation. The order, consistency, or harmony associated with our universe and its micro-macro environments is verifiable through applications of the scientific method. This is not to say that science has all the methods of understanding and explaining the order about us, for "science is not a cumulative body of knowledge which is approaching an ultimate truth at an increasing or decreasing rate. Science is an order men impose upon reality because it is convenient for them to do so" (Abler et al. 1971:25).

Scientific theory establishes through logical means an explanation of physical reality. Thus, theory is not an end but the means to an end. In chapter 2, the basic parallel was drawn between theory and perspective. Just as one's perception of reality is a result of cultural perspective, so a scientist's capacity for identifying and evaluating ordered aspects of reality is in large part attributable to the elegance and relevance of his or her theoretical foundation. Theory aids in ordering facts through the use of various methodologies to resolve specific problems. Commenting on theory, geographer Peter Haggett has stated, "Although . . . theories cannot be proved to be right or wrong in the absolute sense, they can be tested rigorously against the available facts using well established experimental techniques" (Haggett 1966:278).

Theories therefore are constructions — metaphysical bridges designed to span the gap between physical phenomena and our perception of those phenomena. Since theory fulfills this purpose and since scientific inquiry is nonlinear and very diverse due to the range of subjects that can be studied, it should not be surprising that theories occupy a wide range of applicability and relevance. The most pertinent classification for this volume appears to be between those theories referred to as "complete" in contrast to "incomplete" theories. Their definitions are especially pertinent in this frame of reference, as archeologist David L. Clarke has stated:

> Complete theories are those formal and comprehensive networks of defined terms or theorums which may be derived from a complete set of primitive and axiomatic sentences by deduction and tested against reality (e.g., Euclidean geometry). However, most theories in the social and behavioral sciences belong to the group of incomplete theoretical networks and they are often only "quasi-deductive" or "non-formal" theories. Archeological theory in general, and spatial archeological theory in particular, is in the main only quasi-deductive in the

sense that there are difficulties, some of them intrinsic, in establishing precise primitive terms in the initial stages of theory formation and thus a consequent weakness in the deduction process. The same theories are also nonformal since there are often difficulties in testing the theory and its models empirically because of vagueness and ambiguity, limited data, limited capacities for controlled experiment, severe sampling problems and a general lack of suitable evaluation techniques. . . . However, this state of affairs makes it more important for archeology to move as far as possible in reforming its theories towards as complete, formal and deductive a form as may be possible (Clarke 1977:1718).

Clarke's observations provide the nonarcheologist with the insight that scientific research (with respect to contemporary theory development in spatial archeology) is still in its adolescence and will continue to move toward a more mature position — that is, the rigorous application of more formal theories. Thus, the development of understanding through scientific application is a complex and often very slow process. Some aspects of our shared reality are temporarily incapable of being ordered and analyzed with the available research paradigms. When this occurs, the research is static until new paradigms or research perspectives are identified as having the capacity to resolve the old problem. New paradigms often originate in different fields to be later borrowed and implemented when their applicability is realized. For an excellent thesis on this development in science, see Thomas S. Kuhn, *The Structure of Scientific Revolutions* (1962).

Temporal, spatial, and environmental elements in a historical manuscript are aspects of a cultural system. Thus, in its context, any given historic manuscript includes cultural system data, and the Book of Mormon is no exception. Since temporal, spatial, and environmental information relative to settlement distribution can be analyzed using a variety of established systems procedures, it follows that a written history containing settlement and communication route data can be studied using the systemic approach to define its cultural system. The Book of Mormon claims to be a record of ancient peoples and their settlement history; therefore, its settlements and their spatial, temporal, and environmental features are appropriate subjects for rigorous systemic analysis.

## NOTES

1. Systems theory as a scientific paradigm for organizing and evaluating reality was initiated in the 1930s when Ludwig von Bertalanffy sought to understand organization in living organisms. Finding that the current paradigms of the mechanistic and vitalistic schools were inadequate for studying factors of organismic organization—e.g., maintenance, regulation, and competition—this biologist oriented his evaluations to the organismic viewpoint. Eventually the realization that order in living organisms was applicable on a broader scope and in other disciplines resulted in the development of general systems theory. Although von Bertalanffy's first public presentation in systemics was given in 1937, it was not until after the mid-century that the relevance of these concepts began to be understood and used by scientists in other disciplines.

# ADDENDUM TO CHAPTER 8

## STATISTICAL CHARACTERISTICS OF THE AREA SETTLEMENT MODEL

The secondary area network as shown in figure 30 does not permit statistical evaluations of its complexity. The incorporation of the numerous topographic features within its structure preclude its measurement as a settlement model using the techniques that geographers have developed to assess settlement networks.

The basic understanding of the complexity of Book of Mormon settlements is pertinent to any appreciation of the significance of the Area Model. As a result, the secondary area model has been simplified into the area settlement network demonstrated in figure 40. This model incorporates all the settlement vertices, including lands and settlements, with the vertices that symbolize route or path junctions. By applying this abbreviated graph, an analysis of the complexity of the settlements, junctions, and routes of the Book of Mormon can be accomplished using established geographic techniques.

Three studies of the settlement model have been conducted. These studies have analyzed the circuitry, complexity, and connectivity of the network. All three are based on the model's relative structure shown in figure 40, having a total of 66 vertices, or places, and 99 edges or routes.[1] Basic information on the measurement of each index is provided at the end of this addendum.

The initial test for the network is the Beta Index, which geographer Peter Haggett has stated is "the simplest measure of the degree of connectivity of a transport network" (1966:238). The area settlement network contains a rating of 1.5 out of a possible high of 3. This rating shows that the network is a complex system having a medium level of connectivity among its dispersed settlements.

The Gamma Index contains a formula that establishes the complexity of any network. On a scale of 0 to 1, the area settlement network ranks at .52 as a grid type in the medium range of complexity. This study demonstrates that the network is more

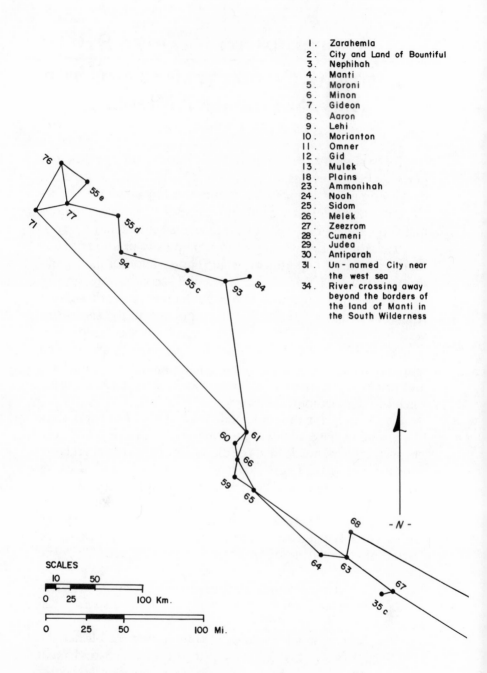

1. Zarahemla
2. City and Land of Bountiful
3. Nephihah
4. Manti
5. Moroni
6. Minon
7. Gideon
8. Aaron
9. Lehi
10. Morianton
11. Omner
12. Gid
13. Mulek
18. Plains
23. Ammonihah
24. Noah
25. Sidom
26. Melek
27. Zeezrom
28. Cumeni
29. Judea
30. Antiparah
31. Un-named City near the west sea
34. River crossing away beyond the borders of the land of Manti in the South Wilderness

SCALES

- N -

FIGURE 40: The Book of Mormon Area Settlement Network

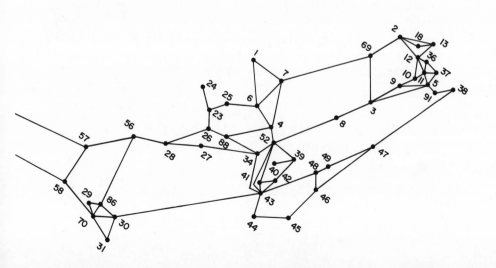

complex than a simple spinal network, with its range of 0 to .49, and much less complex than a delta type network, which ranges from .67 to 1 in the scale of complexity.

The last test involves the Alpha Index, with its scale of 0 to 1 for measuring relative circuitry. In this test, a network that measures 1 is very complex for it contains 100% circuitry or a capacity for unrestricted movement from any given vertex or settlement to any other vertex in the system. The area settlement network measures .26 on this scale, which shows that the network has only about 26% circuitry.

These three studies reveal that the settlement model, although a complex system, is in the moderate range of complexity and has a low level of circuitry, or connectivity, among its diverse settlements. The settlement model therefore is an incomplete model; it is only the remnant of an extensive network of settlements and routes that once existed in southern Mesoamerica. The reasons for its incompleteness are diverse. First, the text does not contain all spatial associations that were used during the 3,000 years of occupation and travel associated with this network; second, the network model provided in figure 40 is a compilation of three separate spatial systems (Jaredite, Nephite land southward, and Nephite land northward) that, although existing within the same territory, were constructed from three separate time periods. Finally, the simplicity of the Jaredite elements within the network's western segment dilute the effect established with the greater complexity of the Nephite elements in the eastern segment, thus reducing the overall connectivity and complexity of the network.

Despite the model's incompleteness, the Book of Mormon area settlement network provides a base from which to launch further inquiry. As research in the field continues, the model will be expanded and will eventually become a closer approximation of the original settlement system of the Book of Mormon.

## MEASURING THE RELATIVE CONNECTIVITY OF THE SECONDARY AREA NETWORK USING THE BETA INDEX

*Basic information on this index (see figure 40):*

Index Scale: 0 to 3. (Indices occurring in the scale from 0 to .999 consist of simple networks called trees or disconnected graphs. Indices from 1 to 3 consist of complex systems containing at least one circuit.)

Index Formula: $\beta$ = e/v

Reference: Haggett 1966:238-39

*Network Size:*
99 edges (e) or routes between vertices
66 vertices (v) or places, including settlements and all non-settlement trail junctions

*Analysis:*
$\beta$ = e/v or 99/66 or $\beta$ = 1.5

*Conclusion:* With a $\beta$ index of 1.5 the Area Settlement Network qualifies as a complex system having a medium level of connectivity.

## MEASURING THE COMPLEXITY OF THE SECONDARY AREA NETWORK USING THE GAMMA INDEX

*Basic information on this index (see figure 40):*

Index Scale: 0 to 1. (Indices occurring in the scale from 0 to .49 consist of simple spinal networks. Indices between .5 to .66 consist of grid type networks that are more complicated, and those from .67 to 1 include the most complex networks of the delta type.)

Index Formula: $\gamma$ = e/3( v-2 )

Reference: Taaffe and Gauthier 1973:101

*Network Size:*
99 edges (e) or routes between vertices

66 vertices (v) or places, including settlements and all non-settlement trail junctions

*Analysis:* $\gamma$ = e/3( v-2 ) or 99/3( 66-2 ) or $\gamma$ = .52

*Conclusion:* With a $\gamma$ index of .52 the Area Settlement Network qualifies as a grid type network having a medium level of complexity.


## MEASURING THE CIRCUITRY OF THE SECONDARY AREA NETWORK USING THE ALPHA INDEX

*Basic Information on this index (see figure 40):*

Index Scale: 0 to 1 with 1 = 100% circuitry
Index Formula: $\alpha$ = e - v + 1/2v - 5

Reference: Taffe and Gauthier 1973:104-5

*Network Size:*
99 edges (e) or routes between vertices
66 vertices (v) or places, including settlements and all non-settlement trail junctions

*Analysis:* $\alpha$ = e - v + 1/2v - 5 or 99 -66 + 1/2 x 66 - 5 or $\alpha$ = .26

*Conclusion:* With an $\alpha$ index of .26 the Area Settlement Network qualifies as a system having 26% circuitry.


### NOTES

1. The more complex series of measuring the distances between the vertices and identifying settlement importance in hierarchical ordering has not been initiated at this stage of model development. Once a more definitive identification of settlement positions in Mesoamerica has been accomplished through field research, such studies analyzing the economic and demographic variables of the settlement model can be initiated.

# APPENDIX A

A Listing of References to Settlements and Topographic Places Used in This Study of the Book of Mormon

## PART 1: A NUMERICAL LISTING OF LOCATIONS

1. Zarahemla
2. City and Land of Bountiful situated in the east sea locality
3. Nephihah
4. Manti
5. Moroni
6. Minon
7. Gideon
8. Aaron
9. Lehi
10. Morianton
11. Omner
12. Gid
13. Mulek
14. River crossing on the east of Zarahemla
15. Hill Amnihu
16. River crossing in the borderlands between Manti and the south wilderness
17. Wilderness zones on the south and on the east of Moroni
18. Plains between city Bountiful and Mulek
19. Wilderness zone west of Mulek
20. Narrow pass near the city Bountiful leading into land northward
21. Land northward from the east sea Bountiful, not identical with the greater land northward accessible to the Nephites and Lamanites along the west sea corridor
22. East Sea
23. Ammonihah
24. Noah
25. Sidom
26. Melek
27. Zeezrom
28. Cumeni
29. Judea
30. Antiparah
31. Unnamed city near the west sea
32. Wilderness of Hermounts
33. Wilderness south of Melek
34. River crossing away beyond the borders of the land of Manti in the south wilderness
35. West Sea

36. Jershon
37. Antionum
38. Siron
39. Helam
40. Amulon
41. Shilom
42. Shemlon
43. Nephi
44. Place or land called Mormon
45. Jerusalem
46. Ani-Anti
47. Middoni
48. Ishmael
49. Midian
50. Narrow strip of wilderness
51. Hill Riplah
52. Passage through the south wilderness
53. Hill north of Shilom
54. Drainage between Shilom and Nephi
55. North Sea
56. Angola
57. David
58. Joshua
59. Jashon
60. Shem
61. Antum
62. Hill Shim
63. City of Desolation
64. Teancum
65. Boaz
66. Jordan
67. Narrow passage in the narrow neck that connected the greater land northward with the land southward
68. Lamanite positions above the city of Desolation
69. Trail junction on the Zarahemla–city Bountiful path linking with the route to Nephihah
70. Trail junction on path between Judea and the unnamed city on the west sea
71. Moron
72. Land of Nehor
73. Heth
74. Valley of Gilgal
75. Plains of Heshlon
76. Wilderness of Akish
77. Plains of Agosh
78. Valley Shurr
79. Valley or land of Corihor
80. Hill Comnor

81. Coriantumr's camp
82. Hill Cumorah/Ramah
83. Place called Ogath
84. Ablom
85. Hill Ephriam
86. Trail Junction on Judea-Antiparah path
87. Valley of Alma
88. Trail junction of the Manti-Judea and Nephi-Nephihah paths
89. Valley west of river crossing in the south wilderness
90. Valley south of hill Riplah, east of the river crossing in the south wilderness
91. Passage through the narrow strip of wilderness linking Moroni with the lands occupied by the Lamanites
92. Battleground on route north from Antiparah and Judea complex
93. Land of Cumorah
94. Land of Corihor

## PART 2: AN ALPHABETICAL LISTING OF LOCATIONS

AARON (8): Nephite settlement
    Alma 8:13                               ca. 82 B.C.
    Alma 50:13, 14                     72 B.C.

ABLOM (84): King Omer's camp
    Ether 9:3                                no date

AGOSH (77): Plains
    Ether 14:11-16                600-580 B.C.

AKISH (76): Wilderness
    Ether 14:3, 4, 11-16         600-580 B.C.

ALMA (87): Valley
    Mosiah 24:20, 24, 25        ca. 120 B.C.

AMMONIHAH (23): Nephite settlement
    Alma 8:6-9, 13, 14, 16,  18    ca. 82 B.C.
    Alma 9:1                          ca. 82 B.C.
    Alma 15:1, 16                 ca. 81 B.C.
    Alma 16:2, 3, 11             81 B.C.
    Alma 25:2                      81 B.C.
    Alma 49:1-12                  72 B.C.

AMNIHU (15): Hill
    Alma 2:15, 17                   87 B.C.

AMULON (40): Settlement
    Mosiah 23:30, 31          ca. 121 B.C.
    Mosiah 24:1               ca. 120 B.C.
    Alma 24:1                  ca. 77 B.C.

ANGOLA (56): Nephite Settlement
    Mormon 2:3-5          A.D. 327-328

ANI-ANTI (46): Lamanite village
    Alma 21:11, 12          90-77 B.C.

ANTIONUM (37): Land of the Zoramites
    Alma 31:3                  ca. 74 B.C.
    Alma 32:4                  ca. 74 B.C.
    Alma 43:4, 5, 15, 18,  22    ca. 74 B.C.

ANTIPARAH (30): Nephite Settlement
    Alma 56:14, 15, 22,  31-36    ca. 64 B.C.
    Alma 57:4                  ca. 64 B.C.

ANTUM (61): Nephite land
    Mormon 1:3              ca. A.D. 322

BOAZ (65): Nephite city
    Mormon 4:20           A.D. 380-375

BOUNTIFUL
  CITY BOUNTIFUL (2)
      Alma 52:17, 20, 27      66-64 B.C.
      Alma 53:3-6           ca. 64 B.C.
      Helaman 1:23         ca. 51 B.C.

| | |
|---|---|
| Helaman 5:14, 15 | ca. 30 B.C. |
| LAND BOUNTIFUL ON THE EAST SEA (2) | |
| Alma 27:22 | 90-77 B.C. |
| Alma 51:28-32 | 67 B.C. |
| Alma 52:9, 15, 18, 22- 24, 39 | 66-64 B.C. |
| Alma 53:3, 4 | ca. 64 B.C. |
| Helaman 1:28, 29 | ca. 51 B.C. |
| LAND BOUNTIFUL ON THE WEST SEA | |
| Alma 22:29-33 | 90-77 B.C. |
| Alma 50:11, 32-34 | 68 B.C. |
| Alma 63:4-7 | 56-55 B.C. |
| Helaman 4:5-7 | 35 B.C. |
| 3 Nephi 3:23 | A.D. 17 |
| 3 Nephi 11:1 | A.D. 34 |
| COMNOR (80): Hill | |
| Ether 14:26-28 | 600-580 B.C. |
| CORIANTUMR'S CAMP (81): Adjacent to hill Ramah | |
| Ether 15:11 | 580-600 B.C. |
| CORIHOR | |
| VALLEY (79) | |
| Ether 14:28 | 600-580 B.C. |
| LAND (94) | |
| Ether 14:26, 27 | 600-580 B.C. |
| CUMENI (28): Nephite settlement | |
| Alma 56:14 | 66 B.C. |
| Alma 57:7-12, 22, 23 | 63 B.C. |
| CUMORAH | |
| HILL CUMORAH (82): Location of final Jaredite and Nephite battles | |
| Mormon 6:2, 4, 6-15 | A.D. 380-385 |
| Ether 15:11 | 600-580 B.C. |
| LAND OF CUMORAH (93): In the greater land northward—contains | |
| hill Cumorah | |
| Mormon 6:2, 4-6 | |
| DAVID (57): Nephite land | |
| Mormon 2:4-6 | A.D. 328 |
| DESOLATION | |
| CITY DESOLATION (63) | |
| Mormon 3:5-8, 10 | A.D. 360-362 |
| Mormon 4:2, 3, 8, 13,   19 | A.D. 363-375 |
| LAND OF DESOLATION: Another term for the greater land northward | |
| Helaman 3:6 | 46 B.C. |
| Ether 7:6 | no date |
| LAND OF DESOLATION ADJACENT TO THE CITY DESOLATION | |
| Alma 22:30-33 | 90-77 B.C. |
| Alma 50:33, 34 | ca. 67 B.C. |
| 3 Nephi 3:23 | A.D. 17 |
| Mormon 3:5 | A.D. 360 |

Mormon 4:1, 2, 19        A.D. 363-375

DRAINAGE AND AGRICULTURAL LANDS BETWEEN NEPHI AND SHILOM (54)

Mosiah 9:14, 15        ca. 187 B.C.

EPHRAIM (85): Hill

Ether 7:9        no date

GID (12): Nephite settlement

Alma 51:24-26        ca. 67 B.C.

Alma 55:7, 16, 20-26        ca. 63 B.C.

Helaman 5:15        ca. 30 B.C.

GIDEON (7): Nephite land, valley and settlement

Alma 2:20, 26        87 B.C.

Alma 6:7, 8        ca. 83 B.C.

Alma 8:1        83 B.C.

Alma 17:1        77 B.C.

Alma 30:21        ca. 74 B.C.

Alma 62:3-7        62 B.C.

GILGAL (74): Valley

Ether 13:27-30        no date

HAGOTH'S SHIPYARD (35c): Nephite settlement? situated on the coastal

lagoon system

Alma 63:5-7        55-54 B.C.

HELAM (39): Nephite settlement in the "middle" land of Nephi

Mosiah 23:4, 19, 20        ca. 121 B.C.

Alma 24:1        ca. 77 B.C.

HERMOUNTS (32): Wilderness

Alma 2:34-37        87 B.C.

HESHLON (75): Plains

Ether 13:28, 29        no date

HETH (73): Land

Ether 8:2        no date

HILL

AMNIHU (15): Hill

Alma 2:15, 17        87 B.C.

COMNOR (80): Hill

Ether 14:26-28        600-580 B.C.

CUMORAH (82): Hill, location of final Jaredite and Nephite battles

Mormon 6:2, 4, 6-15        A.D. 380-385

Ether 15:11        600-580 B.C.

EPHRAIM (85): Hill

Ether 7:9        no date

HILL NORTH OF SHILOM (53)

Mosiah 7:5, 6, 16        ca. 122 B.C.

Mosiah 10:8        ca. 178 B.C.

Mosiah 11:13        150-160 B.C.

RAMAH (82): Jaredite name for the hill Cumorah

Ether 15:11        600-580 B.C.

RIPLAH (51): Hill
    Alma 43:31, 35                     ca. 74 B.C.
SHIM (62): Hill in the land Antum
    Mormon 1:3                     ca. A.D. 322
    Mormon 4:23                  ca. A.D. 379
    Ether 9:3                        no date
ISHMAEL (48): Lamanite land
    Alma 17:19, 26, 34             ca. 90 B.C.
    Alma 18:34                   ca. 90 B.C.
    Alma 20:2                     ca. 90 B.C.
    Alma 23:9-12                90-77 B.C.
JASHON (59): Nephite land and settlement
    Mormon 2:16, 17              A.D. 345
JERSHON (36): Nephite land
    Alma 27:22, 26              ca. 77 B.C.
    Alma 30:1, 19-21           ca. 74 B.C.
    Alma 31:3                     ca. 74 B.C.
    Alma 35:1, 2, 6, 8, 13,  14      74 B.C.
    Alma 43:4, 15, 18, 22,  25    ca. 74 B.C.
JERUSALEM (45): Lamanite city and land
    Alma 21:1, 2, 4, 11            ca. 90 B.C.
    Alma 24:1   —                77-90 B.C.
    3 Nephi 9:7                   A.D. 34
JORDAN (66): Nephite settlement
    Mormon 5:3               A.D. 375-380
JOSHUA (58): Nephite land
    Mormon 2:6-15            A.D. 327-345
JUDEA (29): Nephite settlement
    Alma 56:9, 15               66 B.C.
    Alma 57:11                  63 B.C.
LAND NORTHWARD
  LAND ACCESSIBLE FROM THE EAST SEA LAND OF BOUNTIFUL (21)
    Alma 50:11                   ca. 72 B.C.
    Alma 51:30                   67 B.C.
    Alma 52:2, 9                  66 B.C.
    Helaman 1:22-29             51 B.C.
  LAND ACCESSIBLE FROM WEST SEA LAND OF BOUNTIFUL: Referred to
  in this study as the greater land northward
    Mosiah 8:7-11            125-121 B.C.
    Mosiah 21:25-27          125-121 B.C.
    Helaman 6:6               ca. 29 B.C.
    Helaman 7:1-3              23 B.C.
    3 Nephi 4:23-26           ca. 21 B.C.
LEHI (9): Nephite settlement
    Alma 50:13-15, 25           72-68 B.C.
    Alma 51:24-26            ca. 67 B.C.
    Alma 59:5                 ca. 62 B.C.
    Alma 62:30-32            ca. 60 B.C.

LINE BOUNTIFUL-DESOLATION DEFENSIVE SYSTEM

| | |
|---|---|
| Alma 22:32, 33 | 90-77 B.C. |
| Helaman 4:7, 8 | 34-33 B.C. |
| 3 Nephi 3:23 | A.D. 17 |

MANTI (4): Nephite land and settlement

| | |
|---|---|
| Alma 16:6, 7 | 81 B.C. |
| Alma 17:1 | 77 B.C. |
| Alma 22:27 | 77-90 B.C. |
| Alma 43:22, 24-27, 31-35, 42 | ca. 74 B.C. |
| Alma 56:14, 25 | 66 B.C. |
| Alma 57:22, 30, 31 | ca. 63 B.C. |
| Alma 58:13-30, 39 | ca. 63 B.C. |
| Alma 59:6 | ca. 62 B.C. |

MELEK (26): Nephite land

| | |
|---|---|
| Alma 8:3-6 | 82 B.C. |
| Alma 31:6 | ca. 74 B.C. |
| Alma 35:13 | 74 B.C. |
| Alma 45:18 | 74 B.C. |

MIDDONI (47): Lamanite land

| | |
|---|---|
| Alma 20:2-5, 7, 14-15, 28, 30 | 90-77 B.C. |
| Alma 21:12, 13, 18 | 90-77 B.C. |
| Alma 22:1, 3 | 90-77 B.C. |
| Alma 23:10 | 90-77 B.C. |

MIDIAN (49): Lamanite land

| | |
|---|---|
| Alma 24:5 | ca. 77 B.C. |

MINON (6): Nephite land

| | |
|---|---|
| Alma 2:24 | 87 B.C. |

MORIANTON (10): Nephite land

| | |
|---|---|
| Alma 50:25-31, 36 | 68 B.C. |
| Alma 51:26 | ca. 67 B.C. |
| Alma 55:33 | ca. 63 B.C. |
| Alma 59:5 | ca. 62 B.C. |
| Alma 62:30-32 | 60 B.C. |

MORMON (44): Uninhabited land, place, waters and forest

| | |
|---|---|
| Mosiah 18:4-8, 16, 30, 34 | ca. 147 B.C. |
| Alma 5:3 | ca. 147 B.C. |
| Alma 21:1 | ca. 90 B.C. |

MORON (71): Jaredite capital land

| | |
|---|---|
| Ether 7:5, 6, 17 | no date |
| Ether 14:6, 11, 12 | 600-580 B.C. |

MORONI (5): Nephite settlement and land

| | |
|---|---|
| Alma 50:13-15 | 72 B.C. |
| Alma 51:22-24 | ca. 67 B.C. |
| Alma 59:5 | ca. 62 B.C. |
| Alma 62:25, 32-38 | 60 B.C. |
| 3 Nephi 8:9 | A.D. 34 |
| 3 Nephi 9:4 | A.D. 34 |

MULEK (13): Nephite settlement

| | |
|---|---|
| Alma 51:26 | ca. 67 B.C. |
| Alma 52:2, 17, 20-23 | 65-64 B.C. |
| Alma 53:2, 6 | 64 B.C. |
| Helaman 5:15 | ca. 30 B.C. |

NARROW NECK OF LAND ON THE WEST SEASHORE

| | |
|---|---|
| Alma 22:32 | 90-77 B.C. |
| Alma 63:5 | 55 B.C. |
| Ether 10:20 | no date |

NARROW PASS OR PASSAGE

IN THE VICINITY OF THE CITY BOUNTIFUL ON THE EAST SEA (20)

| | |
|---|---|
| Alma 52:9 | 66 B.C. |

IN THE SOUTH WILDERNESS, SOUTH OF MANTI (52): Hypothetical location based on information contained in Alma 43:22-53 and Alma 44:22.

IN THE SOUTH WILDERNESS, SOUTH OF MORONI (17): Hypothetical location based on information contained in Alma 50:13, Alma 51:22-24 and Alma 62:34.

ON THE WEST SEASHORE IN THE NARROW NECK OF LAND (67)

| | |
|---|---|
| Alma 50:34 | ca. 67 B.C. |
| Mormon 2:29 | A.D. 350 |
| Mormon 3:5 | A.D. 350 |

NEHOR (72): Land

| | |
|---|---|
| Ether 7:4, 9 | no date |

NEPHI (43): Land and settlement occupied by both the Nephites and the Lamanites

| | |
|---|---|
| 2 Nephi 5:7, 8, 16 | 588-570 B.C. |
| Jacob 1:17 | 544-421 B.C. |
| Jacob 2:2, 11 | 544-426 B.C. |
| Omni 12, 13, 27 | 279-130 B.C. |
| Words of Mormon 13 | ca. 130 B.C. |
| Mosiah 7:6-9 | ca. 121 B.C. |
| Mosiah 9:6-8, 14, 15 | 200-187 B.C. |
| Mosiah 11:12 | 160-150 B.C. |
| Mosiah 19:5, 6, 15, 24, 28 | ca. 125 B.C. |
| Mosiah 20:7, 8 | ca. 123 B.C. |
| Mosiah 21:26 | ca. 122 B.C. |
| Mosiah 22:6-8, 11 | ca. 121 B.C. |
| Mosiah 28:1 | ca. 92 B.C. |
| Alma 17:8, 9 | ca. 91 B.C. |
| Alma 18:9 | ca. 90 B.C. |
| Alma 20:2 | ca. 90 B.C. |
| Alma 22:1, 2, 28, 29 | 90-77 B.C. |
| Alma 24:20 | 90-77 B.C. |
| Alma 47:20, 29, 31 | 72 B.C. |
| Alma 49:25 | 72 B.C. |
| Alma 50:7-11, 13 | 72 B.C. |
| Alma 56:3 | 77 B.C. |

| | |
|---|---|
| Alma 58:38 | 63 B.C. |

NEPHIHAH (3): Nephite settlement and land

| | |
|---|---|
| Alma 50:12-15 | 72 B.C. |
| Alma 51:25, 26 | ca. 68 B.C. |
| Alma 56:25 | 65 B.C. |
| Alma 59:5-9 | ca. 62 B.C. |
| Alma 62:14, 18-25, 30 | ca. 60 B.C. |

NOAH (24): Nephite settlement and land

| | |
|---|---|
| Alma 16:3 | 81 B.C. |
| Alma 49:12-15, 18-25 | 72 B.C. |

OGATH (83): A place near the hill Ramah

| | |
|---|---|
| Ether 15:10 | 600-580 B.C. |

OMNER (11): Nephite settlement

| | |
|---|---|
| Alma 51:24-26 | ca. 67 B.C. |

PLAINS BETWEEN MULEK AND CITY BOUNTIFUL (18)

| | |
|---|---|
| Alma 52:20 | 64 B.C. |

RAMAH (82): Jaredite name for the hill Cumorah

| | |
|---|---|
| Ether 15:11 | 600-580 B.C. |

RIPLAH (51): Hill

| | |
|---|---|
| Alma 43:31, 35 | ca. 74 B.C. |

RIPLIANCUM (55c): Sea adjacent to Jaredite battleground

| | |
|---|---|
| Ether 15:8 | 600-580 B.C. |

SEA

  EAST SEA (22)

| | |
|---|---|
| Alma 22:27, 29 | 90-77 B.C. |
| Alma 27:22 | ca. 77 B.C. |
| Alma 31:3 | ca. 74 B.C. |
| Alma 50:7-11, 13-15,   25 | 72-68 B.C. |
| Alma 51:22-26, 32 | ca. 67 B.C. |
| Alma 52:13, 22-39 | ca. 64 B.C. |
| Alma 62:32-34 | 60 B.C. |
| Helaman 3:8 | 46 B.C. |
| Helaman 11:20 | 16 B.C. |

  NORTH SEA (55)

| | |
|---|---|
| Helaman 3:8 | 46 B.C. |
| Ether 9:3 | no date |
| Ether 14:12, 13, 26 | 600-580 B.C. |
| Ether 15:8-10 | 600-580 B.C. |

  SOUTH SEA

| | |
|---|---|
| Helaman 3:8 | 46 B.C. |

  WEST SEA (35)

| | |
|---|---|
| Alma 22:27-33 | 90-77 B.C. |
| Alma 50:11, 32-34 | ca. 67 B.C. |
| Alma 52:11, 12 | ca. 66 B.C. |
| Alma 53:8, 22 | ca. 64 B.C. |
| Alma 56:31 | 65 B.C. |
| Alma 63:4-7 | ca. 55 B.C. |
| Helaman 3:8 | 46 B.C. |

| | |
|---|---|
| Helaman 4:7 | 35 B.C. |
| Helaman 11:20 | 16 B.C. |
| Mormon 2:6 | A.D. 327 |
| Ether 10:19-21 | no date |
| SHEM (60): Nephite land | |
| Mormon 3:20, 21 | A.D. 362 |
| SHEMLON (42): Lamanite land | |
| Mosiah 9:14, 15 | ca. 187 B.C. |
| Mosiah 10:6-8 | ca. 178 B.C. |
| Mosiah 11:12 | 160-150 B.C. |
| Mosiah 19:5, 6 | ca. 145 B.C. |
| Mosiah 20:1, 7 | 145-122 B.C. |
| Mosiah 24:1 | 145-122 B.C. |
| Alma 23:12 | 90-77 B.C. |
| SHERRIZAH : Nephite fortification | |
| Moroni 9:7, 16, 17 | A.D. 327-349 |
| SHILOM (41): Nephite land and settlement | |
| Mosiah 7:5-7, 16, 21 | ca. 121 B.C. |
| Mosiah 9:6-9, 14 | 200-187 B.C. |
| Mosiah 10:8, 9 | ca. 178 B.C. |
| Mosiah 11:12, 13 | 160-150 B.C. |
| Mosiah 22:8, 11 | 145-121 B.C. |
| Mosiah 24:1 | 145-121 B.C. |
| Alma 23:12 | 90-77 B.C. |
| SHIM (62): Hill in the land Antum | |
| Mormon 1:3 | ca. A.D. 322 |
| Mormon 4:23 | ca. A.D. 379 |
| Ether 9:3 | no date |
| SHURR (78): Valley | |
| Ether 14:28 | 600-580 B.C. |
| SIDOM (25): Nephite land | |
| Alma 15:1, 3, 4, 13,  14, 17, 18 | ca. 82 B.C. |
| SIDON : River and river crossings | |
| GENERAL REFERENCES | |
| Alma 4:4 | 86 B.C. |
| Alma 8:3 | 82 B.C. |
| Alma 22:27, 29 | 90-77 B.C. |
| Alma 43:22 | 74 B.C. |
| Alma 50:11 | 72 B.C. |
| Mormon 1:10 | ca. A.D. 322 |
| LOWER CROSSING (14): Ford east of Zarahemla | |
| Alma 2:15, 17, 27, 34,  35 | 87 B.C. |
| Alma 3:3 | 87 B.C. |
| Alma 6:7 | 87 B.C. |
| Alma 16:7 | 87 B.C. |

| | |
|---|---|
| UPPER CROSSING (16): Ford near hill Riplah | |
| Alma 43:27, 32-35, | ca. 74 B.C. |
| 39-41, 50-53 | |
| Alma 44:22 | ca. 74 B.C. |
| Alma 49:16 | 65 B.C. |
| Alma 56:25 | 65 B.C. |
| UPPER CROSSING (34): Ford in south wilderness | |
| Alma 16:6, 7 | 81 B.C. |
| SIRON (38): Lamanite land | |
| Alma 39:3 | ca. 73 B.C. |
| TEANCUM (64): Nephite settlement | |
| Mormon 4:3, 7, 14 | A.D. 363-366 |

TRAIL JUNCTION
- (69): Hypothetical junction of route to Nephihah and the Zarahemla–City Bountiful path
- (70): Hypothetical junction of Judea–Unnamed City path with the Antiparah-Joshua path
- (86): Hypothetical junction of the Judea-Antiparah path with the Antiparah-Angola path
- (88): Hypothetical junction of the Manti–Judea/Joshua path with the Nephi-Ammonihah path

| | |
|---|---|
| UNNAMED SETTLEMENT | |
| CITIES NORTHWARD FROM JUDEA: See Joshua (58) | |
| Alma 56:22-24 | 65 B.C. |
| CITY NEAR JUDEA AND THE WEST SEA (31) | |
| Alma 56:31-33 | 65 B.C. |
| JAREDITE CITY | |
| Ether 10:19-21 | no date |
| VALLEY | |
| ALMA (87): Valley | |
| Mosiah 24:20, 24, 25 | ca. 120 B.C. |
| CORIHOR (79): Valley | |
| Ether 14:28 | 600-580 B.C. |
| GILGAL (74): Valley | |
| Ether 13:27-30 | no date |
| SHURR (78): Valley | |
| Ether 14:28 | 600-580 B.C. |
| VALLEY SOUTH OF THE CROSSING AT THE HILL RIPLAH (90) | |
| Alma 43:31, 35 | ca. 74 B.C. |
| VALLEY ON WEST BANK OF RIVER CROSSING NEAR THE HILL RIPLAH (89) | |
| Alma 43:27, 32, 41, 42, 51-53 | ca. 74 B.C. |
| WILDERNESS | |
| WILDERNESS EAST | |
| Alma 22:29 | 90-77 B.C. |
| Alma 25:5, 8 | 90-77 B.C. |
| Alma 50:7-11 | 72 B.C. |

WILDERNESS OF HERMOUNTS (32)
    Alma 2:34-37          87 B.C.
WILDERNESS, NARROW STRIP OF (50)
    Alma 22:27-34        90-77 B.C.
    Alma 27:14          75 B.C.
    Alma 42:22-24        ca. 74 B.C.
    Alma 50:7-11         72 B.C.
WILDERNESS NORTH OF LAND OF NEPHI (50)
    Mosiah 22:11-13, 16     145-121 B.C.
    Mosiah 24:24, 25       120 B.C.
    Alma 22:27         90-77 B.C.
    Alma 27:14         ca. 75 B.C.
WILDERNESS NORTH AND WEST OF ZARAHEMLA: see Hermounts
   (32)
WILDERNESS SOUTH (50)
    Alma 16:6, 7         81 B.C.
    Alma 22:31        90-77 B.C.
    Alma 31:3          74 B.C.
    Alma 62:34         60 B.C.
WILDERNESS SOUTH OF ANTIONUM (50c)
    Alma 31:3        ca. 74 B.C.
    Alma 43:22         74 B.C.
WILDERNESS SOUTH OF MELEK (33)
    Alma 8:3          82 B.C.
WILDERNESS ON THE SOUTH AND ON THE EAST OF MORONI (17)
    Alma 62:34         60 B.C.
WILDERNESS WEST OF MULEK (19)
    Alma 52:22        ca. 64 B.C.
ZARAHEMLA (1): Nephite land and capital settlement
    Omni :12-16, 21, 28     279-130 B.C.
    Mosiah 1:18       ca. 124 B.C.
    Mosiah 2:1, 4, 6, 7, 26   ca. 124 B.C.
    Mosiah 22:11-13     145-121 B.C.
    Mosiah 24:25      ca. 120 B.C.
    Alma 2:15          87 B.C.
    Alma 15:1, 18        82 B.C.
    Alma 17:1        ca. 75 B.C.
    Alma 17:7-9       ca. 90 B.C.
    Alma 27:14       ca. 75 B.C.
    Alma 31:3        ca. 74 B.C.
    Alma 35:14       ca. 74 B.C.
    Alma 45:18         73 B.C.
    Alma 47:29         72 B.C.
    Alma 48:6          72 B.C.
    Alma 50:7, 11        72 B.C.
    Alma 56:25, 57      65-63 B.C.
    Alma 57:11, 15, 16, 30      63 B.C.
    Alma 58:23, 24        63 B.C.

| | |
|---|---|
| Alma 61:8 | 62 B.C. |
| Alma 62:6, 7, 42 | 62-60 B.C. |
| Alma 63:4 | 55 B.C. |
| Helaman 1:18-28, 33 | ca. 51 B.C. |
| Helaman 3:3, 31 | ca. 43 B.C. |
| Helaman 4:5 | 35 B.C. |
| Helaman 5:16 | ca. 30 B.C. |
| Helaman 6:4 | ca. 28 B.C. |
| Helaman 7:1, 3, 10 | 23 B.C. |
| Helaman 13:2 | 6 B.C. |
| 3 Nephi 3:21-24 | A.D. 17 |
| 3 Nephi 8:8, 24 | A.D. 34 |
| 3 Nephi 9:3 | A.D. 34 |
| 4 Nephi 1:8 | A.D. 36-60 |
| Mormon 1:10 | ca. A.D. 322 |
| Ether 9:31 | no date |
| ZEEZROM (27): Nephite settlement | |
| Alma 56:14 | 66 B.C. |

# APPENDIX B

## BOOK OF MORMON LOCALITIES INCORPORATED INTO THIS STUDY

| Place Name | Site Iden. No. | Place Assoc. Shown in Figure | Place Located in Primary Culture Area | Settlement Type Noted in Book of Mormon | Terrain Type Noted in Book of Mormon | Greater Land Location of Place | Land Designation L=lesser M=middle G=greater | Place was a Battle Site |
|---|---|---|---|---|---|---|---|---|
| Aaron | 8 | 8 | Nephite | City | | Southward | L | Yes |
| Ablom | 84 | 18 | Jaredite | Camp | | Northward | | |
| Agosh | 77 | 18 | Jaredite | | Plains | Northward | | Yes |
| Akish | 76 | 18 | Jaredite | Camp | Wilderness | Northward | | |
| Alma | 87 | 12 | Nephite | Camp | Valley | Southward | | |
| Ammonihah | 23 | 10 | Nephite | City | | Southward | L | Yes |
| Amnihu | 15 | 13 | Nephite | | Hill | Southward | | Yes |
| Amulon | 40 | 12 | Lamanite* | | | Southward | L | |
| Angola | 56 | 16 | Nephite | City | | Southward | L | Yes |
| Ani-Anti | 46 | 12 | Lamanite | Village | | Southward | | |
| Antionum | 37 | 12 | Nephite | | | Southward | L | ? |
| Antiparah | 30 | 10, 12 | Nephite | City | | Southward | | Yes |
| Antum | 61 | 16 | Nephite | | | Northward | L | |
| Battle Site North of Antiparah-Judea | 92 | 20 | Nephite | | | Southward | L | Yes |
| Boaz | 65 | 16 | Nephite | City | | Northward | | Yes |
| Bountiful (East Sea Land and City) | 2 | 8, 12 | Nephite | City | Coastal Rainforest | Southward | M, L | Yes |
| Bountiful (West Sea Land) | See area between 67-58-30 | 20 | Nephite | | Coastal Rainforest | Southward | M | Yes |

| Place Name | Site Iden. No. | Place Assoc. Shown in Figure | Place Located in Primary Culture Area | Settlement Type Noted in Book of Mormon | Terrain Type Noted in Book of Mormon | Greater Land Location of Place | Land Designation L = lesser M = middle G = greater | Place was a Battle Site |
|---|---|---|---|---|---|---|---|---|
| Comnor | 80 | 18 | Jaredite | | Hill | Northward | | Yes |
| Coriantumr's Camp | 81 | 18 | Jaredite | | | Northward | L | |
| Corihor | 79, 94 | 18, 20 | Jaredite | | Valley | Northward | | Yes |
| Cumeni | 28 | 10 | Nephite | | | Southward | L | |
| Cumorah-Ramah | 82, 93 | 18, 20 | Jaredite, Nephite | Camp Camp | Hill | Northward | | |
| David | 57 | 16 | Nephite | City | | Southward | L | Yes |
| Desolation | 63 | 16 | Jaredite, Nephite | Camp | | Borderlands | G, M, L | Yes |
| Drainage North of City Nephi | 54 | 12 | Lamanite* | | | Southward | | Yes |
| Ephraim | 85 | 18 | Jaredite | City | Natural Drainage Hill | Southward Northward | | Yes Yes |
| Gid | 12 | 8 | Nephite | City | Valley | Southward | | Yes |
| Gideon | 7 | 8 | Nephite | City | Valley | Southward | L | Yes |
| Gilgal | 74 | 18 | Jaredite | | | Northward | | Yes |
| Hagoth's Shipyard | 35c | 16 | Nephite | | Coastal Lagoons | Borderlands | | Yes |
| Helam | 39 | 12 | Lamanite* | City | | Southward | L | Yes |
| Hermounts | 32 | 10 | Nephite | | Wilderness | Southward | | Yes |
| Heshlon | 75 | 18 | Jaredite | | Plains | Northward | | |
| Heth | 73 | 18 | Jaredite | | | Northward | L | Yes |
| Hill North of Shilom | 53 | 12 | Lamanite* | City | Hill | Southward | L | Yes |
| Ishmael | 48 | 12 | Lamanite | City | | Southward | L | |
| Jashon | 59 | 16 | Nephite | | | Northward | L | Yes |
| Jershon | 36 | 12 | Nephite | | | Southward | L | Yes |
| Jerusalem | 45 | 12 | Lamanite | City | | Southward | L | |
| Jordan | 66 | 16 | Nephite | City | | Northward | | Yes |
| Joshua | 58 | 16 | Nephite | | | Southward | L | Yes |

| Place Name | Site Iden. No. | Place Assoc. Shown in Figure | Place Located in Primary Culture Area | Settlement Type Noted in Book of Mormon | Terrain Type Noted in Book of Mormon | Greater Land Location of Place | Land Designation L=lesser M=middle G=greater | Place was a Battle Site |
|---|---|---|---|---|---|---|---|---|
| Passage through the Wilderness South of Moroni and Antionum | 91 | 8, 13 | Nephite | | Canyon | Southward | | |
| Plains between Mulek and East Sea City Bountiful | 18 | 8 | Nephite | | Plains | Southward | | Yes |
| Riplah | 51 | 12 Inset | Nephite | | Hill | Southward | | Yes |
| Ripliancum (North Sea) | 55c | 18 | Jaredite, Nephite | | Sea | N/A | | |
| Seashore-East Sea | 22 | 8, 12 | Nephite | | Coastline | N/A | | Yes |
| Seashore-North Sea | 55 | 18 | Jaredite, Mulekite, Nephite | | Coastline | N/A | | Yes |
| Seashore-West Sea | 35 | 10, 16 | Nephite, Lamanite | | Coastline | N/A | | Yes |
| Shem | 60 | 16 | Nephite | City | | Northward | L | Yes |
| Shemlon | 42 | 12 | Lamanite | | | Southward | L | |
| Sherrizah | - | - | Nephite | Defensive Position | Hill | Northward | | Yes |
| Shilom | 41 | 12 | Lamanite* | City | | Southward | L | Yes |
| Shim | 62 | 16, 18 | Nephite | | Hill | Northward | | |
| Shurr | 78 | 18 | Jaredite | Camp | Valley | Northward | | |
| Sidom | 25 | 10 | Nephite | | | Southward | L | |
| Sidon River Crossing East of Zarahemla | 14 | 3, 13 | Nephite | | Ford | Southward | | Yes |
| Sidon River Crossing near Manti | 16 | 12 Inset | Nephite | | Ford | Southward | | Yes |
| Sidon River Crossing beyond the Land Manti in the South Wilderness | 34 | 10 | Nephite | | Ford | Southward | | Yes |

| Settlement | | | Lamanite | | | | | |
|---|---|---|---|---|---|---|---|---|
| Siron | 38 | 8, 12 | Nephite | | | Southward | L | Yes |
| Teancum | 64 | 16 | Nephite | | | Northward | | |
| Trail Junction | 69 | 8 | Nephite | | | Southward | | |
| Trail Junction | 70 | 20 | Nephite | | | Southward | | |
| Trail Junction | 86 | 20 | Nephite | | Valley | Southward | | |
| Trail Junction | 88 | 10 | Nephite | | | Southward | | |
| Unnamed Settlement near Judea | 31 | 10 | Nephite | City | Valley | Southward | | |
| Valley South of the Hill Riplah | 90 | 12 Inset | Nephite | | Mountain Chain & Forest | Southward | | Yes |
| Valley on the West Bank of the Sidon near Manti | 89 | 12 Inset | Nephite | | Mountain Chain & Forest | Southward | | Yes |
| Wilderness, Narrow Strip of | 50 | 12 | Nephite | | Mountains & Forest | Southward | | Yes |
| Wilderness South and also East of Moroni | 17 | 8 | Nephite | | Mountains & Forest | Southward | | |
| Wilderness South of Melek | 33 | 10 | Nephite | | | Southward | | |
| Wilderness West of Mulek | 19 | 8 | Nephite | | | Southward | | |
| Zarahemla | 1 | 10, 12, 16 | Nephite Jaredite? Mulekite, Nephite | City | | Southward | G, M, L | Yes |
| Zeezrom | 27 | 10 | Nephite | City | | Southward | | Yes |

Note: *indicates settlements and lands begun by Nephite peoples but later abandoned and incorported into the Iamanite cultural sphere of influence

# BIBLIOGRAPHY

Abler, Ronald, J.S. Adams and P. Gould
1971 *Spatial Organization: The Geographer's View of the World.*
Englewood Cliffs: Prentice-Hall.

Bertalanffy, Ludwig von
1968 *General System Theory.* New York: George Braziller, Inc.

Binford, Lewis R.
1972 *An Archaeological Perspective.* New York: Seminar Press.

Clarke, David L.
1977 "Spatial Information in Archaeology," in *Spatial Archaeology.*
David L. Clarke, Editor. London: Academic Press.

Dillon, Brian D.
1977 "Salinas de los Nueve Cerros, Guatemala: Preliminary Archaeological Investigations." Socorro, New Mexico: *Ballena Press Studies
in Mesoamerican Art, Archaeology and Ethnohistory,* No. 2.

Dillon, Brian D.
1979 *The Archaeological Ceramics of Salinas de los Nueve Cerros, Alta
Verapaz, Guatemala.* Unpublished Doctoral Dissertation, Berke-
ley: University of California.

Haggett, Peter
1966 *Locational Analysis in Human Geography.* New York: St. Martin's
Press.

Hauck, F. Richard
1973 *The Edzna Hydraulic Complex, Initial Investigation: 1972.* Unpublished Master's Thesis, Provo: Brigham Young University.

Hauck, F. Richard
1975 *Preconquest Mayan Overland Routes on the Yucatan Peninsula
and their Economic Significance.* Unpublished Doctoral Dissertation, Salt Lake City: University of Utah.

Kirchhoff, Paul
1981 "Mesoamerica: Its Geographic Limits, Ethnic Composition and
Cultural Characteristics," in *Ancient Mesoamerica: Selected Read-
ings.* John A. Graham, Editor. Palo Alto: Peek Publications.

Kroeber, A.L. and Clyde Kluckhohn

n.d. *Culture: A Critical Review of Concepts and Definitions.* New York: Vintage Books.

Kuhn, Thomas S.
1962 *The Structure of Scientific Revolutions.* Chicago: The University of Chicago Press—Phoenix Books.

Larsen, Wayne, A. C. Rencher and T. Layton
1980 "Who Wrote the Book of Mormon? An Analysis of Wordprints." Provo: *Brigham Young University Studies,* Vol. 20, No. 3:225-51.

Matheny, Ray T., D. L. Gurr, D. W. Forsyth and F. R. Hauck
1983 Investigations at Edzne Campeche, Mexico. Volume 1, "Part 1: The hydraulic system." *Papers of the New World Archaeological Foundation,* No. 46. Provo: Brigham Young University.

Nibley, Hugh
1952 *Lehi in the Desert and the World of the Jaredites.* Salt Lake City: Bookcraft Publishing Co.

Nibley, Hugh
1976 *Since Cumorah.* Salt Lake City: Deseret Book Company.

Palmer, David A.
1981 *In Search of Cumorah: New evidence for the Book of Mormon from Ancient Mexico.* Bountiful, Utah: Horizon Publishers.

Reynolds, George
1976 *A Complete Concordance of the Book of Mormon.* Salt Lake City: Deseret Book Company.

Smith, Joseph
1830 The Book of Mormon: An Account Written by the Hand of-Mormon, upon Plates Taken from the Plates of Nephi. Palmyra, New York: E. B. Grandin.

Smith, Joseph
1981 The Book of Mormon: An Account Written by the Hand of Mormon upon Plates Taken from the Plates of Nephi. Salt Lake City: The Church of Jesus Christ of Latter-day Saints.

Sorenson, John L.
1985 *An Ancient American Setting for the Book of Mormon.* Salt Lake City: Deseret Book Company.

Taaffe, Edward J. and H. L. Gauthier, Jr.
1973 *Geography of Transportation.* Englewood Cliffs: Prentice-Hall, Inc.

Tregelles, Samual Prideaux
1949 *Gesenius' Hebrew and Chaldee Lexicon to the Old Testament Scriptures.* S. P. Tregelles, Translator. Grand Rapids, Michigan: Eerdmans Publishing Co.

Welch, John W.
1981 "Chiasmus in the Book of Mormon," in *Chiasmus in Antiquity*. John Welch, Editor. Hildesheim: Gerstenberg Verlag.

West, Robert C. and John P. Augelli
1966 *Middle America: Its Lands and Peoples*. Englewood Cliffs: Prentice-Hall, Inc.

Wright, G. Ernest
1960 *Biblical Archaeology*. Westminster Press: Philadelphia.

# INDEX